LIVRARIA LELLO
PORTO

THE LUSIADS

THE LUSIADS

Luís de Camões

LIVRARIA LELLO

PORTO

LIVRARIA LELLO
PORTO

An exclusive edition of
Livraria Lello
Porto – Portugal

Original title: Os Lusíadas
English title: The Lusiads
Author: Luís de Camões
Translation of *The Lusiads* by Richard Francis Burton,
edited by his wife Isabel Burton, London, 1880

Direction: 100Folhas/Imense
Editorial coordination and editing: Teresa Mendonça – BookBug
Editorial advisor: João Carlos Alvim
Foreword: Eduardo Lourenço
Foreword's translator: Silvia Rodrigues
Proofreading: João Carlos Alvim and Teresa Mendonça
Art direction and graphic design: Mariana Pereira – Livraria Lello
Creative direction: Hugo Cardoso – Livraria Lello
Layout: Luís Santos
Cover: *Adamastor*, Palace Hotel de Buçaco, Jorge Colaço, Fábrica
de Sacavém, 1907 (photographed by Nuno M. Dois Branco)

Printed and bound by Esenart Basim Ltd
Registration of copyright: 464812/19
ISBN: 978-989-893-906-7
1st edition: April 2018
2nd edition: December 2019

A UNIQUE EPIC POEM
by Eduardo Lourenço

Little do we know with certainty about the author of *The Lusiads*. Among it is the date when the poem that was destined to become a nation's insignia was published. Camões published it after his return from the East where he spent seventeen years of adventures and miseries, each evoked in some known stages of his epic. The year is 1572, the moment where the empire the Portuguese established in the East at the beginning of the 16th century shows obvious signs of depletion and even downfall. Camões met it in the light of this twilight. His poem shows the signs of this imperial autumn particularly evident for being the opposite of an ancient splendor that has not totally faded yet. Faith left up to him the task of assembling together, when it was still possible to do so, the utmost accomplishments of this extraordinary empire — the first in the West — founded, maintained, for over half a century, thousands of leagues away from the Atlantic shores, by a small European people.

More than the Portuguese nautical accomplishments, even more than the conquest and the warlike and commercial presence in the Indian Ocean, from Ormuz to Malacca, what impelled Camões to write his poem was the awareness he had of the gap between the novelty and greatness of the Lusitanian undertaking and the weakness of the little kingdom that dared to imagine it and carry

5

it out. Only a Portuguese and a poet running away from the bitter and exhilarating knowledge of this weakness — almost madness — could give his people's historical achievements the entirely new epical and even odd expression we find in *The Lusiads*.

Effectively, *The Lusiads* are in many ways a unique epic poem. Only to the Portuguese — especially since the poem became their sublime image — the awareness Camões had of the giant gap between the means and the results of the Portuguese adventure is not surprising. And, however, it was from that amazement that Camões' poem could emerge and therefore assume its epopee nature, nostalgic and voluntarist at the same time. In themselves, the Portuguese nautical accomplishments, achieved over the course of more than a century, were naturally epic not only to the chroniclers that wrote about them, from Zurara to João de Barros, but to the European public opinion, already enticed by everything new and prompted by the universal curiosity of the Renaissance. A great number of humanists, national or foreign, made themselves available to the kings of Portugal to write their own epic interpretation according to ancient canons. Had they been well succeeded we would have today, without a doubt, great machines of poetic rhetoric in which the Renaissance specialized. But we wouldn't have had *The Lusiads*. Camões knew how to fulfill those same "machines" with real poetry changing, from within, the completely formal perspective those same humanists could have of the great Portuguese accomplishments. To them, those feats didn't have a real subject. Camões's outlook gave them one by writing these facts on a story lived both at a personal and national level. He kept the abstract and literary universality of the Renaissance, inflating it with a new sort of patriotic passion that he personally assumed and very suitably came up with. His poem is not only evoked, as he says, by "a love for his homeland so pure and almost eternal that it does not seek a reward" but by the almost romantic consciousness of a connection of that poem with the author himself. In fact, as much as the spirit of the time allowed, beyond the glorified heroes in Vasco da Gama's voyage to India which is the common thread and the narrative's symbolic object, *The Lusiads* real hero is the poet himself. Better yet, the sovereign voice which, from the first to the last stanza, serves as the poem's basis, giving it a rhythm and a tone continuously epic and lyric, a peculiar combination on such a conventional genre like an epopee. Certainly, Ariosto's example, once dominant, could allow all freedoms; but in his poem, specifically meant to get away from that heroic canto model on a marvelous and chivalresque style, things happened in a different way. Camões claims to his poem, by contrasting it with other epic narratives more or less fabulous of that era, the status of truth's chant. Addressing to D. Sebastião, Portugal's young king meant to be a legendary figure, the poet assures the truthfulness of his chant:

> Hark; for with vauntings vain thou shalt not view
> phantastical, fictitious, lying deed
> of lieges lauded, as strange Muses do,
> seeking their fond and foolish pride to feed:
> Thine acts so forceful are, told simply true,
> all fabled, dreamy feats they far exceed;
> exceeding Rodomont, and Ruggiero vain,
> and Roland haply born of Poet's brain.
>
> (Canto I, stanza 11)

However, while reading *The Lusiads* we immediately realize that its epic uniqueness does not rest on, as Camões emphatically highlights from the beginning to the end of the poem, on this transformation into cantos of glorious and real events. The facts he chants are already part of a legend or national memory. His reality itself wouldn't have been enough to bring to life and into shape the genre of epopee he dreams of. In fact, his epopee's progress lives less of the opposition between the heroic chant connected to the fable or fantasy and truth-based chant than of the challenge, characteristic of the Renaissance, the will to surpass ancient models. Just like the Portuguese maritime discoveries surpass Ulysses and Aeneas's accomplishments, so should the poem that celebrates them surpass *The Odyssey* and *The Aeneid*. But this ambition, itself characteristic of the Renaissance rhetoric, trapped in the game of mirrors of these imaginary surpassings, would have been nothing more than a vain desire if Camões hadn't imagined, in order to embody it, a true "poetic machine". This poetic machine, the only one, along with Tasso's, to be able to impose itself as a modern time epopee, is precisely *The Lusiads*. Literally speaking, Camões depicts Gama's voyage, synthesis and symbol of Portugal's faith at a time where its action in the world reaches its apogee. With this mythical voyage, Portugal, a discovering country in charge of broadening the frontiers of the known world "by seas never before sailed" becomes too the bearer of Christ's message to the ends of the earth. In Camões' eyes, his people's particular story then becomes the universal history. According to him, a chant consecrated to the exaltation of faith and the empire has nothing of hyperbolic in it. He surely does not ignore that the Christian Europe at the end of the sixteenth century is a torn world, a Christianity he compares to "Cadmus' teeth", threatened by the Turks who will only see their march detained in Lepanto a few years later. But in the Portuguese East, where he wrote his poem, in the Indian ocean's space where his compatriots negotiate, fight and spread the word of Christ, or in Japan and at

China's gates, the Portuguese epopee as a Christian epopee is familiar to him. Some of *The Lusiads'* interpreters, taking into account its character of highly constructed poem, full of Renaissance's erudition, fascinated despite everything by the cultural power of the classic models, believe that Camões could have written the same poem in Lisbon. It's licit to doubt that thesis. For various titles, it couldn't have been written in a place other than that Christian East in confrontation with a non-Christian culture, the only place where a Portuguese could look at the world, organize his space just like Camões does in the last stanza of his poem. On the contrary, the poem was written to be read in Europe and not in the East. More precisely in Lisbon, where the Renaissance's cultural cannons should still be similar to what they were when Camões – apparently – was forced to leave Portuguese at the beginning of the century's second half. But it was not the case. From the East, he will bring his country a poem still replete with a world's outlook that the Renaissance, with its freedom of spirit and its sensuality perfume, had spread over Europe before he left, and he does that precisely at a time where the sensibility and the ways of thinking at the peninsula where beginning to shape another way, the Counter-Reformation's way.

Faith and empire's epopee, *The Lusiads* seem to, at first sight, by the time they were published, not only follow the values of this Counter-Reformation, but constitute, so to say, its poetical-ideological manifesto. *The Lusiads* are the poem of a people of crusaders. There are numerous passages where Camões urges not only his small country, but Christian Europe, to mobilize against the Turkish and Islam in general. But *The Lusiads* are likewise something else: the unusual and almost inexplicable expression of a sensitivity and a vision of the world still marked by the aesthetic values and philosophical or metaphysical references dear to Renaissance's thought. Only in its pages there's an atmosphere that evokes Angelo Poliziano's, Bembo's and Castiglione's, but more sensual and carnal. *The Lusiads* are not only the poem of the warlike and Christian values of a people but the outmost love poem in Portuguese language. And now that we can no longer read the poem in Mars' cruel light, the power and omnipresence of Venus imposes itself as its most vivid nucleus.

This contradiction, real or apparent, within a catholic-inspired poem, is not the only or the most significant bizarre thing of this unique epopee. It's linked to the curious "poetical machine" that *The Lusiads* are, not on the content's simple plan, meaning or ideology, but in the most decisive plan of its form. Its structure, plan and poetic logic have always caused admiration. At the rationalism's age, the poem was referred to the monstrous or heteroclite domain. During the modern period it was believed to "understand" it better by placing him on the "mannerist" poems. Maybe this is the good solution. But it would also be necessary to find poems that were similar, in particular among the epopees, to circumvent its uniqueness. In fact, we're looking at an epic poem whose explicit aim consists on evoking in heroic and dramatical terms an odyssey no less heroic, Vasco da Gama's journey which then becomes the narrative's formal hero. But what do we find if we read *The Lusiads*? A Vasco da Gama who is essentially a reciter, not an actor – or rarely so – around which the epic action can take place. Furthermore, the actions are not "seen" but recited, evoked, transposed in rhetorical terms: Aljubarrota's episode, death of Inês de Castro, Adamastor's story, evocation of the Portuguese glorious past or memory worthy, described according to the scenes already inscribed on the flags or tapestries. Today, we can consider this method as paradoxically modern or even post-modern, but it doesn't depend on "truth's" logic the author claims for his poem. Poet's contradiction, our reading's maladaptation to what the poem is and intended to be?

The Lusiads are, first of all, not just *a* poem, but *this* unique poem and not any other. Its logic is that of an unreal object that, as such, if it imposes itself as a poem, can't be caught failing. It happens that, in its strangeness, *The Lusiads*, if we allow ourselves to read it at the light of what its culture was, an era's imaginary where we find, at the same time, its expression and enigmatic mirror, speak to us clearly. Camões wanted his epopee to be a chant of "truth". But the truth of his poem couldn't be of the innumerous narratives of veritable feats that the chroniclers of the Indies had already risen to the status of praise worthy events. The epopee — while heroic existence was everywhere — should distance itself from that perspective banally *realistic* to another record, the one of mythical transfiguration that only the poem, as the worlds symbolic form, as a work of art, could reach. It was necessary to *play the card* of real to become ideal. In short, it was necessary to find a way of dramatize the adventure of the discoveries and of the national past which led to those actions of planetary reach. Like that, the epopee — that is, the poem — became possible. Possible as a simulated epopee.

As a poetic object, *The Lusiads* live entirely of this game. Camões imagines that the gods, who in the past were characters that became involved in human events, like the goddess Athena or Venus, intervene now, metaphorically, on the ventures of transcending consequences that the Portuguese, while sailing in the direction of the Indies, are actors. It has always been considered bizarre, and even absurd, that Camões conferred this fiction a "life", a visibility he doesn't grant to human characters, starting with Vasco da Gama himself. And it is even more absurd

11

that, on a poem extolling Catholicism, he trusted to pagan gods that "transcendent" role of explaining what was symbolically "implicated" in the Portuguese epopee. The poet himself seems to somewhat agree with that remark given that, at the end of the poem, he removes the gods from the scene, reducing them to mere figurative expressions of the virtues, mere aesthetical expedient to write "pleasant verses". In fine rigor, the gods, the almost burlesque comedy he makes them play, served to make *the poem* possible. Without them *The Lusiads* wouldn't have been able to be written because it is thanks to this device that the poem acquires a certain distance from its theme that gives freedom to its voice — that is, to itself — to move between the transcendent and devoid of reality world, the world of the gods, ready to serve as a portrait to their feelings' expression or deepest thoughts or wishes and the heroic world excessively overburdened with reality, but unable of showing a meaning if the poet doesn't confer it.

Without paradox, with perfect awareness of the poet's role in the modern world, creator and autonomous sovereign of his creatures, Camões had the need for that mythological fantasy, apparently out of use, to refer the gods and old epopees to their past. But, at the same time, he needed the gods to dream what the reality or the acceptable values and the allowed chants — would have never consented. How could he have given a body of light to love's power, to his natural and irresistible spell, without placing Venus herself at the center of his comedy, promoted to the role of protector of the Portuguese? There are in *The Lusiads* points of exaltation — or melancholy — dedicated to the evocation of facts or deeds of humankind, but none of those verses reveals an intense joy like the ones inspired by the love goddess crossing the skies to ask the father of the gods — her father — audacious fantasy that only fiction authorizes — to help her beloved Portuguese:

The piteous prayer smote the loving ears
of Dionaea fair; her heart was pained;
she left her Nymphs, all bathed in yearning tears,
who by her sudden flight perplext remained:
Now she had thrid the luminous planet-spheres,
now the third Heaven's gateway she had gained;
on, onward still to the sixth sphere, the throne
where high All-Father sits and reigns alone.

And, as her way affronting, forth she hied,
her every gesture such a grace expired,
Stars, Skies and Æther's circumambient tide,
and all that saw her with love-fire were fired. [...]

Wandered the crispy threads of wavy gold
adown a bosom shaming virgin snow:
Her milk-hued breasts with every movement rolled
where Love lay sporting but did nowhere show:
Flames with far-flashing fire the Zone's white fold
wherewith the Boy guaranteed every heart to glow:
while round those columns' polished curves were climbing
Desires, like ivy parent-trunk entwining.

[...]

The while her angel-semblance showed blended
with smiles a sadness in the sweetest way;
like some fair Lady by rude swain offended
incautious rough while playing amorous play;
who laughs and laughing pouts with wrath pretended
passing without pause from grave to gay;
thus she, the Goddess who no rival heeded,
softer than sad before her Father pleaded.

(Canto II, Stanzas 33, 34, 36 and 38)

13

In Camões, the world of the gods is the world of men inverted, the home where the dreams of a humanity who again awakens to the taste of the earthly things — and the discoveries play an obvious role in that — can have a free course. On the other hand, with their labors and sufferings, the humans who excel their strengths and their "forbidden ends of the world" divinize themselves. In the end, they become, on the poem's most famous allegory, worthy of being crowned, in the new Renaissance colorful paradise, as heroes of love. The new Argonauts, on the way back from the royal and initiatory voyage which opens the East and the West and lets us guess nature's secret to the new humanity, celebrate on the Island of Loves the profane and divine glory's nuptials and satisfied desire. It was indeed necessary the East's light — and not only Homer and Ariosto's combined memories — in order to imagine that earthly delight's island in the middle of Counter-Reformation's ocean. After that, the great Captain, more allegoric than ever, can celebrate his royal nuptials with Thetis — betrothal with the sea of a Portugal in that time more powerful than old Venice — and contemplate for a moment the "world's machine", our planet becoming at last object of knowledge and human dominion. Tethys shows Gama this new world's map and the long enumeration of peoples, cultures, of the legends that tell them apart from each other is more eloquent in the eyes of the poet than the description of the prowess, always somewhat embellished by the heroic muse, of those who, among so many disperse nations on the surface of the globe, truly made a world.

This view from above is the symbolic conclusion but also the origin of the epic vision characteristic of *The Lusiads*, as a poem dedicated to the glory of the Portuguese — the first to be able to take advantage of this universal look — but also a poem of an European culture voted to the knowledge of nature and, moreover, eager to let go of its past to make up a new life, to which we call modernity. The amazement felt by this Europe in search of itself before the memories and resurrection of the old world should not deceive us. Imitation was the prelude to emulation and this served as a lever for the invention of a new image, the axiom of the arrival to new stops, not only geographical but also human. No poem is as representative as *The Lusiads* of that moment where the old carries the new in itself and the new still wears the old one. Hence this apparatus of gods, nymphs, not to "simulate the old" but to overcome within the still insuperable horizon a modernity transvestite of antiquity. The mythology in *The Lusiads* is neither an artifice nor an ornament but the still almighty presence of a model that needed to be used as a joke to make the modern myths worthy of comparing them to Rome's praises, Circe's fascination, Dido's tears. The most celebrated passages of *The Lusiads* — the death of Inês, Adamastor's episode, the Old Man of Restelo or the Island of Loves — are not only examples of the irruption of Camões' lyricism in the epic text, but most likely true myths, sublimated reality by the verb that evokes it and offers it to us as an unforgettable moment of a life's vision, neither old, nor modern but simply without subject, like all true poetry. These creations allowed the poem to go beyond a limited, if not narrow, circle — even if its formal object was intended to be of universal interest — from a chant erected to the resplendent, but ephemeral, glory of a people. They really belong to a moment of Europe's history during which it transforms in world history, dialoguing with the poetic memory of a civilization that is opening itself to others. The whole of the poem constitutes itself the first double faced star, ancient and modern, of that time between two worlds or of this world situated between two times, which already navigates among modernity but doesn't dare yet to face, with its bare hands, the loneliness of the new man. Just as Dante didn't dare to walk by himself through the mazes of pain and death, in search of beatitude and asked Virgil to guide him and Beatriz to hold his hand, Camões also crosses the new domains of modern adventure par excellence with his resplendent — some would say baroque — of dead gods, if such gods can die, resurrected by the poet's will, but more by the most uncomfortable demand of an epopee born under the sign of a challenge to the ancient world.

Such is, at least, the appearance of things. In fact, the poet walks alone in and throughout the poem, supported by the passionate love he vows to the people whose deeds he praises. But perhaps even more for a love of another kind, the love of a glory that has no homeland, expression of the new feeling of individuality characteristic to the Renaissance. In particular, the love for the glory of the poets conscious of themselves and supreme guarantors of human dignity, that is, of the Man as son of his works. A particularly well-known passage of *The Lusiads* which inspired the most widespread paraphernalia of images about his fate as a glorious and unhappy poet. It is the one where Camões evokes the shipwreck he suffered at Mekong's mouth during his return from China, shipwreck where he lost all of his belongings but saved the poem:

"This Stream with gentle, bland repose shall greet
in his embrace the Song, that swam to land
from sad and piteous shipwreck dripping wet,
escaped from the reefs and rocks that fang the strand;
from hunger-tortures and the perilous strait,
what time went forth the dour unjust command
on him, whose high sonorous lyre shall claim
such want of Fortune and such wealth of Fame.

(Canto X, stanza 128)

16

Like Moses, *The Lusiads* are a book saved from the water. From the waters of reality that were seldom welcoming to that proud poet who knew really well his "revenge temper" but mostly saved from the dark waters of oblivion, which he often conjures as the worst of all dooms. Along with the poem he saved his memory and, with it — his utmost ambition — the memory of a people who, without his book, wouldn't have a "true homeland", a place with no memory and of all memories, taken from history and time "who dissolves it all". The historical epopee that Camões wrote entered long ago the world of the dead gods. Only the poem that marks it, a chant modeled by passion and bitterness transfigured by the timeless beauty of its stanzas, preserves its memory. And with it, the author's real life, of which we only know it was both fiery and unhappy. Like the one gods grant, according to the old adage, to the ones destined to an immortal life.

E.L.
Providence, November 26 1995

17

CANTO I

1   The feats of Arms, and famed heroick Host,
    from occidental Lusitanian strand,
    who o'er the waters ne'er by seaman crost,
    fared beyond the Taprobane-land,[1]
    forceful in perils and in battle-post,
    with more than promised force of mortal hard;
    and in the regions of a distant race
    rear'd a new throne so haught in Pride of Place:

2   And, eke, the Kings of mem'ory grand and glorious,
    who hied them Holy Faith and Reign to spread,
    converting, conquering, and in lands notorious,
    Africk and Asia, devastation made;
    nor less the Lieges who by deeds memorious
    brake from the doom that binds the vulgar dead;
    my song would sound o'er Earth's extremest part
    were mine the genius, mine the Poet's art.

3   Cease the sage Grecian, and the Man of Troy
    to vaunt long Voyage made in bygone day:
    Cease Alexander, Trajan cease to 'joy
    the fame of victories that have pass'd away:
    The noble Lusian's stouter breast sing I,
    whom Mars and Neptune dared not disobey:
    Cease all that antique Muse hath sung, for now
    a better Brav'ry rears its bolder brow.

19

4 And you, my Tagian Nymphs[2], who have create
in me new purpose with new genius firing;
if 't was my joy whilere to celebrate
your founts and stream my humble song inspiring[3],
Oh! lend me here a noble strain elate,
a style grandiloquent that flows untiring;
so shall Apollo for your waves ordain ye
in name and fame ne'er envy Hippokréné.

5 Grant me sonorous accents, fire-abounding,
now serves ne peasant's pipe, ne lustick reed;
but blast of trumpet, long and loud resounding,
that 'flameth heart and hue to fiery deed:
Grant me high strains to suit their Gestes astounding,
your Sons, who aided Mars in martial need;
that o'er the world be sung the glorious song,
if theme so lofty may to verse belong.

6 And Thou! O goodly omen'd trust, all-dear[4]
to Lusitania's olden liberty,
whereon assured esperance we rear
enforced to see our frail Christianity:
Thou, O new terror to the Moorish spear,
the fated marvel of our century,
to govern worlds of men by God so given,
that the world's best be given to God and Heaven:

7 Thou young, thou tender, ever-flourishing bough,
true scion of tree by Christ belovèd more,
than aught that Occident did ever know,
"Cæsarian" or "Most Christian" styled before:
Look on thy 'scutcheon, and behold it show
the present Vict'ory long past ages bore;
Arms which He gave and made thine own to be
by Him assumèd on the fatal tree:[5]

8   Thou, mighty Sovran! o'er whose lofty reign
    the rising Sun rains earliest smile of light;
    sees it from middle firmamental plain;
    and sights it sinking on the breast of Night:
    Thou, whom we hope to hail the blight, the bane
    of the dishonour'd Ishmaèlitish knight;
    and Orient Turk, and Gentoo-misbeliever
    that drinks the liquor of the Sacred River:[6]

9   Incline awhile, I pray, that majesty
    which in thy tender years I see thus ample,
    E'en now prefiguring full maturity
    that shall be shrin'd in Fame's eternal temple:
    Those royal eyne that beam benignity
    bend on low earth: Behold a new ensample
    of hero hearts with patriot pride inflamèd,
    in number'd verses manifold proclaimèd.

10 Thou shalt see Love of Land that ne'er shall own
    lust of vile lucre; soaring towards th' Eternal:
    For 't is no light ambition to be known
    th' acclaimèd herald of my nest paternal
    Hear; thou shalt see the great names greater grown
    of Vavasors who hail thee Lord Supernal:
    So shalt thou judge which were the higher station,
    King of the world or Lord of such a nation.

11 Hark; for with vauntings vain thou shalt not view
    phantastical, fictitious, lying deed
    of lieges lauded, as strange Muses do,
    seeking their fond and foolish pride to feed:
    Thine acts so forceful are, told simply true,
    all fabled, dreamy feats they far exceed;
    exceeding Rodomont, and Ruggiero vain,
    and Roland[7] haply born of Poet's brain,

12 For these I give thee a Nuno, fierce in fight,
     who for his King and Country freely bled;
     an Egas and a Fuas;[8] fain I might
     for them my lay with harp Homeric wed!
     For the twelve peerless Peers again I cite
     the Twelve of England by Magriço led:
     Nay, more, I give thee Gama's noble name,
     who for himself claims all Æneas' fame.

13 And if in change for royal Charles of France,
     or rivalling Cæsar's mem'ories thou wouldst trow,
     the first Afonso see, whose conque'ring lance
     lays highest boast of stranger glories low:
     See him who left his realm th' inheritance
     fair Safety, born of wars that crusht the foe:
     That other John, a knight no fear deter'd,
     the fourth and fifth Afonso, and the third.

14 Nor shall they silent in my song remain,
     they who in regions there where Dawns arise,
     by Acts of Arms such glories toil'd to gain,
     where thine unvanquisht flag for ever flies,
     Pacheco, brave of braves; th' Almeidas twain,
     whom Tagus mourns with ever-weeping eyes;
     dread Albuquerque, Castro stark and brave,
     with more, the victors of the very grave.

15 But, singing these, of thee I may not sing,
     O King sublime! such theme I fain must fear.
     Take of thy reign the reins, so shall my King
     create a poesy new to mortal ear:
     E'en now the mighty burthen hear I ring
     (and speed its terrors over all the sphere!)
     of singular prowess, War's own prodigies,
     in Africk regions and on Orient seas.

16 Casteth on thee the Moor eyne cold with fright,
   in whom his coming doom he views designèd:
   The barb'rous Gentoo, sole to see thy sight
   yields to thy yoke the neck e'en now inclinèd;
   Tethys, of azure seas the sovran right,
   her realm, in dowry hath to thee resignèd;
   and, by thy noble tender beauty won,
   would bribe and buy thee to become her son.

17 In thee from high Olympick halls behold
   themselves, thy grandsires' sprites; far-famèd pair;[9]
   this clad in Peacetide's angel-robe of gold,
   that crimson-hued with paint of battle-glare:
   By thee they hope to see their tale twice told,
   their lofty memo'ries live again; and there,
   when Time thy years shall end, for thee they 'sign
   a seat where soareth Fame's eternal shrine.

18 But, sithence antient Time slow minutes by
   ere ruled the Peoples who desire such boon;
   bend on my novel rashness favouring eye,
   that these my verses may become thine own:
   So shalt thou see thine Argonauts o'erfly
   yon salty argent, when they see it shown
   thou seest their labours on the raging sea:
   Learn even now invok'd of man to be.[10]

19 They walked the water's vasty breadth of blue,
   parting the restless billows on their way;
   fair favouring breezes breathèd soft and true,
   the bellying canvas bulging in their play:
   The seas were sprent with foam of creamy hue,
   flashing where'er the Prows wide open lay
   the sacred spaces of that ocean-plain
   where Proteus' cattle cleave his own domain:

20   When they who hold Olympick luminous height,
     the Gods and Governors of our human race,
     convened in glorious conclave, all unite
     the coming course of Eastern things to trace:
     Treading the glassy dome of lovely light,
     along the Milky Way conjoint they pace,
     gather'd together at the Thunderer's hest,
     and by old Atlas' gentle grandson prest.

21   They leave the reg'iment of the Firm'aments seven,
     to them committed by his high command,
     his pow'r sublime whose thoughtful will hath given
     Order to skies, and angry seas, and land:
     Then instant gather in th' assize of Heaven
     those who are throned on far Arcturus' strand,
     and those that Auster rule, and Orient tides,
     where springs Aurora and clear Phoebus hides.

22   Reposèd there the Sire sublime and digne,
     vibrates whose hand the fierce Vulcanian ray,
     on seat of starry splendour crystalline,
     grand in his lofty gest of sovran sway:
     Respirèd from his brow such air divine,
     that to divine could change dull human clay;
     bearing the crown and sceptre rutilant,
     of clearer stone than clearest diamant.

23   On sparkling seats, with marquetry inlaid
     of gold and pearl-work, sat in lower state
     the minor Godheads, marshall'd and array'd,
     e'en as demanded reason, rank, and rate:
     Highest the seniors of most honour'd grade;
     lower adown the lower Deities sate:
     When thus high Jove the deathless throng addrest
     with awful accents, dealing gravest hest:

24 "Immortal Peoples of the starlit Pole,
   whose seats adorn this constellated sphere;
   if the stout Race of valour-breathing soul
   from Lusus springing still to thought be dear,
   Your high Intelligences lief unroll
   the writ of mighty Fate: her will is clear,
   this Deed to cold Oblivion's shade shall doom
   the fame of Persia, 'Assyria, Greece, and Rome.

25 "To them't was erst, and well you wot it, given,
   albeit a Pow'r so single, simple, small,
   to see the doughty Moor from 'trenchments driven
   where gentle Tagus feeds and floods the vale:
   Then with the dreadful Spaniard have they striven,
   by boon of Heav'n serene ne'er known to fail;
   and urged their fortune's ever-glorious claim
   to victor-trophies hung in fane of Fame.

26 "Godheads! I leave that antique fame unsaid,
   reft from the race of Romulus their foes;
   when, by their warrior Viriátus led,
   so high in Roman wars their names arose:
   Eke leave I mem'ries which to meritèd
   Honour obligèd when for chief they chose
   that perfect Captain, erst a peregrine foe,
   who feign'd a Dæmon in his milk-white Doe.[11]

27 "Now well you see how steel'd their souls to steer
   a fragile barque through dubious wat'ery way,
   by paths unused, and holding nought in fear
   Notus and Afer's force, wax bolder they:
   How whilom ev'ry region left arear,
   where suns or shorten or draw long the day,
   on wings of stubborn will these men be borne
   to sight the cradles of the nascent Morn.

28 "Promised them Fate's eternal covenant,
     whose high commandments none shall dare despise,
     for years full many they shall rule th' extent
     of seas that see the ruddy suns arise.
     On wavy wastes hard winter have they spent;
     o'erworked they come by travailing emprize;
     't were meet we show them, thus it seemeth me,
     the fair new region which they fain would see.

29 "And as their valour, so you trow, defied
     on aspe'rous voyage cruel harm and sore,
     so many changing skies their manhood tried,
     such climes where storm-winds blow and billows roar;
     my sov'ereign mandate 't is, be theirs to ride
     in friendly haven, on the Blackmoor shore;
     whence shall the weary Fleet, with ev'ry need
     garnisht, once more her long-drawn voyage speed."

30 Thus hearing Jupiter's decree pronouncèd,
     each God responsive spoke, in order due,
     contrasting judgment one and all announced
     giving and taking various divers view.
     But Father Bacchus then and there renouncèd,
     homage to Jove's command, who right well knew
     his deeds on Orient-lond would leave no trace,
     were furth'erance granted to the Lusian race.

31 The Fatal Sisters he had heard declare,
     how from Hispanian bounds a hero-band
     should span the pathless deep, and nought should spare
     wherever Doris batheth Indian strand:
     Should with new vict'ories eve'ry deed out-dare
     done or by his or other stranger hand:
     Profound he sorrows lest he lose the glory,
     the name still cel'ebrate in the Nyssan story.

32 He sees, while Indus he of yore hath tamèd,
   Fortune or favou'ring chance had aye denied
   to hear him India's conqueror acclaimèd
   by bardic men who drain Parnassus' tide:
   And now he dreadeth lest a name so famèd
   be doomed for ever in the mire to hide
   of Lethe-fountain, if on Inde debark
   these vagueing Portingalls so strong and stark.

33 But him opposèd Venus, lovely fair,
   whose heart her Lusian sons had won the more,
   since in them seen the qual'ities high and rare,
   the gifts that deckt her Romans dear of yore:
   The heart of valour, and the potent star,
   whose splendour dazzled Tingitánan shore;
   and e'en the musick of their speech appears
   soft bastard Latin to her loving ears.

34 These causes movèd Cytheréa's sprite;
   and more when learnt she that the Fates intendèd
   the Queen of Beauty should be glorious hight
   where'er their warrior sway her sons extendèd.
   Thus He, who fearèd future stain and blight,
   and She, whose heart to honours high pretended
   urge the debate in obstinate strife remaining;
   with fav'ouring friends each rival right maintaining:

35 As the fierce South, or Boreas in the shade
   of sylvan upland where the tree-boles cluster,
   the branches shatt'ering crash through glooming glade
   with horrid hurry and infuriate fluster:
   Roars all the mountain, Echo moans in dread;
   torn is the leaf'ery, hill-heads boil and bluster:
   Such gusty tumults rise amid the Gods
   within Olympus' consecrate abodes.

36 But Mars, for ever wont t'espouse the part
of his dear Goddess, whatsoe'er the case;
or for old love that flicker'd in his heart,
or for the merits of her fighting race;
forth from the Gods upsprang with sudden start:
Stern melancholy markt his gest and face;
the pond'erous pavoise from his gorget hung
behind his shoulders full of wrath he flung:

37 His beavoir'd helmet of the diamant stone
opeing a little, of his strength right sure,
his sense to speak he strode and stood alone
Jupiter facing, armèd, dour and dure:
Then with hard pen'etrant blow he bore adown
his steely spear-heel on the pavement pure;
quakèd the welkin; and Apollo's ray
waxt somewhat wan as though by cold dismay.

38 And thus: "Omnipo'tent Sire! whose awful reign
perforce obeyeth all thy pow'er hath made;
if these, who seek a new half-world to gain,
whose deeds of brav'ery hast with love survey'd,
thou wouldst not guerdon with a shame and stain,
that erst were favoured through the years that fade
listen no longer thou, sole Judge direct,
to glozing reasons all we Gods suspect:

39 "For, did not Reason in this matter show
herself the victim of unmeasur'd fear,
better beseems it Bacchus love bestow
on Lusus' children, once his comrade dear:
But, let this vain and splen'etick purpose go,
since bred of evil stomach; for 't is clear
that alien envy ne'er shall turn to woes
what weal men merit, and the Gods dispose.

28

40   "And thou, O Sire of surest constancy!
     from the determin'd purpose of thy mind
     turn thee not backwards; weakness 't were in thee
     now to desist thee from the thing design'd.
     Send forth thine agile herald, Mercury,
     fleeter than trimmèd shaft, or winnowing wind,
     and show some happy hythe where Rest shall joy
     all weary breasts with news of India nigh."

41   As thus he said, the Sire of sov'reign might
     assented, nodding grave his awful head
     to Mars' opinion, ever fain of fight,
     and o'er the Council show'ers of nectar shed.
     The Galaxy, the pathway glowing bright,
     the Deities all disparting rose to tread;
     royal obeisance making, and the road
     each took returning to his own abode.

42   While thus it happens in th' æthereal reign,
     Omnipotent Olympick height serene,
     the warrior People cut the curvèd main
     Austral and Oriental course between;
     where fronts the face of Æthiopick plain
     far-famed Saint Lawrence Isle[12] ; Sol's brightest sheen
     upon the water-deities rainèd fire,
     who, changed to fishes, 'scaped Typhoeus' ire.

43   The wafting winds so winsome urged their way,
     As though the smiling heav'ens dear friends defended;
     serene the welkin, and the lucid day
     dawn'ed sans a cloud nor aught of risk portended:
     Astern the leek-green point of Prasum[13] lay
     an olden name where Æthiop coast extended;
     when Ocean op'ening broad a vista show'd
     of islets fondled by the circling flood.

29

44 Vasco da Gama, valiant Capitayne,
for derring-do the noblest volunteer,
of not'able courage and of noble strain,
whom smile of constant Fortune loved to cheer;
seeth no reason why he should remain
where shows the shore-line desert, dark and drear:
Once more determined he to tempt the sea;
but as he willèd Fortune nill'ed it be.

45 For look i appeareth a flotilla yonder,
mosquito-craft that cleave the rolling tide;
and with their flowing sails the surges sunder,
from the small island next the cont'inent side:
The crews rejoicing, in their hope and wonder
could gaze on naught save what their hearts had joy'd.
"Who may be these?" each ask'ed him in amaze;
"What law be theirs, what ruler, what their ways?"

46 The boats appearèd in a manner new
long-built and narrow-beamed, for swiftness plan'd;
mats were the wings wherewith they lightly flew
from certain palm-fronds wove by cunning hand:
The people wore that veritable hue,
Phæton's boon to many a burning land,
when work'ed his rashness on the world such ills:
So Padus knows and Lampethusa feels.

47 They come costumèd all in cotton gear,
of hues contrasting, stripèd, chequed, and white;
one zone-girt cloth around the waist they wear,
other they throw on back in airy plight:
Above the waist-band each brown form is bare;
dag-targe and matchet[14] are their arms of fight:
Scull-cap on head; and, as they wend their way,
shriek shrilly shawms, and harsh-voiced trumpets bray.

48 Waving their raiment and their hands they signèd
the Lusitanian folk to wait awhile:
but our light Prores their course had now inclinèd
to strike where shelter'd by the nearest isle:
Soldiers and sailors in one toil conjoinèd
as though were here the period of their toil:
They take in sail, and strike the lofty spar,
and Ocean, anchor-smit, froths high in air.

49 Nor had they anchor'd, when the stranger race
the shrouds upswarming ready footing gainèd;
joyous they cluster glad of gest and face;
our Captain gracious greeting gives unfeignèd.
He bids incontinent the board to grace
with vinous liquor first Lyæus drainèd;
they crown the chrystal cups, the proffer'd wine
Phæton's scorchèd folk nowise decline.

50 Afeasting cheery all the guests enquirèd
in Arab language, Whence had come their hosts?
Who were they? Where their land? What they desired?
What seas their keels had cut and conn'd what coasts?
The valiant Lusians answered with required
discretion, and eschewing foolish boasts,
"We are the Occidental Portughese;
And, seeking Orient lands, we sail the seas.

51 "We now have coasted, running Ocean o'er,
Callisto's Arctick and th' Antarctick lands;
our course hath circled Africk's winding shore;
strange skies exploring and yet stranger strands:
Ours is a potent King, loved evermore,
and we so prize his praise and his commands,
with mien right joyful, not the sea and sky,
but even Ach'eron Lake we dare defy.

31

52 "And wend we seeking by his royal will
where farthest Indus wat'ereth Eastern plain:
For him through wild wide waves we hoist the sail,
where ugly seals and ores deform the Main.
But Reason tells us that ye may not fail
to answer, an of Truth your souls be fain,
"Who are ye? What this land wherein ye wone?
And sign of India is to you beknown? "

53 "We live," an island-man thus answ'ring said,
"aliens in land and law and eke in blood;
where native races are by nature bred,
a lawless, loutish, and unreasoning brood.
We hold his certain Law, that Holy Seed,
springing from Abram's loins, who hath subdued
the nations subject to his sign'ory true;
by sire a Gentile and by mother Jew,[15]

54 "This little island, where we now abide,
of all this seaboard is the one sure place
for ev'ry merchantman that stems the tide,
from Quiloa[16] or Sofalah or Mombas:
Here, as 'tis necessary, long we've tried
to house and home us, like its proper race:
In fine to find you with the facts you seek,
man calls our little island ' Mozambique.'

55 "And, as far-faring now ye come to view
Indie Hydaspes and his burning board,
hence ye shall bear a Pilot, sure and true,
whose skill the safest guidance shall afford:
'T were also well, ere you your toils renew,
vittaile to ship, and let our island-lord,
who governeth this land, his guests behold,
and stock with needed store each empty hold."

56 His speech thus spake the Moor, and took his leave,
   he and his meiny where the bátels lay:
   formal farewells to chief and crews he gave,
   exchanging congees with due courtesy.
   Now weary Phoebus in the western wave
   had stalled the chrystal chariot of the Day,
   and gave his bright-brow'd sister charge t'illume
   the vast of Earth while lasted nightly gloom.

57 Aboard the way-worn Fleet blithe sped the night
   in careless joyaunce recking nought of fear;
   for the far land which long had 'scaped their sight
   at length gave tidings, and at last lay near.
   Now to take notice 'gins each curious wight
   of the strange people's manners, ways, and gear,
   and much they marvell'ed how the sect misguided
   o'er Earth's broad surface far and wide abided.

58 Rained Luna's radiance shedding rutilant showers
   o'er Neptune's wavelets tipt with silver sheen:
   And like the May-mead fleckt with daisy flowers
   sprent with its sparkling stars the sky was seen:
   The blust'ring storm-winds slept in distant bowers,
   Antres obscure in regions peregrine;
   yet on th' Armada's decks a weapon'd guard
   kept, as so long they wont, good watch and ward.

59 But when Aurora with her marquetry
   'gan strew the glorious honours of her head
   o'er the clear Heav'ens, and oped the ruddy way
   to bright Hyperion rising from his bed;
   lief is the Fleet to dress in brave array
   of flags, and goodly awnings gay to spread,
   that all may greet with holiday and hail
   that island-lord who came with flowing sail.

60 He came right merrily o'er the Main, and sought
to view our nimble Lusitanian fleet;
bringing his country-cates, for t'was his thought
in the fierce foreigner perchance to meet
the race inhuman, which hath ever fought
to change its Caspian caves for happier seat
in Asian cont'inent; and, by Will Divine,
of rule imperial robbèd Constantine.[17]

61 With glad reception our Commander meets
the Moorish chieftain and his whole convóy;
whom with a gift of richest gear he greets
whereof a store was shipped for such employ:
He gives him rich conserves, he gives, rare treats,
the liquors hot which fill man's heart with joy.
Good be the gifts the Moor contented thinks,
but more the sweetmeats prizes, most the drinks.

62 The sailor-people sprung from Lusus' blood
in wond'ering clusters to the ratlines clung;
noting the stranger's novel mode and mood
with his so barb'arous and perplexed tongue.[18]
Sometime the wily Moor confusèd stood
eyeing the garb, the hue, the fleet, the throng;
and asked, with questions manifold assailing,
if they from Turkey-land, perchance, were hailing.

63 He further tells them how he longs to see
what books their credence, law and faith contain;
if these conforming with his own agree
or were, as well he ween'd, of Christian grain:
Nay more, that hidden naught from him may be,
he prayed the Captain would be pleased t' ordain
that be displayèd every puissant arm
wherewith the for'eigners work their foemen harm.

64 To this the doughty Chieftain deals reply,
     through one that óbscure jargon knowing well:
     "Illustrious Signior! I fain will try
     all of ourselves, our arms, our creed to tell.
     Nor of the country, kith or kin am I
     of irksome races that in Turkey dwell;
     my home is warlike Europe and I wend
     Seeking the far-famed lands of farthest Inde.

65 "I hold the law of One by worlds obey'd,
     by visible things and things invisible;
     He who the hemispheres from naught hath made,
     with sentient things and things insensible:
     Who with vitup'erate foul reproach bewray'd
     was doomed to suffer death insufferable;
     And who, in fine, by Heav'n to Earth was given,
     that man through Him might rise from Earth to Heaven.

66 "Of this God-Man most highest, infinite,
     The books thou wouldst behold I have not brought:
     we stand excused of bringing what men write
     on paper, when in sprite 'tis writ and wrought.
     But an with weapons wouldst refresh thy sight,
     As thou hast askèd, I deny thee nought;
     A friend to friends I show them; and I vow
     ne'er wouldst be shown their temper as my foe."

67 This said, he bids his armourers diligent
     bring arms and armour for the Moorman viewer:
     Come sheeny harness, corselets lucident,
     the fine-wove mail-coat and plate-armour sure;
     shields decorate with 'scutcheons different,
     bullets and spingards, th' ice-brook's temper pure;
     bows, quivers furnisht with the grinded pile,
     the sharp-edged partizan, the good brown

68 bill: Brought are the fiery bombs, while they
   prepare
   sulph'urous stink-pots and grenades of fire:
   But them of Vulcan biddeth he to spare
   their dread artill'ery belching flames in ire;
   naught did that gentle gen'erous spirit care
   with fear the few and fearful folk t' inspire,
   and right his reas'oning: 'Twere a boast too cheap
   to play the Lyon on the seely Sheep.

69
   But from whate'er th' observant Moorman heard,
   and from whate'er his prying glance could see,
   a settled deadly hate his spirit stir'd,
   and evil crave of treacherous cowardrie:
   No sign of change he showed in gest or word;
   but with a gay and gallant feigning he
   vowèd in looks and words to treat them fair,
   till deeds his daring purpose could declare.

70
   The Captain prayed him Pilots to purvey,
   his Squadron far as Indian shore to guide;
   so should with wealthy hire and worthy pay
   the labourer's toil and moil be gratified.
   Promised the Moorman sorely led astray
   by ven'omous heart and with such poyson'd pride,
   that Death in place of Pilot, at that hour,
   his hand had given an it had the power.

71
   So hot that hatred, sharp that enmity,
   wherewith his spirit 'gainst his guests was fraught,
   that knew them followers of that verity
   by the Seed of David to our fathers taught.
   Oh darkling secret of Eternity,
   whereof man's judgment may encompass naught!
   Why should they never lack perfidious foe,

36

72 who such fair symbols of Thy friendship show?
    At length, surrounded by his crafty crew,
    the treachour Moorman from our ships took leave,
    on all bestowing bel-accoyle untrue,
    with fair, glad phrase designèd to deceive.
    Soon o'er the narrow way his barquelets flew;
    and, landing safely from Neptunian wave,
    the Moorman, whom his suite obsequious greet,
    regains his homestead and his wonted seat .

73

    From Æther's radiant seat Thebes' mighty son,
    The God two-mother'd, sprung from father-thigh,
    seeing the Lusian host had straight begun
    the Moorman's hate and horror to defy,
    fixt ev'ry project some foul feat upon,
    by which the stranger host might surely die:
    And while the plot his spirit importunèd,
    thus in soliloquy the God communèd:

74

    "Fate hath determinèd in olden time,
    that conquests, fit the self of Fame t' outface,
    these Portingalls shall claim in ev'ry clime
    where India rears her war-ennobled race:
    Shall only I, the son of sire sublime,
    I, whom such gen'erous gifts and guerdons grace,
    suffer that favouring Fate success assure
    to men whose labours shall my name obscure?

75

    "Erst willed the Gods,[19] who willed away the right
    to Philip's son, that o'er this Orient part
    he hold such power, and display such might
    which bound the world 'neath yoke of angry Mart:
    But shall I tamely suffer Fate's despight,
    who lends these weaklings pow'er of arm and art,
    Macedon's hero, Roman brave and I

37

76 before the Lusian name be doomed to fly?
"This must not, shall not be! ere he arrive
this froward Captain at his fancied goal,
such cunning machinations I'll contrive
never shall Orient parts his sight console
And now to Earth! where I will keep alive
the fire of fury in the Moorish soul;
for him shall Fortune with success indue,
who on Occasion keepeth fixèd view."

77

He spoke infuriate, nay, well-nigh insane,
and straight he 'lighted on the Negro shore;
where, mortal gest and human vesture tane,
he made for Prasum Headland famed of yore:
Better to weave his web of wily bane,
he changed his nat'ural shape until it wore
a Moorman's likeness, known in Mozambíque,
a crafty greybeard, favoured of the Shaykh.

78

And, entering him to rede at hour and time
most fitting deemèd for designed wile,
a tale of pyracy he told and crime,
wrought by the strangers harbour'd in his isle:
How all the res'ident nations maritime
bruited reports of battle, death, and spoil,
at ev'ery haven, where the foreigner past
who with false pacts of peace his anchors cast.

79

"And, know thou further" (quoth the Moor) "'tis said,
anent these Christian knaves sanguinolent,
that, so to speak, they garred the waves run red
scathing with fire and steel where'er they went:
Far-framèd plottings, certès, have been laid
against ourselves, for 'tis their whole intent
our homes to rifle, to destroy our lives,

38

80 enchain our children and enslave our wives.
  "I also learnèd how determined be
  forthwith for wat'ering to'ward the land to steer,
  this Captain, with a doughty company;
  for evil purpose ever 'getteth fear.
  Go, too, and take thy men-at-arms with thee,
  waiting him silent in well-ambusht rear;
  so shall his People, landing unawares
  fall ready victims to thy ruse and snares.

81

  "And, even should they by this not'able feat
  fail to be scatter'd, shatter'd, wholly slain,
  I have imaginèd a rare conceit
  of marv'ellous cunning which thy heart shall gain:
  A pilot bid be brought of wily wit
  nor less astute to lay the skilful train,
  who shall the stranger lead where bane and bale,
  loss, death, destruction wait on every sail."

82

  These words of wisdom hardly had he stay'd,
  when the Moor-chieftain, old in fraud and wise,
  fell on his bosom and full glad obey'd,
  such counsel finding favour in his eyes
  Then instant faring forth he ready made
  for the base warfare bellicose supplies;
  so might the Lusians see, when gained the shore,
  the wisht-for waters turned to crimson gore.

83

  And, eke, he seeketh, such deceit to speed,
  a Moslem Loadsman who the prows shall guide,
  shrewd, subtle villain, prompt to wicked deed,
  whereon for dangerous feat he most relied:
  Him he commands the Lusitan to lead,
  and with him hug such coasts and stem such tide,
  that e'en escaping present dangers all

84 he further wend, and whence none rise shall fall.
Already lit Apollo's morning ray
the Nabathæan mounts with rosy light,
when dight was Gama and his stout array
by sea for wat'ering on the land t' alight:
Their boats the soldiers armed for fight and fray
as though they scented tricks of Moslem spite:
Here was suspicion easy, for the wise
bear a presaging heart that never lies.

85

Further, the messenger who went ashore
to claim the promise of the needful guide,
heard tone of battle when replied the Moor,
though none had deemèd he had thus replied.
Wherefore, and recking 'right how sore their stowre
who in perfidious enemy confide,
he fared forearm'd, forewarn'd, and risking nought,
in his three launches, all the boats he brought.

86

But now the Moormen, stalking o'er the strand
to guard the waf'ery stores the strangers need;
this, targe on arm and assegai in hand,
that, with his bended bow, and venom'd reed,
wait till the warlike People leap to land:
Far stronger forces are in ambush hid;
and, that the venture may the lighter seem
a few decoys patrol about the stream.

87

Along the snow-white sandy marge advance
the bellic Moors who beck their coming foes;
they shake the shield and poise the per'ilous lance,
daring the warrior Portughuese to close.
The gen'erous People with impatient glance
the ban-dogs eye who dare their fangs expose:
They spring ashore so deftly no man durst

88 say who the soldier that touch'ed land the first.
    As in the gory ring some gallant gay,
    on his fair ladye-love with firm-fixt eyes,
    seeketh the furious bull and bars the way,
    bounds, runs, and whistles; becks and shouts and cries:
    The cruel monster sans a thought's delay,
    Low'ering its hornèd front, in fury flies
    with eyne fast closed; and, roaring horrid sound,
    throws, gores, and leaves him lifeless on the ground:

89

    Lo! from the launches sudden flash the lights
    of fierce artill'ery with infuriate blare;
    the leaden bullet kills, the thunder frights,
    and hissing echoes cleave the shrinking air:
    Now break the Moormen's hearts and haughtysprites,
    whose blood cold curdleth with a ghastly fear:
    The skulking coward flies his life to save,
    and dies to Death exposed the daring brave.

90

    Withal the Portingalls are not content;
    fierce Vict'ory urging on, they smite and slay:
    The wall-less, undefended settlement
    they shell and burn and make an easy prey.
    The Moors their raid and razzia sore repent,
    who lookt for vict'ory won in cheaper way:
    Now they blaspheme the battle, cursing wild
    th' old meddling fool, and her that bare such child.

91

    Still, in his flight, the Moorman draweth bow,
    but forceless, frighted, flurried by alarms,
    showers of ashlar, sticks, and stones they throw;
    their madding fury 'ministereth arms:
    Now from their islet-homesteads flocking row
    toward the mainland, trembling terr'ified swarms.
    They pass apace and cut the narrow Sound,

41

92 The thin sea-arm, which runs their islet round.[20]
    These ply the deeply-laden almadie,[21]
    those cut the waves and dil'igent swim the Main
    some choke 'neath bending surge of surfy sea,
    some drink the brine, out-puffing it again.
    The crank canoes, wherein the vermin flee,
    are torn by smaller bombards' fiery rain.
    Thuswise, in fine, the Portingalls chastise
    their vile, malicious, treach'erous enemies.

93
    Now to the squadron, when the day was won,
    rich with their warlike spoils the Braves retire,
    and ship at leisure water all their own,
    none meet offence where none t' offend desire.
    The Moors heart-broken vainly make their moan,
    old hatreds 'flaming with renewèd fire;
    and, hopeless to revenge such foul defeat,
    nourish the fairest hopes of fresh deceit.

94
    To proffer truce repentant gives command
    the Moor who ruleth that iniqu'ous shore;
    nor do the Lusitanians understand
    that in fair guise of Peace he proffers War:
    For the false Pilot sent to show the land
    who ev'ry evil will embosom'd bore,
    only to guide them deathwards had been sent;
    such was the signal of what peace was meant.

95
    The Capitayne who now once more inclìne'd
    on wonted way and 'custom'd course to hie,
    fair weather favouring with propitious wind,
    and wend where India's long-wisht regions lie;
    received the Helmsman for his ill design'd
    (who greeted was with joyous courtesy;)
    and, giv'en his answer to the messenger,

96 in the free gale shakes out his sailing gear.
Dismist by such device the gallant Fleet
divideth Amphitritè's wavy way;
the Maids of Nereus troop its course to greet,
faithful companions, debonnair and gay:
The Captain, noways doubting the deceit
planned by the Moorman to secure his prey,
questions him largely, learning all he knows
of gen'eral Inde and what each seaboard shows.

97

But the false Moorman, skilled in all the snares
which baleful Bacchus taught for such emprize,
new loss by death or prison-life prepares,
ere India's seaboard glad their straining eyes:
The hythes of India dil'igent he declares,
to frequent queries off'ring fit replies:
For, holding faithful all their pilot said
the gallant People were of nought afraid.

98

And eke he telleth, with that false intent,
whereby fell Sinon baulked the Phrygian race
of a near-lying isle, that aye had lent
to Christian dwellers safest dwelling-place.
Our Chief, of tidings fain, gave due attent
of ear so gladly to these words of grace,
that with the richest gifts he bade the Guide
lead him to regions where such men abide.

99

E'en so that losel Moorman had designèd,
as the confiding Christian begged and bade;
knowing his islet was of old assignèd
to the malignant sons of Mafamed:
Here he foresees deceit with death combinèd,
for-that in pow'r and force the place outweigh'd
weaker Mozámbic; and that islet's name

43

100 is Quiloa bruited by the blast of Fame.
Thither th' exulting Squadron lief would steer:
but the fair god Cythéra loves to greet,
seeing its certain courses changed to near
the coasts where Doom of Death awaits defeat,
nills that the people, loved with love so dear,
such dreadful fates on shore so distant meet;
and, raising adverse gales, she drives them wide
from the foul goal where guides that felon guide.

101
Now when the caitiff Moor could not but know
that in this matter useless was his guile,
seeking to deal another dev'ilish blow,
and still persistent in his purpose vile,
he urgeth, since the winds' and currents' flow
had borne them on parforce full many a mile,
they near another island, and its race
Christian and Moor hold common dwelling-place.

102
Here too with every word the liar lied,
as by his reg'iment he in fine was bound;
for none who Christ adore could there abide,
only the hounds who worship false Mahound.
The Captain trustful to his Moorish guide,
veering the sails was making for the Sound:
But, as his guardian Goddess leave denieth,
he shuns the river-bar, and outside lieth.

103
So near that Islet lay along the land,
nought save a narrow channel stood atween;
and rose a City thronèd on the strand,
which from the margent of the seas was seen;
fair-built with lordly buildings tall and grand,
as from its offing showèd all its sheen:
Here ruled a monarch for long years high famèd;

104 Islet and City are Mombasah namèd.[22]
  And when the Captain made that happy shore,
  with strangest joyaunce, in the hope to view
  baptizèd peoples, and to greet once more
  dear Christian men, as sware his guide untrue;
  lo! boats come bearing, the blue waters o'er
  their King's good greeting who the stranger knew:
  For long had Bacchus of th' event advisèd,
  in other Moorman's shape and form disguisèd.

105

  Friendly the message which the foemen brought,
  beneath whose surface covered venom lay;
  for deadly hostile was their ev'ry thought
  and soon the hidden fraud uncover'd they.
  Oh dreadful dangers with destruction fraught!
  Oh line of life-tide, never certain way!
  where'er his dearest hope poor mortal hoardeth,
  such scant security life e'er affordeth!

106

  By sea such tempests, such sore injury,
  with Death so often showing near and sure!
  By land such warfare, such foul treachery,
  so much of curst necessities t'endure!
  Ah! where shall weary man take sanctuary,
  where live his little span of life secure?
  and 'scape of Heav'n serene th' indignant storms
  that launch their thunders at us earthen worms?

CANTO II

1   'Twas now the period when the Planet bright,
     whose race distinguisheth the hours of day,
     did at his longed-for, tardy goal alight,
     veiling from human eyne his heav'enly ray;
     and of his Ocean-home, deep hid from sight,
     the God of Night-tide oped the portal-way;
     when the false crafty folk came flocking round
     the ships, whose anchors scarce had bit the ground.

2   'Mid them a villain, who had undertane
     the task of deadly damage, spake aloud:
     "O val'orous Captain, who hast cut the reign
     of Neptune, and his salty plain hast plow'd,
     the King who governeth this island, fain
     to greet thy coming, is so pleased and proud,
     he wisheth nothing save to be thy host,
     to see thee, and supply what need ye most.

3   "And, as he burneth, with extreme desire,
     so famed a pers'onage to behold and greet,
     he prays suspicion may no fear inspire;
     but cross the bar-line, thou and all thy Fleet:
     And, sith by voyage long men greatly tire,
     thy gallant crew by travel-toil is beat,
     he bids thee welcome to refit on land
     as, cèrtes, Nature must such rest command.

4 "And if thou wendest seeking merchandise
   got in the golden womb of the Levant,
   Cinnamon, cloves, and biting spiceries,
   health-dealing drug, or rare and excellent plant,
   or, if thou lust for sparkling stones of price,
   the Ruby fine, the rigid Diamant,
   hence shall thou bear such full, abundant store,
   that e'en thy Fancy shall affect no more."

5 Unto the Herald straight our Chief replieth,
   grateful acknowledging the Royal hest;
   and saith, that seeing Sol now seawards hicth
   he may not enter as becomes a guest:
   But, when returning light shall show where lieth
   the way sans danger, with a fearless breast,
   the Royal orders he will list fulfil,
   a Lord so gracious hath claim higher still.

6 He questions further, an the land contain
   christenèd Peoples, as the Pilot sware:
   The cunning Herald who ne'er speaks in vain
   voucheth that Christian men dwell mostly there.
   Thus doth he banish from our Captain's brain
   the cautious phantasies of doubt and fear:
   Wherefore the Gama straightways 'gan to place
   Faith in that faithless unbeliever-race.[23]

7 And, as condemnèd felons he had brought,
   convíct of mortal crime and shameful deed,
   who might in sim'ilar cases danger-fraught
   be ventured where the common weal had need;
   a twain of wily, well-tried wits he sought,
   bade them the Moorman's craft and trick'eries heed,
   go spy the City's power, and seek to see
   whether desirèd Christians there may be.

8   Fair gifts he gave them for the Royal hand,
    to quit the goodly will the greeting show'd,
    by him held sure and firm and clear and bland,
    whereas 'twas cleanly of a contrary mode.
    Now all the rout perfidious and nefand,
    quitting the Squadron o'er the waters row'd:
    With gladsome, joyous gestures, all deceit,
    The pair of shipmates on the shore they greet.

9   And when in presence of the King convey'd,
    the gifts they gave, and message did present,
    far less they witness'd, as 'bout town they stray'd,
    than what they wanted on their work intent;
    the shrewd sagacious Moors pretences made
    to veil from sight what they to see were sent;
    for where reigns Malice there we ever find
    the fear of Malice in a neighbour's mind.

10   But He,[24] for ever fair, for ever young
    in form and feature, born of mothers twain
    by wondrous birth-rite; and whose wilful tongue
    would work the Navigators' ban and bane—
    dwelt in a house the City-folk among,
    of form and vestment human; who did feign
    to be a Christian priest, and here had raisèd
    a sumptuous altar where he prayed and praisèd.

11   There had he limnèd, figuring aright
    the Holy Ghost's high heavenly portraiture;
    hover'd a Dove, in snowy plume bedight,
    o'er the sole Phoenix, Mary, Virgin pure:
    The Saintly Company was shown to sight,
    the Dozen, in that sore discomfiture,
    as when, taught only by the Tongues that burnt
    with lambent fire, man's varied tongues they learnt.

12 Thither conducted either Comrade went,
    where hateful Bacchus stood in lies array'd;
    and rose their spirits, while their knees were bent
    before the God who sways the worlds He made.
    The perfumed incense by Panchaia sent,
    fuming its richest scent, o'th' altar laid
    Thyóne's Son; and now they view, forsooth,
    the god of Lies adore the God of Truth.

13 Here was receiv'd, for kindly rest at night,
    with ev'ry mode of good and trusty greeting,
    the twain of Christians, who misween'd the rite,
    th'unholy show of holy counterfeiting.
    But soon as Sol returning rained his light
    on sombre Earth, and in one instant fleeting
    forth from the ruddy-dyed horizon came
    the Spouse Tithonian with her front aflame:

14 Return the Moormen bearing from the land
    the Royal licence, with the Christian pair,
    that disembarkèd by our Chief's command,
    for whom the King feign'ed honest friendship fair:
    The Portingall, assured no plot was plan'd,
    and seeing scanty fear of scathe or snare
    when Christian peoples in the place abode,
    to stem the salty river straightway stood.

15 Advised him the scouts dispatcht ashore
    that holy clerk and altars met their sight;
    and how receivèd them the friendly Moor
    while Night's cloud-shadowèd mantle cloaked the light;
    Nay, that both Lord and Liege no feeling bore,
    save what in kindness took a dear delight,
    for, certès, nothing told of doubt or fear,
    where proofs of friendship showè sure and clear.

16 Whereon the noble Gama hied to greet
    gladly the Moors that up the bulwarks plied;
    for lightly trusteth sprite without deceit;
    and gallant souls in goodly show confide.
    The crafty people on the Flagship meet,
    mooring their light canoes along her side:
    Merrily trooped they all, because they wot
    the wisht-for prizes have become their lot.

17 The cautious war-men gather on the land
    arms and'munitions; that whene'er th'Armade
    ride at her anchors near the riv'erine strand
    the work of boarding may be readier made:
    With deepest treachery the traitors plan'd
    for those of Lusus such an ambuscade,
    that reckless of the coming doom they pay
    the blood-debt dating from Mozámbic Bay.

18 Weighed are the biting anchors, rising slow,
    while'customed capstan-songs and shouts resound;
    only the foresails to the gale they throw
    as for the buoyèd bar the Ships are bound:
    But Erycína fair, from ev'ry foe
    aye glad to guard and guide her Race renown'd,
    seen the black ambush big with deadly bane,
    flies from the welkin shaft-swift to the Main.

19 She musters Nereus' maidens fair and blonde,
    with all the meiny of the sea-blue race;
    the Water-princes her commandment own'd,
    for the salt Ocean was her natal place:
    Then, told the reason why she sought the lond,
    with her whole bevy forth she set apace,
    to stay the Squadron ere it reach the bourne
    whence ne'er a Traveller may to life return.

20 On, on they hurry, scattering high the spray,
    and lash with silvern trains the spumy White:
    Doto's soft bosom breasts the briny way
    with hotter pressure than her wonted plight
    Springs Nisé, while Neríne seeks the fray
    clearing the crystal wavelets nimble light:
    The bending billows open wide a path,
    fearing to rouse the hurrying Nereids' wrath.

21 Borne on a Triton's shoulders rides in state
    with fiery gesture, Dionæa fair;
    nor feels the bearer that delicious weight,
    superb his cargo of such charms to bear:
    Now draw they nearer where stiff winds dilate
    the bellicose Armada's sailing gear:
    They part, and sudden with their troops surround
    the lighter vessels in the vayward bound.

22 Girt by her nymphs the Goddess lays her breast
    against the Flagship's prow, and others close
    the harbour-entrance; such their sudden gest
    the breeze through bellied canvas vainly blows:
    With tender bosom to tough timber prest
    she drives the sturdy ship that sternward goes:
    Her circling Nereids raise and urge afar
    the threatened victim from the hostile bar.

23 E'en as to nesty homes the prov'ident Ants,
    their heavy portion'd burthens haling slow,
    drill their small legions, hostile combatants,
    'gainst hostile Winter's war of frost and snow:
    There are their travails given to their wants,
    there puny bodies mighty spirits show:
    Not otherwise the Nymphs from fatal end
    labour the Portughuezes to defend.

24 Their force prevails; astern the Flagship falleth,
   'spite all aboard her raising fearful shout;
   boiling with rage the Crew each yardarm hauleth
   to port and starboard putting helm about:
   Apoop the cunning Master vainly bawleth,
   seeing that right toforn upon his route,
   uprears a sea-girt rock its awful head,
   and present shipwreck fills his soul with dread.

25 But as loud call and clamour 'gan uprise
   from the rude sailor toiling hard and keen;
   the Moors are frighted by th'unusèd cries,
   as though they sighted Battle's horrid scene.
   None know the reason of such hot surprise;
   none know in sim'ilar press whereon to lean;
   they hold their treach'erous felon tricks are known,
   and present tortures must their crime atone.

26 Lo! with a panick fear themselves they flung
   in the swift-sailing barklets which they brought:
   These high uplifted on the billows hung,
   those deep in water diving safety sought:
   Sudden from starboard and from port they sprung,
   by dread of visionary sights distraught;
   for all would rather tempt the cruel tide,
   for none in mercies of their foes confide.

27 Of such a fashion in the sylvan Mere
   the Frogs, a brood of Lycian blood whilòme,
   when fall of coming foot perchance they hear,
   while all incautious left their wat'ery home,
   wake marish-echoes hopping here and there
   to 'scape the perils threat'ening death and doom;
   and, all ensconcèd in the well-known deep
   nought but their small black heads 'bove water peep:

28 So fly the Moors; the Loadsman who alone
    the Ships in deadly imminent risk had led,
    deeming his hateful plans to all beknown,
    plunged in the bitter depths and swimming fled.
    But as her course had missed the steadfast stone,
    where every hope of darling life were dead,
    eftsoons our Amm'irall doth her anchor throw,
    and, near her, furling sail, the rest come to.

29 Observant Gama, seen this sudden sight
    of Moorish strangeness, and surprised to view
    his Pilot flying with accusing flight,
    divines the plottings of that bestial crew:
    And when ne hindrance showèd, ne the might
    of tides that onwards bore, or winds that blew,
    yet that his Flagship forged ahead no more,
    the Marvel hailing thus he'gan implore:—

30 "Oh Chance, strange, passing strange, that gave no sign!
    Oh wondrous Godsend shown so clear, so plain!
    Oh fellest treason baffled inopine!
    Oh hostile Paynims, false, perfidious strain!
    Who of such desp'erate devilish design
    by mortal wisdom could escape the bane,
    unless there throned in Heav'en the Sovran Guard
    to weak humanity strong aid award?

31 "Right well hath provèd Providence on high,
    the scanty safety by these Ports purvey'd:
    Right well appearance showeth every eye,
    how all our confidence hath been betrayed:
    But since Man's wit and wisdom vainly try
    to sound these feints and foils so deeply laid,
    O Thou, Almighty Guard! to guard him deign
    who sans Thine aid himself would guard in vain!

32 "And if Thy holy ruth so condescend
   to save this People peregrine and poor,
   who on Thy grace and goodness sole depend,
   to force salvation from the false fell Moor;
   vouchsafe, O Lord, our weary course shall end
   at some fair Harbour, shelter'd and secure;
   or show the distant shores we pine to see,
   since all this sailing is for serving Thee."

33 The piteous prayer smote the loving ears
   of Dionæa fair; her heart was painèd;
   she left her Nymphs, all bathed in yearning tears,
   who by her sudden flight perplext remainèd:
   Now she had thrid the luminous planet-spheres,
   now the third Heaven's gateway she had gainèd;
   on, onward still to the sixth sphere, the throne
   where high All-Father sits and reigns alone.

34 And, as her way affronting, forth she hied,
   her ev'ry gesture such a grace expirèd,
   Stars, Skies and Æther's circumambient tide,
   and all that saw her with love-fire were firèd.
   Those eyne wherein Dan Cupid aye doth nide,
   such vital spirits in all life inspirèd;
   the frigid Poles with torrid ardours burnèd,
   and spheres of Arctic frost to flame were turned.[25]

35 And with more love to move her Sovereign
   Sire, who aye lov'd her with a constant will,
   herself she shows as to the Trojan swain
   she showed of old on Ida's bosky hill.
   If her the Hunter who the form of man
   lost, seeing Dian in the glassy rill,
   had seen, he ne'er had died by rav'ening hound,
   erst slain by a sorer and a surer wound.

36   Wander'd the crispy threads of wavy gold
     adown a bosom shaming virgin snow:
     Her milk-hued breasts with ev'ry movement roll'd
     where Love lay sporting but did nowhere show:
     Flames with far-flashing fire the Zone's white fold
     wherewith the Boy gar'd ev'ry heart to glow:
     while round those columns' polisht curves were climbing
     Desires, like ivy parent-trunk entwining.

37   A filmy Cendal[26] winds around her waist,
     which del'icate sense conceals by modest veiling;
     and yet not all conceal'd, nor all confest,
     the veil, red-blushing lilies oft revealing:
     With warmer fondness still to 'flame his breast
     she woos his sight with secret charms assailing:
     Now all Olympus shakes with jealous jars,
     rage burneth Vulcan, Love inflameth Mars.

38   The while her angel-semblance showeth blended
     with smiles a sadness in the sweetest way;
     like some fair Ladye by rude swain offended
     incautious rough while playing am'orous play;
     who laughs and laughing pouts with wrath pretended
     passing withouten pause from grave to gay;
     thus she, the Goddess who no rival heedeth,
     softer than sad before her Father pleadeth.

39   "Aye had I deemèd, mighty Father mine,
     in whatsoe'er my loving breast preferrèd,
     to find thee kind and affable and benign,
     e'en though of hostile heart the hate were stirrèd:
     But as I see thine ire to me incline,
     Ire undeserv'ed,— to thee I ne'er have errèd,—
     let Bacchus triumph with his wicked will;
     while in his weal I sit and wail mine ill.

40 "This Folk, these Sons of me, for whom I pour
the tear that trickleth bootless 'fore thy sight,
whose woe, since wish'd them well, I work the more
when my good wishes but thy wrath excite:
For them I weep, for them thine aid implore,
and thus, in fine, with adverse fate I fight:
But now, because my love ill-fortune bears,
I will to will them ill and weal be theirs.

41 "Yet thus to perish by that wild-beast race,
for i have been" [27]*** Whereon, all lovely flows
the burning tear-drop beading down her face,
as pearled with rory dew fresh shines the Rose:
Silent awhile, as though her plea for grace
the portals of her teeth list not disclose
she had pursued; but ere a word she said
the potent Thund'erer further plaint forbade:

42 And, moved to pity by such gentle powers,
pow'ers made to move the heart of Tyger dure,
with beaming smile, as when the sky that lowers
waxeth serene, and clears the lift obscure;
he dries his Daughter's welling tears, and showers
warm kisses on her cheeks and neck snow-pure;
in mode that had the place been lere and lone
a pair of Cupids had Olympus known.

43 And, face approaching to the face he prizèd,
whereat the sobbing tears the faster flow;
e'en as some yeanling by the nurse chastisèd
weepeth caresst with louder feint of woe:
To soothe her troubled bosom he devisèd
the future fortunes of her sons to show,
unripping thus from Fate's impregnate womb
He opes the mysteries of the things to come:—

44 "Thou fairest Daughter mine! throw far thy fear
   lest to thy Lusians happen harm indign;
   nor deem my spirit holdeth aught so dear,
   as the sad waters of these sovereign eyne:
   Thou shalt behold, my Daughter, hear me swear,
   the Greek and Roman dimm'd of all his shine,
   by Gestes illustrious this thy Hero-race
   Shall dare and do in Eastern dwelling-place.

45 "If glib Ulysses e'er to flee was fated
   a life-long slav'ery on Ogygia-shore;
   and if Antenor's fortune penetrated
   Illyric bays, Timavus' fount t' explore;
   e'en if thy pious Æneas navigated
   where seas round Scylla and Charybdis roar;
   thy nobler scions higher grade shall win,
   shall add new worlds to worlds of older men.

46 "Valvartes and cities and the tow'ering wall
   built by their valour, Daughter, thou shalt see:
   Shalt see the Turk, deem'ed bravest brave of all,
   from their dread prowess forcèd aye to flee:
   Shalt see of Inde the free-born monarchs fall
   and own their mightier King's supremacy:
   And when, in fine, they wield the full command
   shall dawn a Higher Law[28] for every land.

47 "Him shalt thou see, who now in hurrièd flight
   fares distant Indus through such fears to find,
   make vasty Neptune tremble with affright,
   and crisp his wavy waste sans breath of wind.
   Oh Chance ne'er seen! Oh wonder-teeming Sight!
   this Quake of Water with plat calm combin'd!
   Oh valiant race, with loftiest thought inbred,
   whom Earth's four El'ements must regard with dread![29]

57

48 "This Land, that water hath to them denied,
shalt see affording surest Hythe, where spent
by their long voyaging, shall rest and ride
Argosies bound from utmost Occident.
In fine, this seaboard all, that futile tried
death-snare to weave, shall pay obedient
toll, tythe, and tribute, knowing vain it were
to beard the Lusian Lyon in his lair.

49 "Shalt see King Erythras' far-famèd Main
permute his nat'ural red to Fear's pale dye:
eke shalt thou see the haughty Hormuz-reign
twice taken, prostrate in their presence lie:
There shalt thou see the furious Moorman slain
pierced by his own deflected archery;[30]
till all ken clearly who thy Sons oppose
by their own deed become their deadliest foes.

50 "Shalt see of Diu[31] th' inexpugnable wall,
two sieges braving, while thy sons defend;
there shall their val'orous worth be shown to all
with feats of arms that every feat transcend:
Envy shalt see in Mars majestical
of Lusian fierceness none shall dare offend.
There shall they sight the Moor with voice supreme
before high Heaven false Mahound blaspheme.

51 "Thou shalt see Góa from the Moslem tane,
and in near future raised to queenly place,
Ladye of Orient land sublimely vain
of triumphs wrested by thy conquering Race.
There, with superb, high, haughtiest disdain
the Gentoo louting low to idols base,
they bit and bridle, mast'ering every land
that 'gainst thy Lusians raiseth head or hand.

58

52 "Thou shalt behold the Fortalice hold out
   of Cananor with scanty garnison:
   Calecut thou shalt see endure sad rout,
   that erst so populous and puissant town;
   shalt in Cochin see one approv'd so stout,
   who such an arr'ogance of the sword hath shown,
   no harp of mortal sang a similar story,
   digne of e'erlasting name, eternal glory.[32]

53 "Ne'er with such Mars-taught art and furious flame,
   was Leucas seen in civil wars to glow,
   when to his Actium-fight Augustus came
   and laid th' injurious Roman captain low;
   whom, deft Aurora's reign and race to tame,
   far-famèd Nyle and Bactrus' Scythic foe,
   despoilèd, 'spite victorious spoils and rare,
   that fair Egyptian not so chaste as fair;[33]

54 "As thou shalt see when Ocean boileth o'er
   with fires enkindled by thy Lusians' bate,
   who captive make the Idol-man and Moor,
   and triumph high o'er many a subject state.
   Till, won rich Aurea-Chersonésus'-shore
   far as far China they shall navigate,
   and each remotest isle of Orient tide
   and every Ocean in their rule shall bide.

55 "'Tis thus, O Daughter mine! thy children's lot
   higher than human vigour to display,
   nowhere shall Brav'ery burn and blaze so hot
   from Ganges' bank to Gaditanian bay;
   nor from the Boreal billows to the gut
   where first an injured Lusian brake the way;[34]
   e'en though their progress o'er the world t' oppose
   the Dead of Ages from their tombs arose."

56 This said, he sendeth Maia's son divine
to visit lowly earth, and there to seek
some harbour's peaceful shelter, with design
that all the Fleet shall ride sans risk of wreck:
And, lest in false Mombasah-land indign
more of delay the valiant Captain make,
'tis Jove's command that be in vision shone
a restful region free from restless fone.

57 Now th' airy space the Cyllenéan span'd,
descending earth with feath'ery feet to tread;
his hand was armèd with the fatal Wand,
which sheds on weary eyne sweet drowsihed;
wherewith he called the sad-eyed shadowy band
from Hades, and obedient breezes sped:
The wingèd basnet on his head he bore;
and thus he sought the Melindanian shore.

58 Fame is his mate who mote aloud proclaim
the Lusitanian's weight and rarest worth;
for mortal breast is won by noble name,
that makes the bearer loved of all on earth.
Thus winning stranger-hearts the Herald came,
and to the mighty bruit gave timely birth:
Anon Desire Melindé burns to see
what mode of men the val'orous People be.

59 Thence to Mombasah takes the God his course,
where the strange vessels rode in fear afar,
to bid the seamen leave, while none the worse,
those lands suspected and that treacherous bar:
For scant availeth human fraud or force
against Infernals waging treach'erous war:
Scant 'vaileth heart and art and judgment staid
when human wisdom lacketh heavenly aid.

60 Already Night had past her middle way,
   and all the starry host with th' alien light
   rained on the breadth of Earth their radiance gay;
   and now was Sleep tired man's supreme delight.
   Th' illustrious Captain weary, wayworn, lay,
   with careful watching through the cares of night,
   a short repose for anxious eyne he snatched:
   The men on duty at their quarters watchèd.

61 When in a vision Maia's son was seen
   And heard to say: "Fly, Lusitanian! Fly
   that wicked Monarch's snares, that only mean
   to draw you forwards where ye surely die:
   Fly, for breathes fair the breeze and smiles serene
   Æther, while stormless sleep the seas and sky;
   in other part another King more benign
   sure shelter offereth unto thee and thine!

62 "Here nought thou findest but the barb'rous rite
   the guest-rite dear to cruel Diomed,
   ill-host that made each miserable wight
   the wonted forage of his stabled steed:
   Those altars which Busiris, infame sprite,
   taught with the stranger's wailing life to bleed,
   here certès wait thee an thou longer dwell:
   Fly, then, this folk perfidious, fierce, and fell!

63 "Steer straight, along this outstretch'd sea-board run,
   another land more leal shalt thou find;
   there near the Belt where th' ever-blazing sun
   to Day and Night hath equal space assign'd:[35]
   There to thy Squadron honour gladly done,
   a King, with many a friendly service kind,
   the surest shelter shall for thee provide,
   and for your India skilful trusty guide."

61

64 Mercury thus; and rousèd from his dreams
    the Captain rising in a stark dismay,
    while pierced the palpable Obscure bright streams
    of sudden light and splendid holy ray:
    Then, seen forthwith that him it best beseems
    in land so vile to make the shortest stay,
    he bade his Master, urged by spirit new,
    to spread the canvas in what breeze there blew.

65 "Hoist sail!" he said, "hoist high in lib'ral air,
    for God commands, and Heav'n affects its friends;
    from yon clear seats was sent a messengèr
    only to speed our steps and shape our ends."
    Meanwhile the sailors to set sail prepare;
    all work and either watch its anchor tends;
    the weighty irons with willing shouts are weighèd,
    and sin'ewy strength, the seaman's pride, displayèd.

66 Now at what time their anchors high uprose,
    lurking in Night's murk shadow rose the Moor,
    stealthy to cut the cables of his foes,
    that all might perish on the rocky shore:
    But watched with lynx-like glances, clear and close,
    the Portingalls prepared for ev'ry stowre:
    Finding his victims wakeful th' enemy fled
    by wings of terror, not by paddle, sped.

67 But now the narrow sharp-cut Prores renew,
    cleaving the humid argent plain, their road;
    blandly the north and eastern Trade-wind blew
    with gentle movement, as in joyous mood:
    Past perils in their talk review'd the Crew,
    for with a fond delay Thought loves to brood
    on dang'rous chances, when to death-in-life
    Life comes so near she scarcely 'scapes the strife.

68 One circle ended Phoebus all aglow,
   and on a second entered, when appearèd
   in the far offing, sailing sure and slow,
   two hulls by gently-breathing Zephyrs steerèd:
   And, as they must be manned by Moorish foe
   our Squadron veering soon her prizes nearèd:
   This one that fearèd fearful ills to brave
   ran straight ashore her crew thereon to save.

69 No sim'lar cunning from such chances led
   her consort, captive of the Lusian hand,
   which, ne by rig'rous Mavors' rage had bled,
   nor felt what furies Vulcan doth command.
   But weakly, master'd by a craven dread,
   the feeble forces which the barquelet man'd
   resistance offer'd none; which haply shown,
   from such resisting greater ills had known.

70 And as the Gama felt him much incline'd
   to seek a Guide for India-land long sought,
   he thought a Helmsman 'mid the Moors to find,
   yet naught to him succeeded as he thought;
   none mote give tidings of the lay of Inde,
   under what tract of heav'n it might be brought:
   But all declare a harbour lies hard by
   Melinde, ready Pilots to supply.

71 Her King's benevolence the Moormen praise,
   conditions lib'ral, breast no guile that knew;
   magnificent, grandiose and gentle ways
   with parts that won respect and honour true.
   All this to heart for fact our Captain lays,
   since to his vision came such view to shew
   the dream-sent Cyllenéan; thus he sped
   whither the vision and the Moorman led.

72 'Twas the glad season when the God of Day
into Europa's rav'isher 'gan return;
when warmèd either point his genial ray
and Flora scattered Arnalthéa's horn:
The hasty Sun, that girds the heavenly way,
brought round the mem'ry of that blessèd morn,
when He, who ruleth all by Will Divine,
upon Creation stampt His seal and sign.[36]

73 At such a time the Squadron neared the part,
where first Melindé's goodly shore was seen,
in awnings drest and prankt with gallant art,
to show that none the Holy Day misween.
Flutter the flags, the streaming Estandart
gleams from afar with gorgeous purple sheen;
tom-toms and timbrels mingle martial jar:
Thus past they forwards with the pomp of war.

74 Men crowd and jostle on Melindé's strand
hasting to sight the stranger's glad Armade;
a folk more truthful far, humane, and bland
than any met on shores their course had made.
Now rides the Lusian Fleet anent the land:
Her pond'rous anchors now the depths invade:
Forthwith a captured Moor they send to greet
the King and mani'fest whence had come the Fleet.

75 The King who well that noble lineage knew,
which to the Portingalls such worth imparts,
prizeth their haib'ring at his Hythe, as due
the praise to Braves so prompt in martial arts:
And, with the spirit ever pure and true
that 'nobleth gen'rous souls and gallant hearts,
he prays by proxy all forthwith may deign
to land and use, as best they choose, his reign.

76 Frank offers these, and made in Honour bright,
    simple the words, undoubted, unprepar'd,
    wherewith the Monarch greets each noble Knight,
    who o'er such seas and lands so far hath fared.
    And eke he sendeth muttons fleecy white
    with many a cramm'd domesticate poulard,
    and tropick fruitage which the markets fill:
    Yet his good gifts are giv'n with better will.

77 A glad and eager ear our Captain lent
    to him who spake his Sovran's speech benign;
    straightway of royal gifts return he sent
    stow'd in his Squadron for such fair design:
    Purple Escarlat,[37] cloth of crimson tint,
    the branchy Coral, highly prized and fine,
    which in deep Water soft and tender grown,
    in Air doth harden to a precious stone.

78 Eke sends he one well known for courtly wit,
    who with the King may pact of peace conclude;
    and prayeth pardon that he could not quit
    his ships at once, and leave the Fleet aflood.
    His trusty Truchman[38] on the land alit,
    and, as before the Monarch's face he stood,
    spake thus in style which only Pallas taught
    when praise and prayer firm persuasion wrought:—

79 "O King sublime! to whom Olympus pure
    of His high justice gave the gift and boon
    to curb and conquer peoples dour and dure,
    to win their love, nor less their fear to own;
    as safe asylum, haven most secure,
    to ev'ry Oriental nation known,
    thee have we come to seek, in thee to find
    the surest med'icine of the Wanderer's mind.

80   "No Pyrates we, who fare on ports to prey,
       and purse-proud cities that in war be weak;
       thieves, who with fire and steel the peoples slay,
       their robber-greed on neighbour-goods to wreak:
       From haughty Europe to the realms of Day
       we sail, and Earth's remotest verge we seek
       of Inde, the great, the rich, for thus ordaineth
       the mighty Monarch who our country reigneth.

81   "What brood so harsh as this was ever bred?
       what barb'arous custom and what usage ban'd
       that can not only men from ports forbid
       but grudge the shelter of their desert sand?
       What of ill Will hold they our hearts have hid,
       that of a folk so few in fear they stand?
       That traps for us they spread and ready snares
       and work their worst whereby we die unwares?

82   "But Thou, wherein full surely we confide
       to find, O King benign! an honest man,
       and hope such certain aid to see supplied,
       as gave Alcino'us the lost Ithacan,
       to this thy Haven sure we stem the tide
       with the Divine Interpreter in van
       For as He sendeth us to thee 'tis clear
       thy heart must e'en be rare, humane, sincere.

83   "And deem not thou, O King! that dreads to land
       our famous Captain thee to serve and see,
       for aught he sees of base or underhand,
       or aught suspects of false and feign'ed in thee:
       But know he acteth by the high command,—
       a law of all obeyed implicitly,—
       his King's own hest, forbidding him t' explore,
       and from his Squadron land at port or shore.

84 "And, since of subjects King may thus require,
   for of the Head should members heed the sway,
   thou, kingly officed, never shalt desire
   the liege his lord's command to disobey;
   but the high ben'efits, and those gifts still higher
   by thee bestow'd, he prom'iseth to repay
   with all that done by him or his can be
   long as the rolling rivers seek the Sea."

85 Thus he; when all conjoint their voices raisèd
   while each to each his separate thoughts convey'd,
   by the high stomach of the Race amazèd,
   who through such seas and skies their way had made.
   Th' illustrious King for loyalty bepraisèd
   the Portingalls, the while his spirit weigh'd
   how high his value, strong his orders are,
   whose Royal word is heard in land so far.

86 And, with a smiling mien and pleasèd face,
   he hailed the Herald, proff'ering high esteem:—
   "All black suspicions from your bosoms chase,
   nor let your souls with frigid terror teem;
   such be your gallant worth, your works of grace,
   the World your deeds shall aye most glorious deem;
   and whoso holdeth right to do you wrong
   ne truth ne noble thoughts to him belong.

87 "That all you warmen may not instant land
   observing 'customèd pre-eminence,
   though sorely grievèd by your King's command,
   yet much we prize so much obedience:
   Yet, as your orders our desire withstand;
   nor we consent to see such excellence
   of heart, such loyalty of soul, belied,
   that our good wishes sole be gratified.

88 "But, as to-morrow's Sun on earth shall shine,
  all our Flotilla shall make holiday;
  to seek your sturdy Fleet is our design
  we have so longed to see full many a day:
  And if your sea-tost vessels bear the sign
  of angry tempests, and their tedious way,
  here they shall find in friendly form and guise
  pilots, munitions, vittaile and supplies."

89 He spake; and 'neath the sea-rim sank to rest
  Latona's son, when home the Herald hied,
  with the fair message to the Fleet addrest,
  in a light canoe that fast outran the tide.
  Now joy and gladness fillèd ev'ery breast,
  all had the perfect cure at length descried,—
  Discov'ery of the Land, long wisht-for sight;
  and thus they festival'd with glee the night.

90 Aboard is foyson of those artful rays,
  whose splendours mock the trem'ulous hairy star:
  Now every bombardier his boast displays,
  till Ocean's thunder answers earth and air.
  The Cyclops' art is shown in various ways,
  in fire-stuffed shells, and burning bombs of war:
  Others with voices which invade the skies,
  make brazen notes from blaring trumps arise.

91 Echoes a loud reply the ready shore.
  with buzzing fireworks forming giddy gyre;
  whirl burning wheels that far in Æther soar;
  sulphurous dust deep-hid explodes in fire;
  Heav'en-high resounds the multitudinous roar;
  the soft blue waters don Flame's red attire
  nor blazeth land the less: 'Tis thus friends greet
  their friends as foemen who in battle meet.

92 Again the restless Spheres revolving sped,
    to olden drudg'ry dooming man anew:
    Again did Memnon's Mother radiance shed,
    and from the sluggard's eyne soft sleep withdrew:
    The latest shadows slowly melting fled,
    on earthly flowerets weeping frigid dew;
    when the Melindan King took boat that he
    might view the Squad that swam the Blackmoor sea.

93 Boiling about him, swarming round the Bay,
    dense crowds glad gather'd and enjoy'd the sight:
    Caftans of finest purple glisten gay;
    glance splendid robes with silken tissue dight:
    In lieu of warrior lance, and harsegaye[39]
    and bow whose burnisht cusps mock Luna's light;
    aloft the revellers bear the palmy bough,
    the fittest crown that decks the conqueror's brow.

94 A spacious stately barge, o'ercanopied
    with dainty silks, of divers teinture stainèd
    beareth Melinde's King, accompanied
    by lords and captains of the land he reignèd.
    Rich clad he cometh with what pomp and pride,
    his country customs and his taste ordainèd,
    a precious Turbant winds around his head
    of cotton wrought with gold and silken thread.

95 Caftan of costly texture Damascene,—
    the Tyrian colour honour'd there of eld;—
    Torque round his collar, shining golden sheen,
    whose wealth of work its wealth of ore excel'd:
    Glitters and gleams with radiance diamantine
    Dag-targe of costly price by girdle held:
    And show, in fine, upon his sandal-shoon
    velvets with seed-pearl and gold-spangle strewn.

96 With silken sunshade, high and round of guise
fast to its handle bound, a gilded spear,
a Minister the solar ray defies
lest hurt of baleful beam the high King bear:
High in the poop his strange glad musick hies,
of asp'erous noise, most horr'ible to the ear,
of archèd trumpets writhed in curious round,
roaring a rough, rude, unconcerted sound.

97 Nor with less garnishment our Lusitanian
swift-sailing galleys from the Squadron bore,
to meet and greet the noble Melindanian,
begirt by goodly company galore.
The Gama cometh dight in dress Hispanian;
but of French work the doublet was he wore,
Satin which Adrian Venice works and stains
crimson, a colour which such prize obtains.

98 Buttons of gold his loopèd sleeves confine,
where solar glancings dazzle gazing eyes:
Hosen of soldier fashion purfled shine
with the rich metal Fortune oft denies:
Points of the same the slashes deftly join,
gored in his doublet, with right del'icate ties:
Gold-hilted sword in mode of Italy:
Plume in his bonnet worn a little wry.

99 I' the suite and escort of the Captain show'd
of the dye murex,— Tyre's surpassing tint,—
the various shades that joy'd men's eyne, and mode
of dress devis'd with fashion different:
Such was th' enamel, and as bright it glow'd
with cunning colours in quaint mixture blent,
as though her rutilant bow had rear'd in air
the Maid of Thaumas, fairest of the fair.

100 Sonorous trumpets manly breasts incite
gladding the heart with martial musick gay:
Churnèd the Moorish keels blue waters white
and awnings sprent with dews of pearly spray:
The horrid-sounding bombards thunder fright
while smoky hangings veil the splendid day;
roar the hot volleys hurtling sounds so loud,
fain close with hands their ears the Moorish crowd.

101 And now the King our Captain's galley sought,
who strainèd in his arms the welcome guest:
He with the courtesy which Reason taught,
his host (who was of Royal rank) addrest.
Noted th' admiring Moor, with marvel fraught,
his visitor's ev'ry mode, and look, and gest,
as one regarding with a huge esteem
Folk who so far in quest of India came.

102 And to him proffers in his phrase high-flown
whatever goods his realm and haven boast;
the while commanding him to hold his own
what store might haply serve his turn the most:
Eke he assures him Fame had made well-known
the Lusian name ere Lusians reached his coast:
for long 'twas rumour'd that in realms afar
it had with peoples of his law waged war.

103 How Africk cont'inent's farthest shores resound,
he told him, with great deeds the warmen did;
whose long campaigns the Conquerors had crown'd
lords of the lands where dwelt the Hesperid.[40]
With long harangue he taught the crowd around
the least deserts the Lusians meritèd,
and yet the most that Fame was fain to teach;
when thus Da Gama to the King made speech:—

71

104 "O thou! who sole hast seen with pit'iful eye,
    benignant King! our Lusitanian race,
    which in such mis'ery dire hath dared defy
    Fate, and the furies of mad seas to face;
    may yon Divine eternity on high,
    that ruleth man, revolving skyey space,
    since gifts so goodly givest thou, I pray
    the Heav'ens repay thee what we never may.

105 "Of all Apollo bronzèd hath thou sole,
    peaceful didst greet us from th' abysmal sea:
    In thee from Æolus' winds that moan and howl,
    we find good, truthful, glad security.
    Long as its Stars leads forth the vasty Pole,
    long as the Sun shall light the days to be,
    where'er I haply live, with fame and glory
    shall live thy praises in my People's story."

106 He spake, and straight the barges 'gin to row
    whither the Moorman would review the Fleet;
    rounding the vessels, one by one, they go
    that ev'ery not'able thing his glance may meet:
    But Vulcan skywards voll'eying horr'ible lowe
    with dire artill'ery hastes the guest to greet,
    while trumpets loud canorous accents blend;
    with shawms the Moorish hosts their answer send.

107 When due attention to the sights had lent
    the gen'erous Moslem, fill'ed with thrilling wonder,
    and hearing, eke, th' unwonted instrument
    that told its dreadful might in fiery thunder;
    he bade the light Batèl wherein he went
    at anchor quiet ride the Flagship under,
    that with the doughty Gama he might hold
    converse of matters erst by Rumour told.

108 The Moor in varied di'alogue took delight,
     and now he prayed the vis'itor would expound
     each war renowned and famous feat of fight
     fought with the races that adore Mahound:
     Now of the peoples he would gain a sight
     that hold our ultimate Hispanian ground:
     Then of the nations who with us confine;
     then of the mighty voyage o'er the brine.

109 "But first, O valiant Captain! first relate,"
     quoth he, "with all the diligence thou can,
     what lands and climes compose your natal state,
     and where your home, recount with regular plan;
     nor less your ancient lineage long and great
     and how your Kingdom's lofty rule began,
     with all your early deeds of derring-do;
     e'en now, tho' know'ng them not, their worth we know.

110 "And, prithee, further say how o'er the Main
     long on this voyage through fierce seas you stray'd,
     seeing the barb'arous ways of alien strain,
     which our rude Africk-land to you display'd:
     Begin! for now the team with golden rein
     draws near, and drags the new Sun's car, inlaid
     with marquetry, from cold Aurora's skies:
     Sleep wind and water, smooth the wavelet lies.

111 "And as th' Occasion such a fitness showeth,
     so is our wish your wondrous tale to hear;
     who dwells among us but by rumour knoweth
     the Lusitanian's labour singular?
     Deem not so far from us removèd gloweth
     resplendent Sol, that need thy judgment fear
     to find Melinde nurse so rude a breed,
     which can ne prize ne praise a noble deed.

73

112 "Vainly the haughty olden Giants vied
   by war to win Olympus clear and pure:
   Pirith and Theseus mad with ign'orance tried
   of Pluto's realm to burst the dread Obscure;
   If in the world such works hath workd pride,
   not less 't is labour excellent and dure,
   bold as it was to brave both Hea'ven and Hell,
   for man o'er raging Nereus to prevail.

113 "With fire consumèd Dian's sacred fane,—
   that master-piece of subtle Ctesiphon,—
   Heróstratus, who by such deed would gain
   of world-wide Fame the high immortal boon:
   If greed of foolish praise and glory vain
   to actions so perverse may urge men on,
   more reason 't is to crown with endless fame
   Deeds that deserve, like Gods, a deathless name."

CANTO III

1 Now, my Calliope! to teach incline
   what speech great Gama for the King did frame:
   Inspire immortal song, grant voice divine
   unto this mortal who so loves thy name.
   Thus may the God whose gift was Medicine,
   to whom thou barest Orpheus, lovely Dame!
   never for Daphne, Clytia, Leucothoe
   due love deny thee or inconstant grow he.

2 Satisfy, Nymph! desires that in me teem,
   to sing the merits of thy Lusians brave;
   so worlds shall see and say that Tagus-stream
   rolls Aganippe's liquor. Leave, I crave,
   leave flow'ry Pindus-head; e'en now I deem
   Apollo bathes me in that sovran wave;
   else must I hold it, that thy gentle sprite,
   fears thy dear Orpheus fade through me from sight.

3 All stood with open ears in long array
   to hear what mighty Gama mote unfold;
   when, past in thoughtful mood a brief delay,
   began he thus with brow high-raised and bold:—
   "Thou biddest me, O King! to say my say
   anent our grand genealogy of old:
   Thou bidd'st me not relate an alien story;
   thou bidd'st me laud my brother Lusians' glory.

75

4 "That one praise others' exploits and renown
is honour'd custom which we all desire;
yet fear I 'tis unfit to praise mine own;
lest praise, like this suspect, no trust inspire;
nor may I hope to make all matters known
for Time however long were short: yet, sire!
as thou commandest all is owed to thee,
maugre my will I speak and brief will be.

5 "Nay, more, what most obligeth me, in fine,
is that no leasing in my tale may dwell;
for of such Feats whatever boast be mine,
when most is told, remaineth much to tell:
But that due order wait on the design,
e'en as desirest thou to learn full well,
the wide-spread Cont'inent first I'll briefly trace,
then the fierce bloody wars that waged my Race.

6 Atwixt the Zone, where Cancer holds command,—
the lucent Sun's septentrional mete,—
and that whose frigid horrors freeze the land
as burn the middle Belt with fervid heat,
lies haughty Europe: On her goodly strand,
facing Arcturus and the Ponent, beat
the briny billows of Atlantis plain,
while free t'wards Auster flows the Midland-main.

7 "That part where lovely Dawn is born and bred,
neighboureth Asia: But the curvèd river,[41]
from far and frore Rhipæan ranges shed,
to feed Mæotis-lake with waves that shiver,
departs them, and the Sea-strait fierce and dread,
that owned the vict'ory of the Greek deceiver,
where now the seaman sees along the shore
triumphant Troja's mem'ories and no more.

8   "There farther still the Boreal Pole below,
    Hyperboréan mountain-walls appear,
    and the wild hills where Æolus loves to blow,
    while of his winds the names they proudly bear:
    Here such cold comfort doth Apollo show,
    so weak his light and warmth to shine and cheer,
    that snows eternal gleam upon the mountains,
    freezeth the sea, and ever freeze the fountains.

9   "Here of the Scythic hordes vast numbers be,
    in olden day a mighty warrior band,
    who fought for honours of antiquity
    with the then owners of the Nylus-land:
    But how remote their claims from verity,
    (for human judgments oft misunderstand),
    let him who seeks what higher lore reveal'd
    ask the red clay that clothes Damascus-field.[42]

10 "Now in these wild and wayward parts be told
    Cold Lapland's name, uncultivate Norwày,
    Escandinavia's isle, whose scions bold
    boast triumphs Italy shall ne'er gainsay.
    Here, while ne frost, ne wintry rigours hold
    in hand the waters, seafolk ply the way,
    over the arm of rough Sarmatic Main
    the Swede, the Brusian,[43] and the shiv'ering Dane.

11 "Between the sea and Tanais-stream we count
    strange races, Ruthens,[44] Moscows, and Livonians,—
    Sarmátæ all of old, — and on the Mount
    Hercynian,[45] Marcomanni, now Polonians.
    Holding the empire Almayne paramount
    dwell Saxons, and Bohemians, and Pannonians;
    and other tribes, wherethrough their currents frore
    Rhine, Danube, Amasis,[46] and Albis pour.

12 "Twixt distant Ister and the famous Strait,
    where hapless Helle left her name and life,
    the Thracians wone, a folk of brave estate,
    Mars' well-loved country, chosen home of strife:
    There Rhódope and Hæmus rue the weight
    of cursèd Othman's rule with horror rife;
    Byzance they hold beneath their yoke indign
    great injury working to great Constantine!

13 "Hard by their side the Macedonians rest,
    whose soil is water'ed by cold Axius' wave:[47]
    Eke ye, of ev'ery choicest realm the best,
    Lands of the free, the wise, the good, the brave,
    that here did breed and bear the facund breast,
    and to the world its wit and wisdom gave,
    wherewith thou, noble Greece! hast reach'ed the stars,
    no less by arts exalt than arms and wars.

14 "The Dalmats follow; and upon the Bay
    where rose Antenor's walls[48] in while of yore,
    superb Venetia builds on wat'ery way,
    Adria's Queen that erst was lowly poor.
    Hence seawards runs a land-arm made to sway
    forceful the sons of many a stranger shore;
    an arm of might, whose Race hath conquer'd time
    nor less by spirit than by sword sublime.

15 "Girdeth her shores the kingdom Neptunine,
    while Nature's bulwarks fence her landward side;
    her middle width departeth Apennine,
    by Mars, her saint and patron, glorified:
    But when the Porter rose to rank divine,
    she lost her prowess, and her bellic pride:
    Humbled she lies with antique puissance spent:
    So Man's humil'ity may his God content!

16 "Gallia can there be seen, whose name hath flown
   where Cæsar's triumphs to the world are told;
   by Séquana⁴⁹ 'tis watered and the Rhone,
   by Rhine's deep current and Garumna⁴⁹ cold:
   Here rise the ranges from Pyréne known,
   the Nymph ensepulchre'd in days of old,
   whence, legends say, the conflagrated woods
   rolled golden streams, and flowèd silvern floods.

17 "Lo! here her presence showeth noble Spain,
   of Europe's body corporal the head;
   o'er whose home-rule, and glorious foreign reign,
   the fatal Wheel so many a whirl hath made:
   Yet ne'er her Past or force or fraud shall stain,
   nor restless Fortune shall her name degrade;
   no bonds her bellic offspring bind so tight
   but it shall burst them with its force of sprite.

18 "There, facing Tingitania's shore, she seemeth
   to block and bar the Med'iterranean wave,
   where the known Strait its name ennobled deemeth
   by the last labour of the Theban Brave.
   Big with the burthen of her tribes she teemeth,
   circled by whelming waves that rage and rave;
   all noble races of such valiant breast,
   that each may justly boast itself the best.

19 "Hers the Tarragonese who, famed in war,
   made aye-perturbed Parthenopé obey;
   the twain Asturias, and the haught Navarre
   twin Christian bulwarks on the Moslem way:
   Hers the Gallego canny, and the rare
   Castilian, whom his star raised high to sway
   Spain as her saviour, and his seign'iory feel
   Bætis, Leon, Granáda, and Castile.

20 "See the head-crowning coronet is she,
    of general Europe, Lusitania's reign,
    where endeth land and where beginneth sea,
    and Phoebus sinks to rest upon the main.
    Willed her the Heavens with all-just decree
    by wars to mar th' ignoble Mauritan,
    to cast him from herself: nor there consent
    he rule in peace the Fiery Continent.

21 "This is my happy land, my home, my pride;
    where, if the Heav'ens but grant the pray'er I pray
    for glad return and every risk defied,
    there may my life-light fail and fade away.
    This was the Lusitania, name applied
    by Lusus or by Lysa, sons, they say,
    of ancient Bacchus, or his boon compeers,
    eke the first dwellers of her eldest years.

22 "Here sprang the Shepherd,[50] in whose name we see
    forecast of virile might, of virtuous meed;
    whose fame no force shall ever hold in fee,
    since fame of mighty Rome ne'er did the deed.
    This, by light Heaven's volatile decree,
    that antient Scyther, who devours his seed,
    made puissant pow'r in many a part to claim,
    assuming regal rank; and thus it came:—

23 "A King there was in Spain, Afonso hight,
    who waged such warfare with the Saracen,
    that by his 'sanguined arms, and arts, and might,
    he spoiled the lands and lives of many men.
    When from Hercùlean Calpè winged her flight
    his fame to Caucasus Mount and Caspian glen,
    many a Knight, who noblesse coveteth,
    comes off'ering service to such King and Death.

24 "And with intrinsic love inflamèd more
    for the True Faith, than honours popular,
    they trooped gath'ring from each distant shore,
    leaving their dear-loved homes and lands afar.
    When with high feats of force against the Moor
    they proved of sing'ular worth in Holy War,
    willèd Afonso that their mighty deeds
    commens'urate gifts command and equal meeds.

25 "'Mid them Henrique second son, men say,
    of a Hungarian King, well-known and tried,
    by sort won Portugal which, in his day,
    ne prizèd was ne had fit cause for pride:
    His strong affection stronger to display
    the Spanish King decreed a princely bride,
    his only child, Theresa, to the count;
    and with her made him Seigneur Paramount.

26 "This doughty Vassal from that servile horde,
    Hagar the handmaid's seed, great vic'tories won;
    reft the broad lands adjacent with his sword
    and did whatever Brav'ery bade be done:
    Him, for his exploits exc'ellent to reward,
    God gave in shortest space a gallant son,
    whose arm to 'noble and enfame was fain
    the warlike name of Lusitania's reign.

27 "Once more at home this conqu'ering Henry stood
    who sacred Hierosol'yma had relievèd,
    his eyes had fed on Jordan's holy flood,
    which the Dear Body of Lord God had lavèd;
    when Godfrey[51] left no foe to be subdued,
    and all Judaea conquered was and savèd,
    many that in his wars had done devoir
    to their own lordships took the way once more.

81

28 "But when this stout and gallant Hun attainèd
  Life's fatal period, age and travail-spent,
  he gave, by Death's necessity constrainèd,
  his sprite to Him who had that spirit lent:
  A son of tender years alone remainèd,
  to whom the Sire bequeath'd his 'bodiment;
  with bravest braves the youth was formed to cope,
  for from such sire such son the world may hope.

29 "Yet old Report, I know not what its weight,
  (for on such antique tale no man relies),[52]
  saith that the Mother, tane in tow the state,
  a second nuptial bed did not despise:
  Her orphan son to disinher'ited fate
  she doomed, declaring hers the dignities,
  not his, with seigniory o'er all the land,
  her spousal dowry by her sire's command.

30 "Now Prince Afonso (who such style had tane
  in pious mem'ory of his Grandsire's name)
  seeing no part and portion in his reign
  all pilled and plunder'd by the Spouse and Dame,
  by dour and doughty Mars inflamed amain,
  privily plots his heritage to claim:
  He weighs the causes in his own conceit
  till firm Resolve its fit effect shall greet.

31 "Of Guimara'ens the field already flow'd
  with floods of civil warfare's bloody tide,
  where she, who little of the Mother show'd,
  to her own bowels love and land denied.
  Fronting the child in fight the parent stood;
  nor saw her depth of sin that soul of pride
  against her God, against maternal love:
  Her sensual passion rose all pow'er above.

82

32 "O magical Medea! O Progne dire!
    if your own babes hi vengeance dared ye kill
    for alien crimes, and injuries of the sire,
    look ye, Teresa's deed was darker still.
    Foul greed of gain, incontinent desire,
    were the main causes of such bitter ill:
    Scylla her agèd sire for one did slay,
    for both Teresa did her son betray.

33 "Right soon that noble Prince clear vict'ory won
    from his harsh Mother and her Fere indign;
    in briefest time the land obeyed the son,
    though first to fight him did the folk incline.
    But reft of reason and by rage undone
    he bound the Mother in the biting chain.
    Eftsoons avenged her griefs the hand of God:
    Such veneration is to parents owe'd.

34 "Lo! the superb Castilian 'gins prepare
    his pow'er to 'venge Teresa's injuries,
    against the Lusian land in men so rare,
    whereon ne toil ne trouble heavy lies.
    Their breasts the cruel battle grandly dare,
    aid the good cause angelic Potencies;
    unrecking might unequal still they strive,
    nay, more, their dreadful foe to flight they drive.[53]

35 "Passeth no tedious time, before the great
    Prince a dure Siege in Guimaraens dree'd
    by passing pow'er, for to 'mend his state,
    came the fell en'emy, full of grief and greed:
    But when committed life to direful Fate,
    Egas, the faithful guardian, he was free'd,
    who had in any other way been lost,
    ail unpreparèd 'gainst such 'whelming host.

36 "But when the loyal Vassal well hath known
how weak his Monarch's arm to front such fight,
sans order wending to the Spanish fone,
his Sovran's homage he doth pledge and plight
Straight from the horrid siege th' invader flown
trusteth the word and honour of the Knight,
Egas Moniz: But now the noble breast
of the brave Youth disdaineth strange behest.

37 "Already came the plighted time and tide,
when the Castilian Don stood dight to see,
before his pow'er the Prince bend low his pride,
yielding the promisèd obediency.
Egás who views his knightly word belied,
while still Castile believes him true to be,
sweet life resolveth to the winds to throw,
nor live with foulest taint of faithless vow.

38 "He with his children and his wife departeth
to keep his promise with a faith immense;
unshod and strippèd,[54] while their plight imparteth
far more of pity than of vengeance:
'If, mighty Monarch! still thy spirit smarteth
to wreak revenge on my rash confidence,'
quoth he, 'behold! I come with life to save
my pledge, my knightly Honour's word I gave.'

39 "'I bring, thou seest here, lives innocent,
of wife, of sinless children dight to die;
if breasts of gen'erous mould and excellent
accept such weaklings' woeful destiny.
Thou se'est these hands, this tongue inconsequent,
hereon alone the fierce exper'iment try
of torments, death, and doom that pass in full
Sinis or e'en Perillus' brazen bull.'

84

40 "As shrifted wight the hangman stands before,
     in life still draining bitter draught of death,
     lays throat on block, and of all hope forlore,
     expects the blighting blow with bated breath:
     So, in the Prince's presence angry sore,
     Egás stood firm to keep his plighted faith:
     When the King, marv'elling at such wondrous truth,
     feels anger melt and merge in Royal ruth.

41 Oh the great Portingall-fidelity
     of Vassal self-devote to doom so dread!
     What did the Persian more for loyalty
     whose gallant hand his face and nostrils shred?
     When great Darius mourned so grievously
     that he a thousand times deep-sighing said,
     far he prefer'd his Zóp'yrus sound again,
     than lord of twenty Babylons to reign.

42 "But Prince Afonso now prepared his band
     of happy Lusians proud to front the foes,
     those haughty Moors that held the glorious land
     yon side where clear delicious Tagus flows:
     Now on Ourique⁵⁵ field was pitched and plan'd
     the Royal 'Campment fierce and bellicose,
     facing the hostile host of Sarrasin
     though there so many, here so few there bin.

43 "Confident, yet would he in nought confide,
     save in his God that holds of Heav'en the throne;
     so few baptizèd stood their King beside,
     there were an hundred Moors for every one:
     Judge any sober judgment, and decide
     'twas deed of rashness or by brav'ery done
     to fall on forces whose exceeding might
     a cent'ury showèd to a single Knight.

44 "Order five Moorish Kings the hostile host
of whom Ismar,[56] so called, command doth claim;
all of long Warfare large experience boast,
wherein may mortals win immortal fame:
And gallant dames the Knights they love the most
'company, like that brave and beauteous Dame,
who to beleaguered Troy such aidance gave
with woman-troops that drained Thermòdon's wave.

45 "The coolth serene, and early morning's pride,
now paled the sparkling stars about the Pole,
when Mary's Son appearing crucified
in vision, strengthened King Afonso's soul.
But he, adoring such appearance, cried
fired with a phrenzied faith beyond control:
'To th' Infidel, O Lord! to th' Infidel.[57]
Not, Lord, to me who know Thy pow'er so well.'

46 "Such gracious marvel in such manner sent
'flamèd the Lusians' spirits fierce and high,
towards their nat'ural King, that excellent
Prince, unto whom love-boon none could deny:
Aligned to front the foeman prepotent,
they shouted res'onant slogan to the sky,
and fierce the 'larum rose, 'Real, real,
for high Afonso, King of Portugal!'

47 "As to the fight by calls defied and cries,
some fierce Molossan on the wooded height,
attacks the rampant Bull, who most relies
on strength of tem'erous horn to force the fight:
Now nips the ear, then at the side he flies
barking, with more of nimbleness than might,
till ripped at last the gullet of his foe
he lays the mighty bulk of monster low:

86

48 "So the new King, inflamed with zeal devout
for God nor less for faithful Lieges' sake,
assails by cunning skill the barb'arous rout
with Braves the fronting phalanx eath to break:
Whereat the ban-dogs 'Allah! Allah!' shout,
and fly to arms; our raging warriors shake
the lance and bow; resound the trumpet tones;
the musick thunders; Echo moans and groans.

49 "E'en as the prairie-fire enkindled on
sun-parched steppe (as winn'oweth upper air
sibilant Boreas), by the blasts swift blown
o'er bush and arid brake rains flame and flare:
The shepherd lads and lasses, idly strown
in rest and gentle slumber, waked by blare
of crackling conflagration blazing higher,
hamlet-wards force their flocks to fly the fire:

50 "Th' astonied Moorman in such startled guise,
snatcheth his weapon hast'ily and sans heed;
yet he awaits the fight, nor ever flies,
nay, spurs his battle-ginnet to its speed.
Meet him as rash and swift his enemies
whose piercing lances gar his bosom bleed:
These fall half-slain, while others flee that can
convoking aidance of their Alcoran.

51 "There may be viewèd 'counters madly rash,
onsets no Serra's sturdy strength could stand,
while charging here and there the chargers dash,—
the gifts of Neptune smiting gravid Land:—
Buffets they deal, and blows that bash and smash,
burneth and blazeth Warfare's blasting brand,
but he of Lusus coat, mail, plate of steel,
hacks, hews, breaks, batters, rives and rends piecemeal.

52 "Men's heads like bullets dance the bloody plain,
   ownerless arms and legs insens'ible lie,
   and quiv'ering entrails tell of mortal pain,
   and faces fade and life's fair colours fly.
   Lost is that impious host, whose heapèd slain
   roll o'er the green'ery rills of crimson dye;
   whereby the grasses lose their white and green
   and nought but glow of crimson gore is seen.

53 "But now the Lusian victor held the field
   his trophies gath'ering, and his gorgeous prey:
   The crusht Hispanian Moor was forced to yield
   while on the plain three days the great King lay.[58]
   And now he chargeth on his virgin shield,
   what still assures this well-won Vict'ory.
   five noble inescutcheons azure-hued,
   signing the Moorish Five his sword subdued.

54 "He paints with bezants five each 'scutcheon,
   the thirty silvers wherewith God was sold,
   and various tinctures make His mem'ory known,
   whose grace and favour did his cause uphold.
   Painted on every cinque a cinque is shown;
   and, that the thirty may be fully told,
   counteth for two the one that central lies
   of the five azures painted crossy-wise.

55 "Some time has passèd, since this gain had past
   of goodly battail, when the high King hies
   to take Leiria, lately tane and last
   conquest that boast our conquer'd enemies.
   Herewith Arronches castled strong and fast
   is jointly gainèd with the noble prize
   Scalabicastro,[59] whose fair fields amene
   thou, chrystal Tagus! bathest all serene.

88

56 "Unto this conquered roll of towns his might
   eke addeth Mafra won in shortest space,
   and in the Mountains which the Moon hath hight
   he clasps frore Cintra to his hard embrace;
   Cintra, whose Naiads love to hide their light
   by hidden founts and fly the honey'd lace,
   which Love hath woven 'mid the hills where flow
   the waters flaming with a living lowe.

57 "And thou, O noble Lisbon! thou encrown'd
   Princess elect of Cities capital,
   rear'd by the facund Rover-King renown'd,
   whose wiles laid low Dardania's burning wall:
   Thou, whose commands oblige the Sea's Profound
   wast taught to bear the Lusitanian's thrall,
   aided by potent navies at what time
   they came crusading from the Boreal clime.[60]

58 "Beyond Germanic Albis and the Rhene,
   and from Britannia's misty margin sent,
   to waste and slay the people Sarracene,
   many had sailed on holy thoughts intent.
   Now gained the Tagus-mouth, our stream amene
   to great Afonso's royal camp they went,
   whose lofty fame did thence the Heav'ns invade
   and siege to Ulysséa's walls they laid.

59 "Five sequent times her front had Luna veilèd,
   five times her lovely face in full had shown,
   when oped her gate the City, which availèd
   no Force 'gainst 'sieging forces round her thrown.
   Right bloody was th' assault and fierce th' assailèd,
   e'en as their stubborn purpose bound them down;
   asp'erous the Victor, ready all to dare,
   the Vanquisht, victims of a dire despair.

89

60 "Thus won she yielded and, in fine, she lay
    prostrate that City which, in days of old,
    the mighty meiny never would obey
    of frigid Scythia's hordes immanely bold:
    Who could so far extend their savage sway,
    till Ebro saw 't, and Tagus trembling roll'd,
    and some o'er Bætis-land, in short, so swept
    that was the region Vandalia 'clept.

61 "What might of city could perchance endure
    prowess which proud Lisbóa might not bear?
    Who mote resist the powers dure and dour
    of men, whose Fame from earth invadeth air?
    Now yield obedience all Estremadure,
    Obidos, Torres Vedras, Alemquer,
    where softly plash the musick-murmuring waves,
    'mid rocks and reefs whose feet the torrent laves.

62 "Eke ye, Transtagan lands! ye justly vain
    of flavous Ceres' bien and bonny boon,
    yielded to might above the might of men
    the walls and castles by his valour won:
    Thou, too, Moor-yeoman! hopest hope insane,
    those riant regions long as lord to own;
    for Elvas, Moura, Serpa, well-known sites,
    with Alcacer-do-Sal must yield their rights.

63 "The noble City and sure seat behold,
    held by Sertorius, rebel famed whilòme;
    where now the nitid silv'ery waters cold,
    brought from afar to bless the land and home,
    o'erflow the royal arches hundredfold,
    whose noble sequence streaks the dark-blue dome;
    not less succumb'd she to her bold pursuer,
    to Giraldó, entitled 'Knight Sans Peur.'[61]

64 "Fast towards Beja city, vengeful prest,
    to slake his wrath for spoilt Trancoso's wrong,[62]
    Afonso, who despiseth gentle rest
    and would brief human life by Fame prolong.
    Feebly resisteth him and his be
    the City, falling to his arms ere long,
    and nought of life within her walls but feel
    the raging victor's edge of merciless steel.

65 "With these Palmella yielded to the war,
    piscous Cezimbra, eke, her finny spoils;
    then, aided onwards by his fortunate star,
    the King a pow'erful force of foemen foils:
    Felt it the City, saw 't her Lord afar,
    who to support and aid her spares no toils,
    along the hill-skirt marching all unware
    of rash encounter lackt he heed and care.

66 "The King of Bad'ajoz was a Moslem bold,
    with horse four thousand, fierce and furious Knights,
    and countless Peons, armed and dight with gold,
    whose polish't surface glanceth lustrous light.
    But as a savage Bull on lonely wold,
    whom jealous rage in hot May-month incites,
    sighting a stranger, mad with love and wrath
    the brute blind lover chargeth down the path:

67 "So doth Afonso, sudden seen the foes
    that urge their forward march securely brave,
    strike, slay, and scatter, raining doughty blows;
    flies the Moor King, who recks but self to save:
    Naught save a panick fear his spirit knows;
    his foll'owers eke to follow only crave;
    while ours, who struck a stroke so sore, so fell,
    were sixty horsemen told in fullest tale.

68 "Victory swift pursuing, rest disdaineth
     the great untiring King; he must'ereth all
     the lieges of his land, whom nought restraineth
     from ever seeking stranger realms to 'thrall.
     He wends to 'leaguer Bad'ajoz, where he gaineth
     his soul's desire, and battleth at her fall
     with force so fierce, and art and heart so true
     his deeds made others fain to dare and do.

69 "But the high Godhead, who when man offends,
     so long deservèd penalties delays,
     waiting at times to see him make amends,
     or for deep myst'ery hid from man's dull gaze;
     if He our valiant King till now defends
     from dangers, facèd fast as foes can raise,
     lends aid no longer, when for vengeance cries
     the Mother's curses who in prison lies;

70 "For in the City which he compast round,
     encompast by the Leoneze was he,
     because his conquests trespasst on their ground,
     which of Leon and not of Port'ugale be.
     Here was his stubborn will right costly found,
     as happeth oft in human history,
     an iron maims his legs, as rage-inflamèd
     to fight he flies and falls a captive maimèd.

71 "O famous Pompey! feel thy Wraith no pain
     to see the fate of noble feats like thine;
     nor mourn if all-just Nemesis ordain
     thy bays be torn by sire-in-law indign;
     though Phasis frore and parcht Syéné-plain
     whose perpendic'ular shadows ne'er decline,
     Bootes' ice-bergs, and Equator-fires,
     confess the terrors which thy name inspires;

92

72 "Tho' rich Arabia, and the brood ferocious
　　Heniochs, with Colchis-region known of yore
　　for Golden Fleece; and though the Cappadoces
　　and Júdeans who One only God adore;
　　tho' soft Sophénes,[63] and the race atrocious,
　　Cilician, with Armenia whence outpour
　　the twain of mighty streams, whose farthest fount
　　hides in a higher and a holier Mount;[64]

73 "And though, in fine, from far Atlantic tide
　　E'en to the Taurus, Scythia's tow'ring wall,
　　all saw thee conquer; fearless still abide
　　if none save Emath-field beheld thee fall:
　　Thou shalt behold Afonso's ovant pride,
　　lie subjugate, that subjugated all.
　　Such fate Celestial Counsel long foresaw
　　thine from a sire, his from a son-in-law.

74 "Returned the King sublime, in fine, with sprite
　　by the just doom of Judge divine chastisèd,
　　and when of Santarem in pride of might
　　the Saracen a bootless siege devisèd;
　　and when of Vincent, martyr benedight,
　　the precious Corse by Christian people prizèd,
　　from Sacrum Promontorium[65] was conveyed
　　and reverent-wise in Ulysséa laid:

75 "Faster to push the projects still in hand,
　　the toil-spent Father sent his stout young son,
　　bidding him pass to Alemtejo's land,
　　with warlike gear and soldiers many a one.
　　Sancho, a sov'ereign wielder of the brand,
　　straight forward passing, gore-red gars to run
　　the stream[66] whose waters feed Seville and flood,
　　dyed by the brutish Moormen's barb'rous blood.

76 "With hunger whetted by this new success,
   now resteth not the Youth till sight his eyes
   another slaughter, sore as this, oppress
   the barb'rous host that circling Beja lies:
   Not long the Prince whom fortune loves to bless,
   waits the fair end where leads his dear emprize.
   But now the routed Moors to vengeance cleave,
   their only hope such losses to retrieve.

77 "They crowd the mighty Mount whereof Meduse
   robbèd his body who the skies upbore:
   They flock in thousands from Cape Ampeluse
   and from Tangier, Antæus' seat of yore.
   Abyla's[67] dweller offereth scant excuse;
   who with his weapon hasteth him the more,
   when heard the Moorish clarions shrilly-tonèd,
   and all the reign high Juba whilom ownèd.

78 "The Mir-almuminin,[68] who led the throng,
   from the Dark Continent past to Portugal:
   Thirteen Moor kings he led, high, haught, and strong,
   to his Imperial sceptre subject all:
   Thus wreaking forceful every tyrant Wrong,
   wherever easy Wrong mote sate his gall,
   Sancho in Santarem he flies t' invest,
   yet his was hardly of success the best.

79 "Gives asp'erous battle, righting fury-fraught
   the hateful Moor a thousand feints designing;
   ne horrid catapult avails him aught,
   ne forceful batt'ering-ram, ne hidden mining:
   Afonso's son, conserving force and thought,
   and firm resolve with warlike skill combining,
   foreseeth all with prudent heart and art,
   and stern resistance brings to every part.

94

80 "But now the Vet'ran,— doomed by years to ease
and gentle rest, from life of toil and teen,
be'ing in the city,[69] down whose pastured leas
Mondego's wavelets kiss the hem of green;—
when learnt how close his son beleaguer'd is
in Santarem by Moormen blind with spleen,
forth from the City flies the fone to meet,
age-idless spurning with fast eager feet.

81 "He heads his army, tried in war and known,
his son to succour; and his well-led host
shows wonted Port'ingall-fury all their own,
till in brief time the Moor is broke and lost.
The Battle-plain,— whose blood-stained front is strown
with steely coats, and caps of varied cost,
horse, charger, harness, rich and worthy prize,—
heaped with their owners' mangled corpses lies.

82 "Forth fares the remnant of the Paynimry
from Lusitania, hurled in headlong flight:
But Mir-almuminin may never flee,
for ere he flee his life hath fled the light.
To Him whose arm vouchsafed such Victory
in praise and stintless prayer our hosts unite:
Chances so passing strange make clear to ken
God's arm smites sorer than all arms of men.

83 "Such crown of conquest still bedeckt the brow
of old Afonso, Lord of lofty fame;
when he, in fine, who ever foiled his foe,
was foiled by antient Time's unyielding claim:
Past the death-sickness o'er his pallid brow
its frigid hand, and wrung his feeble frame;
and thus the debt on mortal shoulders laid
his years to gloomy Libitína paid.

84 "His loss the lofty Promontories mourn,
  and from the wavy rivers floods of grief
  with lakelets overspread the fieldèd corn,
  and trickling tears are sorrow's sole relief:
  But ring so loud o'er Earth's extremest bourne
  the fame and exploits of our great lost chief,
  that evermore shall Echo for his reign
  'Afonso!' 'Afonso!' cry, and cry in vain.

85 "Sancho, his lusty son, the worthy heir
  of his great Father's valour, force and might,
  as did his early doings clear declare,
  when Bætis[70] fled ensanguin'd from the fight,
  and from Andalusía forced to fare
  the barb'arous King and peoples Ishmælite;
  and more, when they who vainly Beja girt
  of his shrewd blows themselves had borne the hurt:

86 "After he had been raised to Royal hest,
  and held for years a few his father's land,
  he wends the city Sylves to invest,
  plowèd whose plain the barb'arous peasant's hand:
  With allies val'orous was his daring blest
  the sturdy Germans, whose Armada man'd
  by furnisht host was flying o'er the wave,
  the lost Judæa to regain and save.

87 "To join in holy enterprise they went
  Red Frederick, who did first to move begin
  his mighty armament and succour sent
  to ward the town where Christ had died for men;
  When Guy, whose Croisers were by thirst bespent,
  yielded his sword to gallant Saladin
  there, where the Moslem host was well supplied
  with wat'ery store to those of Guy denied.[71]

88 "But that majestical Armade that came
     by dint of storm-wind o'er the Lisbon bar,
     would aid our Sancho the foul foe to tame,
     all being bounden for the Holy War:
     As to his Father, happed to him the same;
     and Lisbon fell to fortunes similar;
     aided by Germans, Sylves town he takes
     and the fierce dweller slays or subject makes.

89 "And if so many trophies from Mahound
     his valour snatchèd, eke denies his pride
     the Leoneze in peace to till their ground,
     whom Mart with martial usage loved to guide:
     Till on the bended neck his yoke he bound
     of haughty Túi and all its country-side;
     where many a city felt the dreaded blow
     which with thine arms thou, Sancho! broughtest low.

90 "But 'mid his many palms this Prince waylaid
     the stroke of tem'erous Death; his heir prefer'd
     was that esteemèd son whom all obey'd,
     second Afonso, of our Kings the third.
     He reigning, Alcacér-do-Sal was made
     ours, snatcht for ever from the Moorish herd;
     that erst was taken by the Moor beset,
     and now parforce he pays of Death the Debt.

91 "Afonso dying, straight to him succeedeth
     a second Sancho, easy-going soul,
     who in his weakling idlesse so exceedeth,
     the rulèd rule their ruler and their tool
     He lost the Reign, for which another pleadeth,
     by private preference deprived of rule;
     since, govern'd only by his minions' will
     he made him partner in their works of ill.

92 "Yet ne'er was Sancho, no, such profl'igate pest
    as was that Nero wedded with a boy,
    who in foul incest showing horrid zest
    his mother Agrippina dared enjoy;
    Ne'er with strange cruel arts did he molest
    the liege, nor gar'd the torch his town destroy;
    he was no waster, no Heliogabálus,[72]
    no woman-king like soft Sardanapálus.

93 "Ne'er was his tyr'annised people so chastisèd
    as wretched Sicill by her tyrant bane;
    ne like the despot Phálaris, he devisèd
    novel inventions for inhuman pain:
    But his high-hearted realm, which ever prizèd
    lords of the highest hopes and sovran strain,
    would ne'er whole-soulèd such a King obey,
    who showed not fittest for the kingly sway.

94 "Hence came the gov'ernance of the reign to right
    the County Bolognese; and he arose
    at length to kingship, when from life took flight
    his brother Sancho sunk in soft repose.
    This, whom the 'Brave Afonso' subjects hight,
    when fenced his kingdom from internal foes,
    strives to dilate it; what his Sire possest
    is worlds too narrow for so big a breast.

95 "Of both Algarves, given to his hand
    in gift of bridal dowry, greater part
    his arm recovers, and outdrives the band
    of Moors ill-treated now by hostile Mart.
    He freed and made the Mistress of her Land
    our Lusitania, such his bellic art;
    till final ruin whelmed the mighty hordes
    where'er Earth owned Lusus' subjects lords.

96 "See, next that Diniz comes in whom is seen
the 'brave Afonso's' offspring true and digne
whereby the mighty boast obscurèd been,
the vaunt of lib'eral Alexander's line:
Beneath his sceptre blooms the land serene
(already compast golden Peace divine)
with constitution, customs, laws and rights,
a tranquil country's best and brightest lights.

97 "The first was he who made Coimbra own
Pallas-Minerva's gen'erous exercise;
he called the Muses' choir from Helicon
to tread the lea that by Mondego lies:
Whate'er of good whilere hath Athens done
here proud Apollo keepeth ev'ery prize:
Here gives he garlands wove with golden ray,
with perfumed Nard and ever-verdant Bay.

98 "Brave towns and cities reared his hand anew,
stout fortalice, and strongly-castled mure,
while his well-nigh reformèd kingdom grew
with stalwart towers and lofty walls secure:
But when dure Atropos cut short the clew,
and shore the thin-spun thread of life mature,
arose, to filial duty nidering
the fourth Afonso, yet a brave good King.

99 "This proud Castile's bravades with equal pride
despised, of soul and breast serenely grand;
for aye the Lusitanian's sprite defied
fear of the strongest, though the smaller band:
But when the Mauritanian races hied
to win and wear Hesperia's winsome land,
and marchèd boldly to debel Castile
superb Afonso went to work her weal.

100   "Ne'er did Semiramis such myriads see
     who o'er the wide Hydaspick prairie trod;
     nor Attila,— who daunteth Italy
     with dreadful boast, self-titled 'Scourge of God,'
     hurried such Gothick hosts to victory,
     as the wild Saracens' stupendous crowd,
     with all th' excessive might Granáda yields
     that flockt to battle on Tartessus' fields.

101   "When saw Castilia's monarch, high and haught,
     such force inexpugnable fain of strife,
     dreading lest all Hispania come to naught,
     once lost ere this,[73] far more than loss of life;
     aid of our Lusian chivalry he sought
     and sent the summons by his dearest wife,
     his spouse who sends her, and the joy and pride
     of the fond Father to whose realm she hied.

102   "Entered Maria, fairest of the fair,
     her Father's palace-halls of tow'ring height;
     lovely her gest though joy was crusht by care
     that brimmed her beauteous eyes with tears that blight:
     and waved her glorious wealth of golden hair
     o'er neck and shoulders iv'ory-smooth and white:
     Before her gladly-greeting Sire she stood,
     and told her mission in this melting mood:—

103   "'Whatever various races Earth hath borne,[74]
     the fierce strange peoples of all Africk-land
     leadeth Marocco's mighty Monarch, sworn
     our noble Spain to conquer and command:
     Power like this ne'er met beneath the Morn
     since bitter Ocean learnt to bathe the strand:
     They bring such fierceness and a rage so dread
     the Living shake and quake the buried Dead.

104 "'He to whose arms thou gavest me to wife,
　　his land defending when such foes invade,
　　offers himself, o'erfeeb le for the strife,
　　to the hard mercies of the Moorish blade;
　　if, Sire! thou deign not aid that all-dear life
　　me shalt see from out the kingdom fade,
　　widowèd, wretched, doomed to lot obscure,
　　sans realm, sans husband, e'en sans life secure.

105 "'Wherefore, O King! of whom for purest fear,
　　Mulucha's[75] currents in their course congeal;
　　cast from thee dull delay, rise, swift appear
　　a second Saviour to our sad Castile:
　　If this thy count'enance, beaming love so dear,
　　set on a Father's fond proud heart its seal,
　　haste, Father! succour, an thou hasten not,
　　haply he faileth who thy succour sought.'

106 "Not otherwise fear-filled Maria spake
　　her Sire, than Venus when, in saddest strain,
　　she pled to great All-Father for the sake
　　of her Æneas tossing on the Main;
　　and in Jove's breast could such compassion 'wake,
　　his dreadful thunders from his hand fall vain:
　　The clement Godhead all to her concedeth
　　and mourneth only that no more she needeth.

107 "But now the squadded warriors muster dense
　　on Eborensian plains with fierce array;
　　glint in the sun-glare harness, sword, spear, lance,
　　and richly furnisht destriers prance and neigh;
　　The banner'd trumpets with a blast advance,
　　rousing men's bosoms from the gentle sway
　　of holy Peace to dire refulgent arms,
　　and down the dales reverb'erate War's alarms.[76]

108 "Majestic marcheth, girt by powers,
th' insignia of his Royal state among,
valiant Afonso, and his tall form towers
by neck and shoulders taller than the throng;
his gest alone embraves the heart that cowers,
in his stout presence wax the weaklings strong:
Thus to Castilia's realm he leads his band,
with his fair daughter, Ladye of the Land.

109 "In fine when met the Kings, Afonsos twain,[77]
upon Tarifa's field, they stand to front
that swarming host of stone-blind heathen men,
for whom are small the meadows and the mount.
No sprite there liveth of so tough a grain,
but feels its faith and trust of small account,
did it not clearly see and fully know,
Christ by His servants' arms shall smite the foe.

110 "The seed of Hagar laughing, as it were,
to view the Christian pow'er so weak, so mean;
begins the lands, as though their own, to share
ere won, among the conquering Hagarene;
such forgèd title and false style they bear
claiming the famous name of Saracene:
Thus with false reck'oning would they strip and spoil
calling it theirs, that noble alien soil.

111 "E'en so the barb'arous Giant huge and gaunt,
with cause to royal Saul so dread appearing
when seen the swordless Shepherd stand afront,
armed but with pebbles and with heart unfearing;
launchèd his sneer of pride and arr'ogant taunt
at the weak youngling's humble raiment jeering,
who, whirled the sling, soon read the lesson well,
how much shall Faith all human force excel:

112 "Thus do the Moormen, traitor-souls, despise
   our Christian forces, nor can understand
   how Heav'en's high fortress wonted aid affies,
   which e'en horrific Hell may not withstand:
   On this and on his skill Castile relies,
   falls on Marocco's King, strikes hand to hand:
   The Portingall, who holds all danger light,
   makes the Granádan kingdom fear his might.

113 "Behold! the brandisht blade and lance at rest,
   rang loud on coat and crest, a wild onsèt!
   They cried, as each his several law confest,
   these 'Sanct' Thiago!' and those 'Mahomet!'
   The cries of wounded men the skies opprest,
   whose flowing blood in ugly puddles met,
   where other half-slain wretches drowning lay,
   who dragged their shatter'd limbs from out the fray.

114 "With such prevailing force the Lusian fought
   the Gránadil, that in the shortest space
   an utter ruin of his host was wrought;
   ne fence, ne steely plate our strokes could face
   With such triumphant Vict'ory cheaply bought
   unsatisfied, the Strong Arm[78] flies apace,
   and timely aids Castilia's toiling pow'er,
   still mixt in doubtful conflict with the Moor.

115 "Now brightly burning Sol had housed his wain
   in Thetis' bower, and his slanting ray
   sank westward, bearing Hesper in his train,
   to close that rare and most memorious day:
   When of the Moors those valiant Sovrans twain
   the dense and dreadful squadrons swept away,
   with such fell slaughter as ne'er told of Man
   the page of Story since the world began.

116 "Ne'er could strong Marius e'en the quarter show,
of lives here victim'd by victorious Fate;
when to the river, red with gory glow,
he sent his thirsty Braves their drouth to sate:
Ne yet the Carthaginian, asp'erous foe
to Roman pow'er and cradled in her hate,
when slain so many Knights of noble Rome,
of their gold rings he sent three bushels home.

117 "And if sole thou so many souls to flit
couldst force, and seek Cocytus' reign of night,
when thou the Holy City didst acquit
of the base Júdean, firm in olden rite;
'twas that Jehovah's vengeance thus saw fit,
O noble Titus! not thine arm of might;
for thus inspirèd men had prophesied,
and thus by Jesu's lips 'twas certified.

118 "Accomplishèd his act of arms victorious,
home to his Lusian realm Afonso sped,
to gain from Peace-tide triumphs great and glorious,
as those he gained in wars and battles dread;[79]
when the sad chance, on History's page memorious,
which can unsepulchre the sheeted dead,
befel that ill-starr'd miserable Dame
who, foully slain, a thronfed Queen became.

119 "Thou, only thou, pure Love, whose cruel might
obligeth human hearts to weal and woe,
thou, only thou, didst wreak such foul despight,
as though she were some foul perfidious foe.
Thy burning thirst, fierce Love, they say aright,
may not be quencht by saddest tears that flow;
nay, more, thy sprite of harsh tyrannick mood
would see thine altars bathed with human blood.

120 "He placed thee, fair Ignèz! in soft retreat,
　　culling the first-fruits of thy sweet young years,
　　in that delicious Dream, that dear Deceit,
　　whose long endurance Fortune hates and fears:
　　Hard by Mondego's yearned-for meads thy seat,
　　where linger, flowing still, those lovely tears,
　　until each hill-born tree and shrub confest
　　the name of Him deep writ within thy breast.[80]

121 "There, in thy Prince awoke responsive-wise
　　dear thoughts of thee which soul-deep ever lay;
　　which brought thy beauteous form before his eyes,
　　whene'er those eyne of thine were far away:
　　Night fled in falsest, sweetest phantasies,
　　in fleeting, flying reveries sped the Day;
　　and all, in fine, he saw or cared to see
　　were memories of his love, his joys, his thee.

122 "Of many a dainty dame and damosel
　　the coveted nuptial couches he rejecteth;
　　for nought can e'er, pure Love! thy care dispel,
　　when one enchanting shape thy heart subjecteth.
　　These whims of passion to despair compel
　　the Sire, whose old man's wisdom aye respecteth,
　　his subjects murmuring at his son's delay
　　to bless the nation with a bridal day.

123 "To wrench Ignèz from life he doth design,
　　better his captured son from her to wrench;
　　deeming that only blood of death indign
　　the living lowe of such true Love can quench.
　　What Fury willed it that the steel so fine,
　　which from the mighty weight would never flinch
　　of the dread Moorman, should be drawn in hate
　　to work that hapless delicate Ladye's fate?

124 "The horr'ible Hangmen hurried her before
the King, now moved to spare her innocence;
but still her cruel murther urged the more,
the People swayed by fierce and false pretence.
She with her pleadings pitiful and sore,
that told her sorrows and her care immense
for her Prince-spouse and babes, whom more to leave
than her own death the mother's heart did grieve:

125 "And heav'enwards to the clear and chryst'alline skies,
raising her eyne with piteous tears bestainèd;
her eyne, because her hands with cruel ties
one of the wicked Ministers[81] constrainèd:
And gazing on her babes in wistful guise,
whose pretty forms she loved with love unfeignèd,
whose orphan'd lot the Mother filled with dread,
unto their cruel grandsire thus she said,—

126 "If the brute-creatures, which from natal day
on cruel ways by Nature's will were bent;
or feral birds whose only thought is prey,
upon ærial rapine all intent;
if men such salvage be'ings have seen display
to little children loving sentiment,
e'en as to Ninus' mother did befall,
and to the twain who rear'd the Roman wall:

127 "O thou, who bear'st of man gest and breast,
(an it be manlike thus to draw the sword
on a weak girl, because her love imprest
his heart, who took her heart and love in ward);
respect for these her babes preserve, at least!
since it may not her òbscure death retard:
Moved be thy pitying soul for them and me,
although my faultless fault unmoved thou see!

128   "'And if thou know'est to deal in direful fight
        the doom of brand and blade to Moorish host,
        know also thou to deal of life the light
        to one who ne'er deserved her life be lost:
        But an thou wouldst mine inn'ocence thus requite,
        place me for aye on sad exilèd coast,
        in Scythian sleet, on seething Libyan shore,
        with life-long tears to linger evermore.

129   "'Place me where beasts with fiercest rage abound,—
        Lyons and Tygers, there, ah! let me find
        if in their hearts of flint be pity found,
        denied to me by heart of humankind,
        there with intrinsic love and will so fond
        for him whose love is death, there will I tend
        these tender pledges whom thou see'st; and so
        shall the sad mother cool her burning woe.'

130   "Inclin'ed to pardon her the King benign,
        moved by this sad lament to melting mood;
        but the rude People and Fate's dure design
        (that willed it thus) refused the pardon sued:
        They draw their swords of steely temper fine,
        they who proclaim as just such deed of blood:
        Against a ladye, caitiff, felon wights!
        how showed ye here, brute beasts or noble knights?

131   "Thus on Polyxena, that beauteous maid,
        last solace of her mother's age and care,
        when doom'd to die by fierce Achilles' shade,
        the cruel Pyrrhus hasted brand to bare:
        But she (a patient lamb by death waylaid),
        with the calm glances which serene the air,
        casts on her mother, mad with grief, her eyes
        and silent waits that awesome sacrifice.

132 "Thus dealt with fair Ignèz the murth'erous crew,
in th' alabastrine neck that did sustain
the charms whereby could Love the love subdue
of him, who crown'd her after death his Queen;
bathing their blades; the flow'ers of snowy hue,
which often water'ed by her eyne had been,
are blood-dyed; and they burn with blinding hate,
reckless of tortures stor'd for them by Fate.

133 "Well mightest shorn of rays, O Sun! appear
to fiends like these on day so dark and dire;
as when Thyestes ate the meats that were
his seed, whom Atreus slew to spite their sire.
And you, O hollow Valleys! doomed to hear
her latest cry from stiffening lips expire,—
her Pedro's name,— did catch that mournful sound,
whose echoes bore it far and far around!

134 "E'en as a Daisy sheen, that hath been shorn
in time untimely, floret fresh and fair,
and by untender hand of maiden torn
to deck the chaplet for her wreathèd hair;
gone is its odour and its colours mourn;
so pale and faded lay that Ladye there;
dried are the roses of her cheek, and fled
the white live colour, with her dear life dead.

135 "Mondego's daughter-Nymphs the death obscure
wept many a year, with wails of woe exceeding;
and for long mem'ry changed to fountain pure,
the floods of grief their eyes were ever feeding:
The name they gave it, which doth still endure,
revived Ignèz, whose murthered love lies bleeding,
see yon fresh fountain flowing 'mid the flowers,
tears are its waters, and its name "Amores!"[82]

108

136 "Time ran not long, ere Pedro saw the day
of vengeance dawn for wounds that ever bled;
who, when he took in hand the kingly sway,
eke took the murth'erers who his rage had fled:
Them a most cruel Pedro did betray;
for both, if human life the foemen dread,
made concert savage and dure pact, unjust as
Lepidus made with Anth'ony and Augustus.

137 "This in his judgments rig'orous and severe,
plunder, advoutries, murtherers supprest:
To stay with cruel grasp Crime's dark career,
bred sole assurèd solace in his breast:
A Justiciary, not by love but fear,
he guarded Cities from haught tyrant-pest;
their doom more robbers dree'd by his decrees
than Theseus slew, or vagueing Hercules.

138 "Pedro, the harshly just, begets the bland,
(see what exceptions lurk in Nature's laws!)
remiss, and all-regardless prince, Fernand,
who ran his realm in danger's open jaws:
For soon against the weak, defenceless land
came the Castilian, who came nigh to cause
the very ruin of the Lusian reign;
for feeble Kings enfeeble strongest strain.

139 "Or 'twas the wages Sin deserves of Heaven,
that filchèd Léonor from marriage bed,
by false, misunderstood opinions driven
another's wife, a leman-bride to wed;
Or 'twas because his easy bosom given
to vice and vileness, and by both misled,
waxèd effeminate weak; which may be true,[83]
for low-placed loves the highest hearts subdue.

140 "Of such offences ever paid the pain
    many, whom God allowed or willèd He;
    those who fared forth to force the fair Helèn;
    Appius and Tarquin, eke, such end did see:
    Say, why should David of the saintly strain
    so blame himself? What felled th' illustrious tree
    of Benjamin? Full well the truth design a
    Pharaoh for Sara, Sichem for a Dinah.

141 "But if so weakeneth forceful human breast
    illicit Love, which spurns the golden mean,
    well in Alcmeré's son we find the test
    as Omphalé disguis'ed to hero-quean.
    Anthony's fame a shade of shame confest,
    to Cleopatra bound by love too keen;
    nor less thou, Punick victor! wast betray'd
    by low allegiance to some Puglian maid.

142 "Yet say who, peradventure, shall secure
    his soul from Cupid armed with artful snare
    'mid the live roses, human snow so pure,
    the gold and alabaster chrystal-clare?
    who 'scapeth Beauty's wiles and per'egrine lure,
    the true Medusa-face so awful fair,
    which man's imprison'd, witch-bound heart can turn
    no, not to stone, but flames that fiercely burn?

143 "Who se'eth a firm-fixt glance, a gesture bland,
    soft promises of angel-excellence,
    the soul transforming aye by charmed command;
    say, who from pow'er like this can find defence?
    Pardie, he scantly blameth King Fernand
    who pays, as he did, Love's experience:
    But human Judgment would, if fancy-free,
    adjudge his laches even worse to be.

CANTO IV

1 "After the horrors of the stormy Night,
   i with gloom, and lightning-gleams, and hiss of wind,
   breaks lovely Morning's pure and blessèd light,
   with hope of haven and sure rest to find:
   Sol banisheth the dark obscure from sight,
   laying the terror of man's timid mind:
   Thus to the doughty kingdom it befel,
   when King Fernando bade this world farewell.

2 "For, if so many with such hopes were firèd
   for one whose potent arm their harms could pay
   on those, that wrought their wrongs with soul untirèd,
   nerved by Fernando's heedless, feeble way;
   in shortest time it happed as they desired,
   when ever-glorious John arose to sway,
   the only heir that did from Pedro spring,
   and (though a bastard) every inch a King.

3 "That such accession came from Heaven divine
   proved 'special marvels, God His truth proclaiming,
   when Ev'ora city saw the choicest sign,
   a babe of age unspeech'd the ruler naming;
   and, but to show the Heav'en's supreme design,
   she raised her cradled limbs and voice, exclaiming,—
   'Portugal! Portu'ugal!' high uplifting hand,
   'for the new King, Dom John, who rules the land.'

4 "Changèd in sprite were all within the Reign,
   old hatreds firing hearts with novel flame;
   absolute cruelties none cared restrain
   popular Fury dealt to whence it came:
   Soon are the friends and kith and kinsmen slain
   of the adult'erous County and the Dame,
   with whom incont'inent love and lust unblest,
   the wappen'd widow showèd manifest.

5 "But he, dishonour'd and with cause, at last
   by cold white weapon falls before her eyes,
   and with him many to destruction past;
   for flame so kindled all consuming flies:
   This, like Astyanax, is headlong cast
   from the tall steeple ('spite his dignities);
   whom orders, altar, honours, nought avail;
   those through the highways torn and stript they trail.

6 "Now long Oblivion veils the deeds accurst
   of mortal fierceness, such as Rome beheld,
   done by fierce Marius, or the bloody thirst
   of Sylla, when parforce his foe expel'd.
   Thus Léonor, who mortal vengeance nurst
   for her dead County gars, with fury swell'd,
   Castilia's force on Lusitania fall,
   calling her daughter heir of Portugal.

7 "Beatrice was the daughter, interwed
   with the Castilian, who for kingship greedeth,
   putative offspring of Fernando's bed,
   if evil Fame so much to her concedeth.
   Hearing the voice, Castile high raiseth head,
   and saith this daughter to her sire succeedeth;
   for warfare must'ereth she her warrior bands
   from various regions and from various lands.

8 "They flock from all the Province, by one Brigo[84]
   (if such man ever was) yclept of yore;
   and lands by Ferd'inand won, and Cid Rodrigo
   from the tyrannick gov'ernance of the Moor.
   Little in fear of warlike feat doth he go
   who with hard plowshare cleaving lordeth o'er
   the champaign Leonèze, and boasts to be
   the blight and bane of Moorish chivalry.

9 "In Valour's ancient fame the Vandal host,
   confident still and stubborn, 'gan appear
   from all Andalusía's head and boast,
   laved by thy chrystal wave, Guadalquivir!
   the noble Island[85] eke, whilere the post
   of Tyrian strangers, to the war drew near,
   bringing insignia by renown well known,
   Hercules' Pillars on their pennons shown.

10 "Eke come they trooping from Toledo's reign,
   City of noble, ancient or'igin, span'd
   by Tagus circling with his sweet glad vein,
   that bursts and pours from Conca's[86] mountain-land.
   You also, you, all craven fear disdain
   sordid Gallegos! hard and canny band,
   for stern resistance fast to arms ye flew,
   warding their doughty blows whose weight ye knew.

11 "Eke War's black Furies hurried to the fight
   the fierce Biscayan folk, who clean despise
   all polish't reasons, and ne wrong ne slight
   of stranger races bear in patient guise.
   Asturias-land and that Guipusc'oan hight,
   proud of the mine which iron ore supplies,
   with it their haughty sworders armed and made
   ready their rightful lords i' the war to aid.

113

Luís de Camões

12 "John in whose bosom Peril only grows
    the strength Jew Sampson borrow'd of his hair,
    though all he hath be few to fight his foes,
    yet bids his few for battle-gage prepare:
    And, not that counsel fails when danger shows,
    with his chief lords he counsels on th' affair,
    but drift of inner thoughts he seeks and finds;
    for 'mid the many there be many minds.

13 "Nor lack their reas'onings who would disconcert
    opinions firmly fixt in pop'ular will,
    whose weal of ancient valour is convèrt
    to an unusèd and disloyal ill:
    Men in whose hearts Fear, gelid and inert,
    reigneth, which faith and truth were wont to fill:
    Deny they King and Country; and, if tried,
    they had (as Peter did) their God denied.

14 "But ne'er did such denial-sin appear
    in noble Nuno Alv'ares, nay, instead,—
    although his brothers show'd default so clear,—
    he fiercely chid the fickle hearts misled;
    and to the lieges steeped in doubt and fear,
    with phrase more forceful than fine-drawn he said,
    too fere for facund, as he bared his glave,
    threating Earth, seas, and sphere with ban and brave:—

15 "'What! 'mid the noble sons of Portugale
    that nills to strike for freedom beats a heart?
    What! in this province which the nations all
    crowned War's princess in ev'ry earthly part
    breathes, who his aid denies, such nid'ering thrall?
    renaying faith and love, and force and art
    of Portingall; and, be whate'er the cause,
    would see his country keep the stranger's laws?

114

16   "'What! flows not still within your veins the blood
       of the brave soldiers who 'neath banners borne
       by great Henriques[87] fierce with hero-mood,
       this valiant race in war did ever scorn?
       When tane so many banners, and withstood
       so many foemen, who such losses mourn,
       that seven noble Yarls were forced to yield
       their swords besides the spoils that strewed the field?

17   "'Say you, by whom were alway trodden down
       these, now who seem to tread adown on you;
       for Diniz and his son of high renown,
       save by your sires' and grandsires' derring-do?
       Then if by sin or sore neglect o'erthrown
       so could your olden force Fernand undo,
       to you fresh forces this new King shall bring;
       an it be sooth that Subjects change with King.

18   "'Such King ye have, that an ye courage have
       equal his kingly heart ye raised to reign,
       all en'emies shall ye rout so be ye brave,
       much more the routed, eath to rout again:
       But an such noble thought no more may save
       your souls from pen'etrant Fear to bosom tane,
       the craven hands of seely terrors tie,
       this stranger's yoke I, only I, defy.

19   "'I with my vassals only, and my brand
       (this said, his dreadful blade he bared mid-way)
       against the high and hostile force will stand,
       that threats a kingdom strange to stranger sway:
       By virtue of my Liege, my mourning Land,
       of Loyalty denied by you this day
       I'll conquer all, not only these my foes,
       but whatsoever durst my King oppose.'

115

20 "E'en as the Youths who 'scaping Cannæ-field,—
    its only remnants,— to Canusium fled
    despairing, and well-nigh disposed to yield,
    and hail the Carthaginian vict'ory-led,
    the young Cornelius to their faith appeal'd,
    and took his comrades' oath upon his blade
    the Roman arms t' uphold as long as life
    hold, or hath pow'er to 'scape the mortal strife:

21 "Forceth the Folk enforcèd in such wise
    Nuno, and when his final words they hear,
    th' ice-cold and sullen humour sudden flies,
    that curdled spirits with a coward fear:
    To mount the beast Neptunian all arise,
    charging and tossing high the lance and spear;
    they run and shout with open-mouthèd glee,—
    'Long live the famous King who sets us free!'

22 "O' the pop'ular classes not a few approve
    the War their natal land and home sustains:
    These fare to furbish armours, and remove
    injurious rust, of Peace the biting stains;
    they quilt their morions, plates for breast they prove;
    each arms himself e'en as his fancy fain 's;
    while those on coats with thousand colours bright,
    the signs and symbols of their loves indite.

23 "With all this lustrous Company enrol'd
    from fresh Abrantès sallies John the Brave,
    Abrantès, fed by many a fountain cold
    of Tagus rolling sweet abundant wave.
    The vanguard-knights commands that warrior bold
    by Nature fittest made command to have
    of th' Oriental hordes withouten count,
    wherewith Sir Xerxes crost the Hellespont:

24 "I say Don Nuno, who appearèd here
　　the proudest scourger of that prideful Spain,
　　as was in olden days the Hun so fere,
　　curse of the Frankish, of Italian men.
　　Followed another far-famed cavalier
　　who led the dexter phalanx Lusitane,
　　apt to dispose them, prompt to lead his fellows,
　　Mem Rodrigues they call de Vasconcéllos.

25 "While of the Knights in corresponding flank
　　Antám Vasqués d'Almáda hath command,
　　to Avranches' Earldom rose anon his rank,
　　who holds the Lusian host's sinistral hand
　　Nor far the banner from men's notice shrank
　　in rear, where Cinques by Castles[88] bordered stand
　　with John the King, who shows a front so dread
　　E'en Mars must learn to hide his 'minished head.

26 "Linèd the rempart[89] groups trembling fair,
　　whom hopes and fears alternate heat and freeze,
　　mothers and sisters, wives and brides in pray'er,
　　with fasts and pilgrim-vows the Heav'ens to please.
　　And now the Squadrons wont the war to dare,
　　affront the serrièd hosts of enemies,
　　who meet this onset with a mighty shout;
　　while all are whelmed in dreadful direful doubt.

27 "Messenger-trumpets to the cries reply,
　　and sibilant fife, and drum, and atambor;
　　while Antients wave their flags, and banners fly
　　with many-colour'd legends 'broidered o'er.
　　'Twas fruity August when the days be dry,
　　and Ceres heaps the peasant's threshing-floor,
　　August, when Sol Astrsæa's mansion reigneth;[90]
　　and the sweet must of grapes Lyæus straineth.

28 "Sudden Castilia's trump the signal gave
    horribly fearful, sounding tem'erous dread:
    Heard it the Hill Artábrus;[91] and his wave
    Guadiana rollèd backwards as he fled:
    O'er Douro and Transtagan lands it drave;
    Tagus sore agitated seaward sped;
    while mothers trembling at the terr'ible storm
    embraced with tighter arm each tiny form.

29 "How many faces there wan waxt and white,
    whose fainting hearts the friendly life-blood cheerèd!
    For in dire danger Fear hath more of might,—
    the fear of danger,— than the danger fearèd:
    If not, it seemeth so; when rage of fight
    man's sprite to quell or kill the foe hath stirrèd,
    it makes him all unheed how high the cost
    were loss of limb, or dear life rashly lost.

30 "Battle's uncertain work begins; and move
    right wings on either part to take the plain;
    these fighting to defend the land they love,
    those eggèd on by hope that land to gain:
    Soon great Pereira, who would foremost prove
    the knightly valour of his noble strain;
    charges and shocks, and strews the field till sown
    with those who covet what is not their own.

31 "Now in the dust-blurred air with strident sound
    bolts, arrows, darts and man'ifold missiles fly;
    beneath the destrier's horny hoof the ground
    quaketh in terror, and the dales reply;
    shiver the lances; thundereth around
    the frequent crash of fellèd armoury;
    foes on the little force redoubling fall
    of Nuno fierce, who makes great numbers small.

32 "See! there his brethren meet him in the fray:
    (Fierce chance and cruel case!) But dreads he nought,
    right little were it brother-foe to slay,
    who against King and Country trait'orous fought:
    Amid these ren'egades not a few that day
    war in the foremost squadrons fury-fraught
    against their brethren and their kin (sad Fate!)
    as in great Julius' warfare with the Great.[92]

33 "O thou, Sertorius! O great Coriolane!
    Catiline! all ye hosts of bygone age,
    who 'gainst your Fatherland with hearts profane
    ragèd with rav'ening parricidal rage;
    if where Sumánus holds his dismal reign
    most dreadful torments must your sin assuage,
    tell him, that e'en our Portugal sometimes
    suckled some traitors guilty of your crimes.

34 "Here doth the foremost of our lines give way,
    so many foemen have its force opprest:
    There standeth Nuno, brave as Ly'on at bay,
    where Africk Ceita rears her hilly crest;
    who sees the 'circling troop of cavalry,
    over the Tetu'an plain to chace addrest;
    and raging as they couch the deadly spear
    seems somewhat stirred, but hides all craven fear:

35 "With sidelong glance he sights them, but his spleen
    ferine forbids the King of Beasts to show
    a craven back; nay, rather on the screen
    of plumping lances leaps he as they grow.
    So stands our Knight, who stains and soils the green
    with alien gore-streams: On that field lie low
    some of his own; howe'er with valour dowerèd;
    hearts lose their virtue by such odds o'erpowerèd.

36 "John felt the danger and the dure affront
   of Nuno; straight like Captain wise and ware,
   he rushed afield, viewed all, and in the brunt
   with words and works taught men fresh deeds to dare.
   As nursing Ly'oness, fere and fierce of front,
   Who, left for chase her whelps secure in lair,
   findeth while for'aging for their wonted food
   Massylian[93] hind hath dared to rob her brood:

37 "Runs, frantick raging, while her roar and moan
   make the Seven-Brother Mountains[94] shake and rave.
   So John with other chosen troop hath flown
   forward his dexter wing t' enforce and save:
   'Oh strong Companions! Souls of high renown!
   Cavaliers braver than what men hold brave,
   strike for your country! now all earthly chance,
   all hope of Liberty is on your lance!'

38 "'Behold me here, your Comrade and your King,
   who 'mid the spear and harness, bolt and bow,
   foremost I charge and first myself I fling;
   smite, ye true Portughese, deal yet one blow!'
   Thus spake that great-soul'd Warrior, brandishing
   four times his lance before the final throw;
   and, thrusting forceful, by that single thrust
   lanceth such wounds that many bite the dust.

39 "For, see, his soldiers brent with ardour new,
   honoured repentance, honourable fire,
   who shall display most courage staid and true,
   and dare the dangers dealt by Mars his ire
   contend: The steel that catcheth flamey hue,
   aims first at plate, then at the breast aims higher;
   thus, wounds they give and wounds they take again;
   and, dealing Death, in Death they feel no pain.

40 "Many are sent to sight the Stygian wave,
   into whose bodies entered iron Death:
   Here dieth Sanct' Iágo's Master brave,
   who fought with fiercest sprite till latest breath;
   another Master dire of Calatrave,
   horrid in cruel havock, perisheth:
   Eke the Pereira foully renegate
   die God denying and denouncing Fate.

41 "Of the vile, nameless Vulgar many bleed;
   flitting with Gentles to the Gulf profound;
   where hungers, rav'ening with eternal greed,
   for passing human Shades the three-head Hound:
   And humbling more that haughty, arr'ogant breed,
   and better taming enemies furibund,
   Castilia's Gonfanon sublime must fall
   beneath the forceful foot of Portugall.

42 "Here⁹⁵ wildest Battle hath its cruel'est will,
   with deaths and shouts, and slash and gory shower;
   the multitud'inous Braves, who 're killed and kill,
   rob of their proper hues the bloom and flower:
   At length they fly! they die! now waxeth still
   War's note, while lance and spear have lost their power:
   Castilia's King the fate of pride must own,
   seeing his purpose changed, his host o'erthrown.

43 "The field he leaveth to the Conqueror,
   too glad his life had not been left in fight:
   Follow him all who can; and panick sore
   lends them not feet, but feather'd wings for flight:
   Their breasts are fillèd with a wild dolòur,
   for Deaths, for Treasure waste in wanton plight;
   for woe, disgust, and foul dishonour's soil
   to see the Victor rev'elling in their spoil.

121

44 "Some fly with furious curses, and blaspheme
him who the World with Warfare made accurst;
others that cov'etous breast all culp'able deem
for Greed enquicken'd by his selfish thirst.
That, alien wealth to win, with sore extreme
he plunged his hapless folk in woes the worst;
leaving so many wives and mothers, lorn
of sons and spouses, evermore to mourn.

45 "Campèd our conqu'ering John the'customed days
on foughten field, in glory of the brave;
then with vowed pilgrimage, gift, pray'er, and praise,
he gave Him graces who such vict'ory gave.
But Nuno, willing not by peaceful ways
on human memory his name to 'grave,
but by his sovran feats of war, commands
his men pass over to Transtágan lands.

46 "His gallant project favoureth Destiny,
making effect commensurate with cause;
the Lands that bordered by the Vandals lie
yielding their treasures bow before his laws:
Now Bætic banners which Seville o'erfly,
and flags of various princes, without pause,
all trail foot-trampled; naught their force availeth
whate'er the forceful Portingall assaileth.[96]

47 "By these and other Victories opprest,
Castilia's lieges long deplored their woes;
when Peace by all desired and gentle Rest,
to grant their vanquisht fone the Victors chose;
then seemed it good to His almighty hest
that the contending Sovrans should espouse
two royal Damsels born of English race,
Princesses famed for honour, form, and grace.

48 "Nills the brave bosom, used to bloody broil,
the lack of foeman who his force shall dree;
and thus, Earth holding none to slay and spoil,
he carries conquest o'er the unconquer'd Sea.
First of our Kings is he who left the soil
patrial, teaching Africk's Paynimry,
by dint of arms, how much in word and deed
the Laws of Christ Mafamed's laws exceed.

49 "See! thousand swimming Birds the silv'ery plain
of Thetis cleave, and spurn her fume and fret,
with bellied wings to seize the wind they strain,
where his extremest mete Alcides set:
Mount Abyla, and dight with tow'er and fane
Ceita, they seize, ignoble Mahomet
they oust: and thus our gen'eral Spain secure
from Julian-craft,[97] disloyal and impure.

50 "Death granted not to Portugal's desire
Hero so happy long should wear the crown;
but soon th' angelick Host and heav'enly Choir
a home in highest Heaven made his own:
To ward his Lusia, and to raise her higher,
He who withdrew him left the goodly boon,—
building our country on her broadest base, —
of noble Infants a right royal Race.

51 "Noways so happy was Duarte's fate,
what while he rose the royal rank to fill:
Thus troublous Time doth ever alternate
pleasure with pain, and temper good with ill.
What man hath lived through life in joyous state,
who firmness finds in Fortune's fickle will?
Yet to this Kingdom and this King she deignèd
spare the vicissitudes her laws ordainèd.

52 "Captive he saw his brother, hight Fernand,
the Saint aspiring high with purpose brave,
who as a hostage in the Sara'cen's hand,
betrayed himself his 'leaguer'd host to save.
He lived for purest faith to Fatherland
the life of noble Ladye sold a slave,
lest bought with price of Ceita's potent town
to publick welfare be preferred his own.

53 "Codrus, lest foemen conquer, freely chose
to yield his life and, conqu'ering self, to die;
Regulus, lest his land in aught should lose,
lost for all time all hopes of liberty;
this, that Hispania might in peace repose,
chose lifelong thrall, eterne captivity:
Codrus nor Curtius with man's awe for meed,
nor loyal Decii ever dared such deed.

54 "Afonso, now his kingdom's only heir,—
a name of Victory on our Spanish strand,—
who, the haught fierceness of the Moor's frontier
to lowest mis'ery tamed with mighty hand,
pardie, had been a peerless cavalier
had he not lusted after Ebro-land:
But still shall Africk say, 't were hopeless feat
on battle-plain such terr'ible King to beat.

55 "This could pluck Golden Apples from the bough,
which only he in Tiryns born could pluck:
He yoked the salvage Moor, and even now
the salvage Moorman's neck must bear his yoke.
Still palms and greeny bays begird his brow
won from the barb'arous raging hosts that flock,
Alcacer's fortèd town with arms to guard,
Tangier the pop'ulous, and Arzille the hard.

56 "All these by gallant deeds, in fine, were gainèd,
and low lay ev'ry diamantine wall
anent the Portingalls, now taught and trainèd
to throw the Pow'er that lists to try a fall:
Such extreme marvels by strong arms attainèd,—
right worthy el'oquent scripture one and all,—
the gallant Cavaliers, whose Gestes of glory
added a lustre to our Lusian story.

57 "But soon, ambition-madded, goaded on
by Passion of Dominion bitter-sweet,
he falls on Ferdinand of Aragon,[98]
Castile's haught kingdom hoping to defeat.
The swarming hostile crowds their armour don,
the proud and various races troop and meet,
from Cadiz fast to tow'ering Pyrenee,
who bow to Ferdinand the neck and knee.

58 "Scornèd an idler in the realm to rest
the youthful John; who taketh early heed
to aid his greedy father with his best,
and sooth, came th' aidance at the hour of need.
Issued from bloody battle's terr'ible test
with brow unmoved, serene in word and deed
maugre defeat, the Sire, that man of blood,
while 'twixt the rivals Vict'ory doubtful stood:

59 "For-that of valiant princely vein his son,
a gentle, stalwart, right magnan'imous Knight,
when to th' opponents he such harm had done,
one whole day campèd on the field of fight.
Thus from Octavian[99] was the vict'ory won,
while Anthony, his mate, was Victor hight,
when they the murth'erers who the Cæsar slew,
upon Philippi-field the deed made rue.

60 "But as thro' gathered shades of Night eterne
Afonso sped to realms of endless joy,
the Prince who rose to rule our realm in turn
was John the Second and the thirteenth Roy.
This, never-dying Glory's meed to earn,
higher than ventured mortal man to fly,
ventured; who sought those bounds of ruddy Morn,
which I go seeking, this my voyage-bourne.

61 "Envoys commiss'ioneth he, who passing o'er
Hispania, Gaul, and honoured Italy,
took ship in haven of th' illustrious shore
where erst inhumèd lay Parthenopè;
Naples, whose Dest'iny was decreed of yore,
the var'ious stranger's slave and thrall to be,
and rise in honour when her years are full
by sovereign Hispania's noble rule.

62 "They cleave·the bright blue waves of Sic'ulan deeps;
by sandy marge of Rhodes-isle they go;
and thence debark they where the cliffy steeps
are still enfam'd for Magnus here lain low:[100]
To Memphis wend they, and the land that reaps
crops which fat Nylus' flood doth overflow;
and climb 'yond Egypt to those Æthiop heights
where men conserve Christ's high and holy rites.

63 "And eke they pass the waters Erythréan,
where past the shipless peoples Israelite;
remain arear the ranges Nabathéan,
which by the name of Ishmæl's seed are hight:
Those odoriferous incense-coasts Sabsæan,
dainty Adonis' Mother's dear delight,
they round, and all of Happy Ar'aby known,
leaving the Waste of Sand and Reign of Stone.

64 "They push where still preserveth Persic Strait,
    confusèd Babel's darkling memory;
    there, where the Tygre blendeth with Euphràte,
    which from their head-streams hold their heads so high.
    Thence fare they his pure stream to find, whose fate
    'twill be to deal such length of history,
    Indus, and cross that breadth of Ocean-bed
    where daring Trajan never darèd tread.

65 "Strange tribes they saw, and through wild peoples past
    Gedrosian, and Carmanian, and of Inde;
    seeing the various custom, various caste,
    which ev'ry Region beareth in her kind.
    But from such asp'erous ways, such voyage vast
    man finds not facile safe return to find:
    In fine, there died they and to natal shore,
    to home, sweet home, returned they nevermore.[101]

66 "Reserved, meseemeth, Heav'en's clear-sighting will
    for Man'oel, worthy of such goodly meed,
    this arduous task, and stirred him onward still
    to stirring action and illustrious deed:
    Man'oel, who rose the throne of John to fill,
    and to his high resolves did eke succeed,
    forthwith when taken of his realm the charge,
    took up the conquest of the Ocean large:

67 "The same, as one obliged by a noble Thought,
    the debt of Honour left as 'heritance
    by predecessors, (who in life aye fought
    their own dear land's best interests to advance)
    ne'er for a moment failèd of his fraught,—
    Obligement;— at what hour Day's radiance
    pales, and the nitid Stars on high that rise,
    with falling courses woo man's sleep-worn eyes;

68 "Already being on bed of gold recline'd
    where Fancy worketh with prophetick strain;
    revolving matters in his restless mind,
    the bounden duties of his race and reign;
    Sleep, soft restorer, comes his eyne to bind,
    while thought and mem'ory both unbound remain;
    for, as his weary lids sweet slumber sealeth,
    Morpheus in varied forms himself revealeth.

69 "Here seems the King so high to soar away,
    that touched his head the nearest primal Sphere,[102]
    where worlds of vision 'neath his glances lay,
    nations of vasty numbers, strange and fere:
    and there right near the birthplace of the Day,
    unto his outstretched eyne began appear,
    from distant, olden, cloud-compelling mountains
    flowing, a twain of high, deep, limpid fountains.

70 "Birds of the feral kind, and kine, and flocks,
    'bode in the shadows of the shaggy wood:
    A thousand herbs and trees with gnarled stocks,
    barring the paths of passing mortals stood.
    Adverse had ever been those mountain-rocks
    to human intercourse, and clearly show'd,
    never since Adam sinned against our days,
    brake foot of man this breadth of bosky maze.

71 "From out the Fountains seemed he to behold
    for him inclining, with long hasty stride,
    two Men, who showèd old and very old,
    of aspect rustick yet with lordly pride:
    Adown their twistèd pointed locks slow roll'd
    gouts which their bodies bathed on ev'ry side;
    the skin of earthy texture, dark and dull;
    the beard hirsute, unshorn, but long and full.

72 "These hoary Fathers round their foreheads bore
tree-boughs, with unknown shrub and herb entwine'd;
and one a worn and wearied aspect wore,
as though from regions lying far behind:
And thus his waters which did slower pour
seemèd adown the further side to wind:
E'en thus Alpheus from Arcádia fled
to Syracuse and Arethusa's bed.

73 "This, who with graver gait and gesture came,
thus from a distance to the Monarch crieth:
'O thou! Whose sceptre and whose crown shall claim,
of Earth a mighty part that guarded lieth;
we twain, who fly through mouths of men by Fame,
we, whose untamèd neck man's yoke defieth,
warn thee, O King! 'tis time to send commands,
and raise large tribute from our natal lands.

74 "'Illustrious Gange am I, whose farthest fount
in realms celestial, heav'nly heights, I trace:
And yon stands Indus, King, who on the mount
which thou regardest, hath of birth his place.
Thou shalt hard warfare wage on our account;
but, still insisting ev'ry fear to face,
with ne'er seen conquests, and sans soil or stain,
the tribes thou viewest thou shalt curb and rein.'

75 "No more that holy noble River said;
both in a moment fade and disappear:
Awaketh Manoel in novel dread,
and big o'erchargèd thoughts ybred of fear.
Meanwhile his glitt'ering mantle Phoebus spread
upon the sombre somn'olent hemisphere;
Dawn comes and o'er the gloomy welkin showers
blushings of modest rose, and fiery flowers.

129

76 "The King in counsel calls his lords to meet,
   and of the vision'd figures news imparts;
   the holy Elder's words he doth repeat,
   which with a mighty marvel heaves their hearts.
   All straight resolve t' equip a sturdy fleet,
   that men, well skilled in navigator-arts,
   should cut the stubborn Main and forth should fare
   in search of novel climes and novel air.

77 "I, who right little deemed, forsooth, to find
   myself attaining hopes my Sprite desirèd;
   yet mighty matters of such cunning kind
   my heart presaging promised and inspirèd;
   e'en now ken not, or how or why design'd,
   or for what happy chance in me admirèd,
   that famous Monarch chose me, gave to me
   of this grave, gracious enterprize the key.

78 "And with fair offer coucht in courteous phrase,—
   lordly command obliging more than laws,—
   he said: 'In exploits dure and daring ways
   who woo most perils win the most applause:
   Riskt life enfameth man with highest praise
   or lost in honour's, not in honours', cause;
   And, when to blighting Fear it never bends,
   short it may be, yet more its length extends.

79 "'Thee from a chosen host have chosen I
   the dangers claimed by thee to undergo:
   'Tis heavy travail, hard, heroick, high;
   which love of me shall lighten, well I trow.'
   I could not suffer more:— 'Great King!' I cry,
   'to face the steel-clad host, sward, lance, fire snow,
   for thee were thing so slight, my sole annoy
   is to see trivial life so vain a toy.

80 "'Imagine ev'ry wildest aventure,
   such as Eurystheus for Alcides plan'd:
   Cleone's Lyon, Harpies foul and dour,
   and Boar of Erymanth and Hydra ban'd;
   in fine to seek those empty shades obscure
   where Styx surrounds of Dis the dire Dead-land;
   the greatest danger and the deadliest brunt,
   for thee, O King! this soul, this flesh would front.'

81 "His thanks and costly gifts on me bestows
   the King, whose reason lauds my ready will;
   for Valour fed on praises lives and grows,
   Praise is the noble Spirit's spur and spell.
   At once to share my fortunes doth propose,
   whom friendship and fraternal love compel,
   nor less resolved to win him name and fame, a
   dear trusty brother namèd Paul da Gama.

82 "Eke Nicholas Coelho volunteers,
   trainèd to toilsome tasks and sufferings long;
   both are in valour and in counsel peers,
   in arms experienced, and in battle strong.
   Now choicest hands in Youthtide's gen'erous years,
   lusting for Bravery's meed around me throng;
   doughty, high-mettled, as doth best become
   advent'urous manhood that would tempt such doom.

83 "All these by Man'oel's hand remun'erate were,
   that Love through Duty might the more increase;
   and with high words each heart was fired to bear
   adventures, peradventure, sans surcease.
   Thus did the Minyæ for their feat prepare,—
   to gain the glories of the Golden Fleece,—
   orac'ulous Argo-ship, that dared the first
   through Euxine waves her vent'urous way to burst.

84 "Now in famed Ulysséa's haven man'd,
    with raptures worthy of the great design
    (where his sweet liquor and his snowy sand
    our Tagus blendeth with Neptunian brine),
    ride the ships ready. Here my strong young band
    by fear unbridled glad in labour join;
    for those of Mars and Neptune,[103] one and all,
    the world would wander did I only call.

85 "Fast by the foreshore comes the soldiery
    in various colours prankt with various art;
    nor less enforced by inner force are they
    to seek and see Earth's unexplorèd part.
    Round the good Navy gentle breezes play
    and blithely waves each airy estandart:
    They[104] swear, gazing brine, on the breadth of brine,
    'mid stars Olympick Argo-like to shine.

86 "When all prepared according to this sort
    with what of wants such lengthy way demandeth,
    our souls we did prepare for Death's disport
    who before seaman's eyne for ever standeth:
    To the Most Highest, throned in Heaven's court
    which He sustains, whose glance this globe commandeth,
    that He, our guard and guide, His aidance lend,
    we prayed, and see our incept to its end.

87 "Thus we departed from the saintly Shrine[105]
    built on the margent of the briny wave,
    named, for all mem'ory, from the Land Divine,
    where God incarnèd came the world to save.
    King! I assure thee when this mind of mine
    remem'b'ereth how 'twas ours those shores to leave,
    filled are my sprite and heart with doubts and fears,
    and eyes can hardly stay their trickling tears.

88 "The City-people on that saddest day
(these for their bosom-friends, and those for kin,
and others but spectators) thronged the way
sad and down-hearted at the dreary scene:
We, winding through the virtuous array
a thousand monks and priests of rev'erend mien,
praying, in solemn pageant, to the Lord,
afoot set forth the ready barques to board.

89 "On such long dubious courses sent to steer,
us deemed the people den'izens of the tomb;
the wailing women shed the piteous tear,
and sadly sighed the men to sight our doom:
Wives, sisters, mothers (most their hearts must fear
whose love is foremost) added to the gloom
Despair; and shudder'd with a freezing fright
lest we, their loved ones, aye be lost to sight.

90 "This, following, saith: 'O son! I ever held
coolth of my sorrows and the sweet relief
of mine already weary way-worn eld
so soon to sink in glooms of need and grief;
why leave me thus to want and woe compel'd?
Why fly my love, fond child? whose days so brief
shall set in darkness, and in briny grave
shalt feed the fishes of the greedy wave.

91 "That, with loosed locks: 'O douce and dearest spouse,
lacking whose love Love willeth not I live;
why risk, when daring Ocean's wrath to rouse,
thy life, my life which is not thine to give?
How canst forget our fond fair marriage-vows?
Why face the waves a homeless fugitive?
Our love, our vain content shall nought avail
Thrown to the breezes as they blow the sail?'

92 "With such and sim'ilar words that spake the tongue
of love and human nature's yearning woe,
followed our seaward path both old and young,
life's two extremes by Time made weak and slow.
Sad Echo wailèd the near wolds among,
as though hard hills were movèd grief to show:
And tears the snowy shore suchwise bedewd,
drops rivall'd sands in equal multitude.

93 "Of us the Company, ne'er raising eye
on wife or mother, marcht in such a state,
we feared our hearts fall faint, and fain we fly
our fixt resolves, repenting all too late:
Thus I determined straight aboard to hie,
sans 'Fare-thee-wells' by custom consecrate;
which, though they be dear love's own lovely way,
redouble grief to those who go or stay.

94 "But now an agèd Sire of reverend mien,[106]
upon the foreshore throngèd by the crowd,
with eyne fast fixt upon our forms was seen,
and discontented thrice his brow he bow'd:
His deep toned accents raising somewhat keen,
that we from shipboard hear him speak aloud,
with lore by long experience only grown,
thus from his time-taught breast he made his moan:—

95 "'Oh craving of Command! Oh vain Desire!
of vainest van'ity man miscalleth Fame!
Oh fraud'ulent gust, so easy fanned to fire
by breath of vulgar, aping Honour's name!
What just and dreadful judgment deals thine ire,
to seely souls who overlove thy claim!
What deaths, what direful risks, what agonies
wherewith thou guerd'onest them, thy fitting prize!

134

96 "'Thou dour disturber of man's sprite and life,
    fount of backsliding and adultery,
    sagacious waster, and consummate thief
    of subjects, kingdoms, treasure, empery:
    They hail thee noble, and they hail thee chief,
    though digne of all indignities thou be;
    they call thee Fame and Glory sovereign,
    words, words, the heart of silly herd to gain!

97 "'What new disaster dost thou here design?
    What horror for our realm and race invent?
    What unheard dangers or what deaths condign,
    veiled by some name that soundeth excellent?
    What bribe of gorgeous reign, and golden mine,
    whose ready offer is so rarely meant?
    What Fame hast promised them? what pride of story?
    What palms? what triumphs? what victorious glory?

98 "'But oh! race 'gendered by his sin insane,
    whom disobedience of the high command,
    not only chasèd from the heav'enly reign,
    and doomed to distant and exilèd land;
    but, eke, from other state too blest for men
    where Peace with Innocence fared hand in hand,
    that olden golden Age, his victims hurl'd
    into an iron and an armèd world:

99 "'Since by this gustful Van'ity led astray,
    lighter thou makest man's light phantasy;
    since his brute fierceness and his lust of prey
    bear honoured names of Strength and Valiancy;
    since thou wilt price and prize, in wildest way,
    despisal of man's life, which aye should be
    esteemed of mortals, nay, held doubly dear,
    when He who gave it, gave it up with fear:

100 "'Neighbours thee not the hateful Ishmælite,
with whom abundant strife shalt ever hold?
Follows he not th' Arabian's law unright,
an thou wouldst fight to fill of Christ the fold?
A thousand cities, regions infinite,
are they not his, an cov'etest earth and gold?
Is he not strong in warfare, high in name,
if Honour be, not greed of gain, thine aim?

101 "'Dost leave the foeman breeding at thy gate
who wendest foreign far-off fone to seek;
whereby this antique realm lies desolate;
whose strength, o'erstretchèd, waxeth ruinous weak?
Seekest thou dark and dubious chance of fate,
who hearest Fame with honey'd accents speak,
lauding thy lot, and hailing thee seignior
of Inde, Perse, Arab and Æthiopia-shore?

102 "Oh, curst the Mortal, who the first was found
teaching the tree to wear the flowing sheet!
worthy th' eternal pains of the Profound,
if just that justest law I hold and greet.
Ne'er may man's judgment lofty and renown'd,
nor genius rare, nor harp sonorous sweet,
requite such gift with mem'ory, honour, fame;
perish thy glory, perish e'en thy name!

103 "'Iápetus' daring Son from Heaven brought
the fire he added human breast to bless;
fire, that inflamed to wars a world distraught,
with death and eke disgrace: (ah, sad distress!)
How better far for us and ours hadst wrought
Prometheus! and with loss of life the less;
had thy famed Statue never felt the fire
of great designs that 'gender great desire!

104 "'Ne'er had the Stripling, miserably brave,
    'tempted his Sire's high car, nor empty Air
    the mighty Mason and his boy, who gave
    names which the Sea-gulf and the River bear.
    No fierce emprize and fell, by land and wave,
    through fire, steel, water, wind, frost, heat, to fare,
    wherein the human race loves not to range.
    Sorrowful sort! condition strangest strange!'

CANTO V

1 "Such words that agèd Sire of honoured mien
   still was exclaiming, as we spread the wing
   to catch the sea-breath gentle and serene,
   and from the well-known Port went sorrowing:
   After the manner of far-faring men,
   when loosed the sail we garred the welkin ring
   crying 'Boon Voyage!' whereupon the breeze
   made every trunk glide off with 'customed ease.

2 "'Twas in the season when th' Eternal Light
   entered the Beast that workt Nemæa's woe;[107]
   and rolled our Earth, consumed by Time's long flight,
   in her sixth epoch, feeble, cold and slow:
   Now, in the wonted way, had met her sight
   the suns that fourteen hundred courses show,
   with seven and ninety more, wherein she ran,
   as o'er the seas th' Armada's course began.

3 "Slow, ever slower, banisht from our eyne,
   vanisht our native hills astern remaining:
   Remained dear Tagus, and the breezy line
   of Cintran peaks, long, long, our gaze detaining:
   Remainèd eke in that dear country mine
   our hearts with pangs of mem'ory ever paining:
   Till, when all veilèd sank in darkling air,
   naught but the welkin and the wave was there.

138

4 "Thus fared we opening those wastes of tide,
no generation openèd before;
sighting new islands and new airs we hied,
which gen'erous Henry had the heart t' explore:
Past Mauritanian hills and homes we plied,
the realm Antæus ruled in times of yore,
leaving to larboard; on our dexter hand
lay nothing surer than suspected land.[108]

5 "Hard by the great Madeiran Isle we past,
whose wealth of woodland won her chryssome name;
where first our people did their fortunes cast,
for name more famous than for classick fame:
But not the least, although 'twas found the last,
the smiles of Venus shall this Island claim:
Nay, an 'twere hers, scant cause it had to fear a
Cnidos or Cyprus, Paphos or Cythéra.

6 "We left Massylia's seaboard, sterile waste,
where Azenéguan[109] herds their cattle feed;
a folk that never soft sweet waters taste,
nor doth the meadow-math suffice their need;
a land no luscious fruit'ery ever graced,
where birds spoil iron in their maws of greed,
a soil where nought save horrid Want abounds,
parting the Berber's from the Blackmoor's grounds.

7 "We past the limit where, his southing done,
Sol guides his chariot t'oward his northern goal;
where lie the Races whence Clyméné's son
the clear bright colour of the daylight stole;
Here laving strangest peoples loves to run
black Sanagá in tropick summer cool;
where th' Arsenarium Cape its name hath lost,
yclept Cape Verd by us that keep the coast.

8 "Now past Canaria's archipelago,—
'Fortunate Isles' of olden mariners these,—
the waves that play around the Maids we plow
of agèd Hesper, hight Hesperides:[110]
Lands ever new, whose wonders greater grow
upon the sight, uprose our eyne to please:
Then with a prosp'rous wind we took the port,
to take provision of the wonted sort.

9 "Now at his Island was the harbour tane,
that warrior Sanct 'Iago's name did take;
a Saint who often holp the sons of Spain
brave slaught'ering of the Moorish man to make.
Hence while a favouring Boreas fanned the Main,
once more we sped to cut the vasty lake
of briny Ocean, while beneath the wave
settled the shore that sweet refreshment gave.

10 "Compast our courses thence the greater part
of Africk, eastward left her continent:
The province Joloff which, disposed athwart,
departs in tribes the Negro 'habitant;
mighty Mandinga-land by whose good art
the rich and lucid ore for us is sent,
which curvèd Gámbia's wealth of waters drinketh
ere in Atlantis' breadth his current sinketh:

11 "We past the Dorcades,[111] those isles assign'd
of the Weird Sisters erst the home to be,
who born of several vision reft and blind,
made single eye-ball serve for all the three:
Thou, only thou, whose crispy locks entwin'd
frore Neptune fired'st in his realm, the sea,
than ev'ry foulest monster fouler still
the burning sand with viper-brood didst fill.

12 "In fine with pointed Prow t'oward Austral shore
across the vastest Guinea Gulf we stray'd,
leaving the rugged Range where Lyons roar
and Cape of Palmas called from palmy shade:
The Rio Grande,[112] where the thund'erous Bore
roars on our noted coasts, we left and made
that goodly Island named from him who tried
to thrust his finger in the God-man's side.[113]

13 "There the broad shores of Congo kingdom show,
whilom by us convert to faith of Christ,
where long Zaïre's deep clear waters flow
River by men of old unseen, unwist:
And now in fine the wide-spread seas I plow,
far from Callisto's well-known Pole, and list
to pass the torrid heats beneath the Line,
which doth the centre of our Sphere define.

14 "And now our vision had afront descried,
there in the new half-heav'en a meteor new,
unseen by other men, who or denied,
or held it doubtful, an 'twere false or true:
We saw the Firm'ament's darker, duller side,
aye scant of stellar light where stars be few,
and the fixt Pole where man may not agree
if other land begìn, or end the sea.

15 "Thus passing forward we the regions gain,
where twice Apollo's yearly passage lies,
twin winters making, and of summers twain,
while he from Pole to Pole alternate flies:
Through calms and storms, caprices of the Main,
of angry Æolus sea-sent tyrannies,
we saw the Bears, despite of Juno, lave
their tardy bodies in the boreal wave.

16 "To tell the many dangers of the deep,
    sea-changes landsman never apprehendeth,
    sudden Tornados, storms the seas that sweep,
    Levens, whose fire the depths of air accendeth;
    black nights when Heav'en in rain-flood seems to weep,
    and Thunders bellowing till the welkin rendeth,
    were but lost labour, and would do me wrong,
    e'en were I dower'd with an iron tongue.

17 "Portents I witness'd, which rude mariners
    by long experience wont their lore to try,
    vouch for veracious, while each one avers
    things must be truthful when they meet his eye:
    These the sound judgment of the Sage prefers;—
    or taught by Science or pure Wits to 'spy
    the hidden secrets which in Nature brood,—
    to judge misfacts, or facts mis-understood.

18 "I saw, and clearly saw, the living Light,[114]
    which sailor-people hold their Patron-saint,
    in times of trouble and the winds' rude fight,
    and sable orcan when man's heart is faint.
    Nor less to one and all 'twas exquisite
    marvel, surpassing power of wonderment,
    to see the sea-based clouds, with bulky shaft,
    upheaving Ocean's depth with sucking draught.

19 "Certès I saw it (nor can I presume
    my sight deceivèd me) as high it grew,
    an airy vapourlet, a subtle fume
    which, caught by windy currents, whirling flew:
    Thence tow'ering tall to circumpolar gloom
    a Tube appeared so thin, so faint of hue,
    that man's unaidèd sight could hardly see it:
    Yet of some cloudy substance seemed to be it.

142

20 "Little by little growing high in air,
   with bigger girth than biggest mast it loomèd;
   here slim its middle, broad its bosom, where
   great gulps of water were in floods enwombèd:
   The wave of ev'ry Wave it seemed to share;
   while gathered vapours o'er its summit gloomèd;
   increasing ever more, and overchargèd
   as the huge water-load its bulk enlargèd.

21 "E'en as a ruddy Leech sometimes is seen
   fixt on the lips of beeve (that careless stood
   to drink on frigid fountain's hem of green),
   slaking her fire of thirst with alien blood:
   Sucking, she rounds her form with hunger lean;
   and swills and swells till full of gory food:
   Thus the grand column greater volume gaineth
   itself, and heavier weight of cloud sustaineth.

22 "But, when 'twas wholly filled, and fully fed,
   withdrawn the footing planted on the Main,
   athwart the welkin pouring floods it fled,
   with water bathing 'jacent watery plain;
   and all the waves it suckt in waves it shed;
   wherein no salty savour mote remain.
   Now let our Sages deft in Script expose
   what mighty secrets these which Nature shows.

23 "Had the Philosophers, who fared of eld
   so far the Wonders of the World to find,
   the Miracles which I beheld, beheld;
   the canvas spreading to such divers wind;
   what many weighty volumes had they fill'd!
   what pow'er to Stars and Signs had they assign'd!
   what growth to knowledge! what rare qualities!
   and all the purest Truth that scorneth lies.

24 "Five times the Planet, which maintains her place
   in the first sky, her swifter course had made,[115]
   now showing half and then her full of face,
   while over Ocean our Armada sped:
   When poised on topmost yard, in giddy space,
   'Land!' shouts a lynx-eyed sailor, 'land ahead!'
   Hurry the crews on deck in huge delight
   and over Orient sky-rim strain their sight.

25 "In misty manner 'gan their shapes to show
   the highland-range attracting all our eyes;
   the pond'erous anchors stood we prompt to throw,
   and furl the canvas which now useless lies:
   And that with surer knowledge mote we know
   the parts so distant which before us rise,
   with Astrolàbos, novel instrument,
   which safe and subtle judgment did invente:

26 "We landed, lost no time, on long and wide
   Bight,[116] and the seamen scattered 'bout the shore,
   to see what curious things be there descried,
   where none descried or ever trod before:
   But with my Pilots I retired aside
   on farther sands, our landfall to explore;
   and lief the solar altitude would span,
   and map the painted world in chart and plan.

27 "Here had our wand'ering course outrun, we found,
   of Semi-capran Fish the final goal,[117]
   standing atween him and the gelid round,
   Earth's austral portion, the more secret Pole.
   Sudden I see my crew a man surround,
   complexion'd sooty as the charrèd coal,
   tane as he hied him far from home to take
   combs of rich honey from the hilly brake.

144

28 "He comes with troubled gest and gait, as though
    he ne'er had found him in such fell extreme;
    nor he our speech, nor we his jargon know,
    a salvage worse than brutal Polypheme:
    Of the fine fleecy store to him I show
    the Colchos-treasure, gentle ore supreme,
    the virgin silver, spices rich and rare,
    yet seemed the Sylvan nought for these to care.

29 "Then bade I baser things be brought to his view,
    bunches of glassy beads transparent bright,
    of little tinkling falcon-bells a few,
    a cap of cramoisie that glads the sight.
    By signs and signals then I saw and knew,
    in such cheap trash he takes a child's delight:
    I bid them loose him with his treasures all,
    when off he hurries for the nearest kraal.

30 "His friends and neighbours on the following day,
    all mother-nude, with night-entinctur'd skin,
    adown their asp'erous hillocks fand their way,
    lárgesse and gifts their mate had won, to win:
    In crowds they gather'd and so tame were they,
    the show of softness bred much daring in
    Fernam Velloso's brain to see the land,
    and thread the bushes with the barbarous band.

31 "Now doth Velloso on his arm rely
    and, being arr'ogant, weens to wend secure;
    but when already overtime goes by
    wherein no sign of good I can procure;
    standing with face upturned in hope to 'spy
    the bold Adv'enturer, lo! adown the dure
    hillocks appears he, making for the shore,
    with more of hurry than he showed before.

32 "Coelho's galley lightly rowed for land
to take him off, but ere the shore she made
a burly Blackmoor cast a bully hand
on him, for fear their prisoner evade:
Others and others coming, soon the band
grappleth Velloso, who finds none to aid;
I haste, our gallant oarsmen strenuous working,
when shows a Negro flock[118] in ambush lurking.

33 "Now from the clashing cloud a rattling rain
of shafts and stones began on us to pour,
nor did they hurtle through the lift in vain,
for thence my leg this hurt of arrow bore.
But we, like men with causes to complain,
send such thick-woven answer strong and sore
that from their exploit gainèd some, perhaps,
a blush of honours crimson as their caps.

34 "And, saved Velloso from such imm'inent fate,
fast to the Squadron both the boats retirèd,
seeing the rude intent and ugly hate
of brutes by bestial rage and malice firèd;
from whom no better tidings could we 'wait
anent that India-land, the dear-desirèd,
save it lay far, far, far, the fellows said:—
Once more the canvas to the breeze I spread.

35 "Then to Velloso quoth a mate in jest
(while all with meaning smile the jibe attend),
'Holá, Velloso! sure that hilly crest
is hard to climb as easy to descend.'
'Yea, true!' the daring volunteer confest;
'but when so many curs afar I ken'd
packing, I hurried, for I 'gan to doubt me
ill-luck might catch you were ye there without me.'

36 "He then recounted how, when duly made
   that wooded Mount, the blacks of whom I speak,
   his further travel o'er the land forbade
   threat'ening unless he turn death-wrong to wreak:
   Then, straight returning, ambuscade they laid,
   that we when landing a lost mate to seek,
   might straight be banisht to the Reign obscure,
   that at more leisure they the loot secure.

37 "But now five other suns had come and gone,
   since from our landfall went we forth to plow
   seas to the seaman still unseen, unknown,
   while from astern the breezes favouring blow;
   when, as a night closed in, all careless strown
   the Crew kept watch upon the cutting Prow,
   deep'ening the welkin's darkling hues, a cloud
   sails high o'erhead, and seems the sky to shroud.

38 "It came so chargèd with such tem'erous stride
   in every falt'ering heart blank fear it bred:
   Roars from afar and raves the sombre tide
   as though vain thunder'ing on some rocky head:
   'Almighty Pow'r, o'er worlds sublime! I cried,
   'what threat from Heaven, or what secret dread,
   shall now this climate and this sea deform,
   what greater horror than the natural storm?'

39 "These words I ended not, when saw we rise
   a Shape in air, enormous, sore the view o'it;
   a Form disformèd of a giant size;
   frownèd its face; the long beard squalid grew o'it;
   its mien dire menacing; its cavern'd eyes
   glared ghastly 'mid the mouldy muddy hue o'it;
   stainèd a clayey load its crispy hair
   and coal-black lips its yellow tusks lay bare.

40   "So vast its eerie members, well I can
     assure thee, all the double deemed to sight
     of Rhodes' Colossus, whose inord'inate span
     one of the world's Seven Wonders once was hight.
     But when its gross and horrent tones began
     to sound as surged from Ocean's deepest night:
     ah ! crept the flesh, and stood the hair of me
     and all, that gruesome Thing to hear and see.

41   "'O rasher, bolder Race:' —'twas thus it Spoke,—
     'than all whose daring deeds have tempted Fate;
     thou, whom no labours tame nor war's fell stroke,
     nor rest wilt grant on human toils to 'wait:
     Since these forbidden bounds by thee are broke
     who durst my Virgin Seas to violate,
     which long I guardèd, where I ne'er allow
     plowing to foreign or to native prow:

42   "'Since the dark secrets com'st thou here to 'spy
     of Nature and her humid element,
     which from Man's highest lore deep hidden lie,
     on noble or immortal mission sent;
     from me the Terrors which ye dare defy
     hear now, the sequence of thy rash intent,
     o'er ev'ry largest Sea, o'er ev'ry Land
     which still thy cruel conquest shall command.

43   "'This know, what ships shall sail my waters o'er
     and brave, as brav'est thou me, to work my worst;
     to them assurèd foe shall prove my shore,
     where blow the storm-winds and the tempests burst:
     Hear! the first Squadron[119] that shall dare explore
     and through my restless waves shall cleave the first,
     such improvisèd chastisement shall see,
     more than all dangers shall the damage be.

44   "'An Hope deceive not, here I hope to deal
     consummate vengeance on th' Explorer's head;[120]
     nor he the latest shall my fury feel
     by pertinacious confidence ybred;
     nay, ye shall ev'ery year see many a keel
     (if me my judgment here hath not misled)
     such wrecks endure, shall see such fate befall,
     that Death shall seem the lightest ill of all.

45   "'And to the first illustrious Leader[121] whom
     Fame's favour raiseth till he touch the skies,
     I will give novel and eternal tomb,
     by the dark sentence of a God all-wise:
     Here of hard Turkish fleet that dree'd his doom,
     he shall depose the prideful prosp'erous prize;
     here shall at length my wrath and wrack surpass a
     Quíloa in ruins and a rent Mombasah.

46   "'Shall come Another, eke of honour'd fame,[122]
     a Knight of loving heart and liberal hand,
     and he shall bring his dainty darling Dame,
     Love's choicest treasure bound by Hymen's band:
     Ah, sore the sorrow, dark the day when came
     the pair to this my hard and hateful land,
     condemn'd from cruel wreck their lives to save
     and, suffer'ed toils untold, to find a grave.

47   "'Shall see slow starving die their children dear,
     sweet pledges bred of love, in fond love born;
     shall see the Caffres, greedy race and fere,
     strip the fair Ladye of her raiment torn:
     Shall see those limbs, as chrystal light and clear,
     by suns, and frosts, and winds, and weather worn,
     when cease to tread, o'er long drawn miles, the heat
     of sandy waste those delicatest feet.

48 "'And, more, shall see their eyne, whom Fate shall spare
    from ills so dreadful, from so dire a blow,
    the two sad lovers left in mis'ery, where
    implac'able thorns and terr'ible thickets glow:
    There, when the stones wax soft at their despair,
    shown by their ceaseless woe, sigh, groan, tear, throe,
    in a last strained embrace their souls exhale
    from out the fairest, fondest, saddest jail.'

49 "The fearful Monster would more ills unfold,
    our doom disclosing, when aloud cried I:—
    'Who art thou, whose immense stupendous mould,
    pardie, is mighty miracle to mine eye?'
    His lips and dingy orbs he wreathed and roll'd,
    and with a sudden frightful wailing cry,
    in slow and bitter accents he replied
    as though the question probed and galled his pride:

50 "'I am that hidden mighty Head of Land,
    the Cape of Tempests fitly named by you,
    which Ptol'emy, Mela, Strabo never fand,
    nor Pliny dreamt of, nor old Sages knew:
    Here in South Ocean end I Africk strand,
    where my unviewèd Point ye come to view,
    which to the far Antarctick Pole extendeth;
    such he your daring rashness dire offendeth.

51 "'Encelados, and Terra's Titan brood,
    Ægæon and the Centiman, the line
    of me, who Adamástor hight, withstood
    the hand that hurleth Vulcan's bolt divine:
    Hill upon hill to pile was not my mood;
    to conquer Ocean-waves was my design;
    I went to seek, as Captain of the Main,
    the fleet of Neptune which I sought in vain.

52 "'For Peleus' high-born spouse my burning love
   lurèd me rashly to such rude emprize;
   the belles of heaven ne'er my breast could move
   mine Ocean-Empress filled my yearning eyes:
   One day I saw her with the Nereids rove,
   all bare and beauteous, 'neath the summer skies:
   and in such manner she bewitcht my will
   no other feeling can my bosom fill.

53 "'But as my Ladye's grace I could not gain
   for being homely, huge of form and face,
   I sware by forceful rape my want t' obtain
   and so to Doris I disclosed my case:
   In dread she told her child my loving pain
   when modest Thetis, with her merry grace,
   replied:— 'What Nymph can boast, whate'er her charms,
   the strength to wrestle in a Giant's arms?

54 "'Algates, that Ocean may once more be free
   from this sad Warfare, I some mode will find,
   to gar mine honour with his suit agree;'
   thus was the message to mine ear consign'd.
   I, who no treach'erous snare in aught could see,
   (for lovers' blindness is exceeding blind)
   felt with a buoyant hope my bosom bound,
   and hopes of passion by possession crown'd.

55 "'Love madden'd, moonstruck, now I fled the war,
   and kindly Doris named the trysting-night;
   at length my lovely love I saw appear,
   my winsome Thetis, in her robeless white:
   Like one possest I hurried from afar
   opeing mine arms to clasp the life and sprite
   of this my body, and hot kisses rain
   upon her cheeks, her locks, her glorious eyne.

151

56 "'Ah! how it irks to tell my sad disgrace!
thinking my lover in these arms to hold,
mine arms a rugged Mountain did embrace,
yclad with bramble bush, a horrid wold:
Before this rock, upstanding face to face,
which for that Angel front I did enfold,
no more was I a Man, no! lorn and lone
a rock, a stone, I stood before a stone.

57 "'Oh Nymph! the loveliest born that bare the Main,
alb'eit my presence ne'er by thee was sought,
how could my poor delusion cause thee pain?
Why not be mountain, cloud, rock, vision, nought?
Raging I wandered forth well-nigh insane
for yearning grief with foul dishonour fraught,
to seek another world, where none could see
my trickling tears, and scoff at them and me.

58 "'Meanwhile my brethren, who the conquest lost,
crusht in extremest conquer'd mis'ery pinèd;
whom, for more surety, that vain-glorious host
of upstart Gods 'neath various Mounts consignèd:
And, as Immortals scoff at mortal boast,
I, to my sorrows in no wise resignèd,
felt Fate, mine awful foe, begin to shape
a dreadful vengeance for my daring rape.

59 "'My flesh slow hardens into solid earth,
to rocks and horrid crags enstone my bones;
these limbs thou seest and this mighty girth,
extend where desert Ocean raves and moans:
In fine the giant-stature of my birth
to this far Headland sprent with rocks and stones
the Gods debased; and doubling all my woes,
round me white, winsome, watery Thetis flows.'

60 "Thus parlied he; and with appalling cry,
   from out our sight the gruesome Monster died;
   the black cloud melted, and arose on high
   sonorous thunders rollèd by the tide.
   To th' Angel-choirs with hands upraisèd, I—
   invisible Controuls so long our guide,—
   prayed God in pity would those Ills withhold,
   by Adamástor for our Race foretold.

61 "Now Pyroeis and Phlegon 'gan appear
   with th' other pair that hale the radiant wain,
   when the tall heights of Table Mount we spere,
   which from the mighty Giant form hath tane:
   Standing along now easting shores we steer,
   and cleave the waters of the Lévant main,
   the coast-line hugging with a northing Prow,
   and sight a second landfall o'er the bow.[123]

62 "The native owners of this other land,
   the burnisht livery of Æthiops wore,
   yet was their bearing more humane and bland,
   than those who so mistreated us before.
   With dance and joyous feasts, a merry band
   approacht us tripping on the sandy shore,
   bringing their Women and fat herds that grace
   the pastures, gentle kine of high-bred race.

63 "The bronzèd Women, scorcht by burning clime,
   astraddle rode the slow-paced gentle Steer,
   beasts which their owners hold of beeves the prime,
   better than any of the herds they rear:
   Pastoral canticles, or prose, or rhyme,
   concerted in their mother-tongue we hear;
   and to the rustick reed sweet tunes they teach,
   as Tit'yrus chaunted 'neath his spreading beech.

64 "These, who seemed glad to see the guest abide
amid them, greeted us with friendly mood,
and many a fatted fowl and sheep supplied,
their goods exchanging for the things deemed good:
But though my comrades tried, they vainly tried,
for not a word in fine was understood
that of our search a signal might convey:—
Anchor I weighéd, and I sailed away.

65 "Now here in mighty gyre our flight had flown
round Blackmoor Africk shore; and now regainéd
our Prores the torrid heat of Middle Zone,
while Pole Antarctick far in rear remainéd:
We left astern an Islet a first made known
by the first Squadron whose long toils attainéd
the Cape of Tempests; and, that Islet found,
ended her voyage at its bourne and bound.[124]

66 "Thence drave we, cutting for a length of days,—
where storms and sadd'ening calms alternate range,—
undreaméd Oceans and unpathéd ways,
our sole conductor Hope in toils so strange:
Long time we struggled with the sea's wild maze,
till, as its general Law is changeless Change,
we met a current[125] with such speed that sped,
against the flow 'twas hard to forge ahead.

67 "Of this prevailing flood the puissant force,
which lo the southward our Armada hove,
such set opposéd to our northing course,
the winds to waft us onwards vainly strove:
Till Notus fashed to find us fare the worse,
(it seems) in struggle with the drift that drove,
enforced his blasts, and with such choler blew
maugre the mighty current on we drew.

68 "Reducèd Sol that famed and sacred Day,
    wherein three Kings in Orient region crown'd,
    a King came seeking who belittled lay,
    a King in whom three Kings in One are bound:
    That morn to other hythe we made our way
    finding the peoples that before we found,
    by a broad River, and we gave it name
    from the high hol'iday when to port we came.[126]

69 "Sweet food we barter'd from their scanty store,
    sweet water from their stream; but natheless here
    gained we no tidings of that Indian shore,
    from men to us that almost dumblings were.
    See now, O King! what distant regions o'er
    of Earth we wandered, peoples rude and fere,
    nor news nor signal had our labours earnèd
    of the fair East for which our spirits yearnèd.

70 "Imagine, prithee, what a piteous state
    must have been ours when all save life was gone,
    by hunger broken and the storm's wild hate,
    and curst by novel climes and seas unknown:
    Our hearts despaired of Hope deferred so late,
    ill dull Despair had marked us for her own;
    toiling beneath those strange unnat'ural skies,—
    our northern nature's fellest enemies.

71 "And now decayed and damaged waxt our food,
    sore damaging the wasted frame of man,
    without one comfort, sans one gleam of good,
    not e'en Hope's flatt'ering tale nor Fancy vain:
    Dost think that Sailor of the sturdiest mood,
    or any Soldier save the Lusitan,
    perchance, had loyalty so long preservèd
    both for his King and for the Chief he servèd?

72 "Dost think, the wretches had not mutinied
against the Head who with their mood had striven,
parforce becoming Pyrats, turned aside
from duty, by despair, want, hunger driven?
In very sooth these men were sorely tried,
since from their hearts ne moil ne toil hath driven
Portingall-excellence, abounding still
in leal valour and obedient will.

73 "Leaving in fine that Port of fair sweet flood,
and, dight once more to cut the salty spray;
off from the coast-line for a spell we stood,
till deep blue water 'neath our kelsons lay;
for frigid Notus, in his fainty mood,
was fain to drive us leewards to the Bay
made in that quarter by the crookèd shore,
whence rich Sofála sendeth golden ore.

74 "This Sea-bight passing far, the nimble helm,
by men to saintly Nicholas assignèd,
where roaring Ocean raves on Terra's realm,
this and that vessel's prore eftsoons inclinèd:
And now from hearts which hopes and fears o'erwhelm,
hearts in such faith t' a fragile plank resignèd,
as hope grew hopeless, esperance despair,
good sudden tidings banisht cark and care.

75 "And thus it happed, as near the shore we went
where beach and valley lay in clearest view,
a stream whose course in ocean there was spent,[127]
showèd of sails that came and went a few.
Good sooth, to greatest joyaunce all gave vent,
when first we sighted mariners who knew
mariner-practice; for we here were bound
to find some tidings which, indeed, we found.

156

76   All Æthiopians are yet 'twould appear,
    they held communion with men better bred:
    Some words of Arab parlancè here we hear
    imported sounds their mother-speech amid:
    A flimsy wrapper of tree-wool they wear
    a-twisted tight about each kinky head;
    while other pieces dipt in azure tinct,
    are round their middles and their shame precinct.

77   "In Arab language, which they little know,
    but which Fernam Martins well comprehendeth,
    ships great as ours, they say, scud to and fro
    piercing the waters with the beak that rendeth:
    But there where Phoebus leaps in air, they go
    whither the broad'ening coast to south extendeth,
    then from south sunwards;[128] and a Land is there
    of folk like us and like the daylight fair.

78   "Here was each bosom with rare gladness cheerèd
    by the good people, and their news much more:
    From all the signals in this stream appearèd,
    'Stream of Good Signals' christened we the shore:
    A marble column on this coast we rearèd
    whereof, to mark such spots, a few we bore;
    its name that lovely Angel-youth supplied[129]
    who did Thobias to Gabáel guide.

79   "Of shells and oysters, and the weedy load,
    the noisome offspring of the Main profound,
    we cleansed our kelsons which the long sea-road
    brought to careening cloggèd and immund:
    Our blameless Æthiops, who not far abode,
    with pleasing jocund proffers flockt around
    supplying maintenance we mainly sought,
    pure of all leasing, free from feigning thought.

80 "Yet from our esp'erance great, our hopes immense
bred by this seaboard, was not pure and true
the joy we joyed; nay, cruel recompense
dealt us Rhamnúsia, sorrows strange and new.
Thus smiling Heav'en mixt favours doth dispense;
in such condition dark and dure man drew
the breath of Life; and, while all Ills endure,
Good changeth often, Good is never sure.

81 "And 'twas that sickness of a sore disgust,[130]
the worst I ever witness'd, came and stole
the lives of many; and far alien dust
buried for aye their bones in saddest dole.
Who but eye-witness e'er my words could trust?
of such disform and dreadful manner swole
the mouth and gums, that grew proud flesh in foyson
till gangrene seemèd all the blood to poyson:

82 "Gangrene that carried foul and fulsome taint,
spreading infection through the neighb'ouring air:
No cunning Leach aboard our navy went,
much less a subtle Chirurgeon was there;
but some whose knowledge of the craft was faint
strove as they could the poisoned part to pare,
as though 'twere dead; and here they did aright;—
all were Death's victims who had caught the blight.

83 "At last in tangled brake and unknown ground,
our true companions lost for aye, we leave,
who 'mid such weary ways, such dreary round,
such dread adventures aidance ever gave.
How easy for man's bones a grave is found!
Earth's any wrinkle, Ocean's any wave.
whereso the long home be, abroad, at home,
for ev'ery Hero's corse may lend a tomb.

158

84 "When from that Haven we resumed our way
while brighter hopes with darker hearts combine'd,
we opèd Ocean where the down coast lay,
expecting surer signal e'er to find:
At last we rode in rude Mozámbic Bay,
of whose vile leasing, and whose villain kind
thou must have knowledge; and the foul deceit
wherewith Mombásah would her guests defeat.

85 "Until safe anchored in thy harbour, rife
with all the gracious guest-rites that bestow
health on the living, on the dying life,
God in His pity pleased the way to show:
Here rest, here sweet repose from grief, toil, strife,
new Peace appeasing ev'ry want and woe
thou gavest us: Now, if hast heard me well
told is the tale thou badest me to tell.

86 "Judge then, O King! an over Earth e'er went
men who would 'tempt such paths of risk and dread?
Dost deem Æneas or e'en eloquent
Ulysses, fared so far this Earth to tread?
Did any dare to see the Sea's extent
howe'er the Muse their Gestes hath sung or said,
as I by force of will and skill have seen
and still shall see; or e'en the eighth, I ween?

87 "This, who so deeply drank of Fount Aonian,
o'er whom contend in conquest peregrine
Rhodes, Ios, Smyrna, with the Colophonian
Athens and Argos and the Salamine:
And that, the lustre of the land Ausonian,
whose voice altis'onous and whose lyre divine
his native Mincius hearing, sinks to sleep,
while Tyber's waves with pride and pleasure leap:

88   "Sing, laud and write they both in wild extremes
     of these their Demigods, and prowess vaunt
     on fabled Magians, Circes, Polyphemes,
     and Sirens lulling with the sleepy chaunt:
     Send them to plow with oar and sail the streams
     of Cicons; on th' oblivious lands descant
     where slumb'erous Lotus-eaters dazed and died;
     e'en be their Pilot whelmed in Ocean-tide:

89   "Storms let them loosen from the Bags of Wind,
     create Calypsos captivate by love;
     make Harpies' touch contam'inate all they find,
     and in sad Hades make their Heroes rove;
     however much o'er much they have refin'd
     such fabled tales, which Poet's fancy prove,
     the simple naked truth my story telleth
     all their grandiloquence of writ excelleth."

90   Fast on our Captain's facund lips depends
     as drunk with wonder, all that soul-wrapt crowd;
     until at length his travel-story ends;
     his tale that told of noble deeds and proud.
     The high-conceiv'ed intent the King commends
     of Kings to not'able feats of warfare vow'd:
     Their Lieges' old and val'orous strain extols,
     their loyal spirits and their noble souls.

91   Th' admiring audience to recount are fain
     each case, as each one best could understand:
     None from the hardy Folk could turn their eyne
     who by such long-drawn ways the waves had span'd.
     Now, as the Delian youth turns round the rein
     Lampetia's brother held with feeble hand,
     and in the Thetian arms way-weary falls;
     the King hies sea-borne to his royal halls.

160

92 How pleasant sound the praise and well-won glory
   of man's own exploits as man hears them chime!
   for noble travail, actions digne of story,
   that dim or equal those of passèd Time.
   Envy of famous feats untransitory
   hath 'gendered thousand deeds sublime:
   The Brave who loves to tread in Valour's ways
   pants for the pleasure of his fellows' praise.

93 Achilles' glorious feats could not so 'flame,
   nor Alexander's soul to fight inspirèd;
   as he who sang in numbered verse his name;
   such praise, such honour most his soul desirèd.
   Nought but the trophies of Miltiades' fame
   could rouse Themistocles with envy firèd;
   who owned his highest joy, his best delight,
   came from the voices which his feats recite.

94 Vasco da Gama striveth hard to prove
   that these old travels in world-song resounding
   merit not glory nor men's hearts may move
   like his sore travails Heav'en and Earth astounding.
   Yes ! but that Hero, whose esteem and love
   crownèd with praise, prize, honours, gifts abounding
   the Lyre of Mantua, taught her Bard to chaunt
   Æneas' name and Rome's high glories vaunt.

95 Scipios and Cæsars giveth Lusia-land,
   gives Alexanders and Augusti gives;
   but she withal may not the gifts command
   whose want rears rough and ready working-lives:
   Octavius, prest by Fortune's heaviest hand,
   with compt and learned verse her wrong survives.
   Nor, certés, Fulvia shall this truth deny,
   Gláphyra's[131] wit entrapt her Anthony.

96 Goes Cæsar subjugating gen'eral France
    yet worked his arms to Science no offence;
    this hand the Pen compelling, that the Lance
    he vied with Cicero's gift of eloquence:
    What most doth Scipio's name and fame enhance
    is of the Com'edy deep experience:
    What Homer wrote that Alexander read,
    we know, whose roll ne'er left his couch's head.

97 In fine, the nations own no Lord of Men
    that lackt a cultured learnèd phantasy,
    of Grecian, Latian, or barbarian strain;
    only the Lusian lacking it we see.
    Not without shame I say so, but 'twere vain
    to hope for high triumphant Poesy
    till men our Rhymes, our Songs shall lay to heart;
    for minds Art-ign'orant aye look down on Art.

98 For this, and not for Nature's fault, be sure,
    Virgil nor Homer rise to strike the lyre;
    nor shall rise ever, an this mode endure,
    pious Æneas or Achilles dire.
    But,—worst of all,— it maketh man so dour
    austere, rough, frigid to poetic fire;
    so rude, so heedless to be known or know,
    few heed the want and many will it so.

99 Let grateful Gama to my Muse give grace,
    for the great patriot-love that gars her sound
    the Lyre for all her Sons, and aye retrace
    the name and fame of ways and wars renown'd:
    Nor he, nor they who call themselves his race
    e'er in Calliope a friend so found,
    or from the Tagus-maidens boon could claim,
    to leave their golden webs and hymn his name.

100　Because fraternal love and friendly will
　　　that deals to every Lusian Brave his meed
　　　of laud, this thought, these resolutions fill
　　　my gentle Tagides; and this their creed.
　　　Yet ne'er let human bosom cease to thrill
　　　with Hope to dare and do some mighty deed,
　　　since or by these or, haply, other ways,
　　　he ne'er shall forfeit prizes, value, praise.

CANTO VI

1 Scant could devise how best to entertain
the pagan King our Voyagers renown'd,
firm friendship of the Christian King to gain
and folk so puissant proved, so faithful found:
Grieveth him greatly, that his rule and reign
be placed so distant from Europa's bound
by lot, nor let him neighbour that abode
where opened Hercules the broad sea-road.

2 With games and dances, gentle, honest play
e'en as accorded with Melindan style,
and fishing frolicks, like the Lageian gay[132]
delighted Anthony with gladde'ning guile,
rejoiced that famous Sovran every day,
the Lusitanian host to feast and fill
with banquets rich, rare meats and unknown dishes
of fruit and flesh, of birds, and beasts, and fishes.

3 But when the Captain saw him still detainèd
far more than seemèd meet, while the fresh breeze
to sail inviteth; and he had obtainèd
the Negro Pilots and the new supplies;
no longer list he tarry; for remainèd
long paths to plow through salt and silvern seas;
To the good Pagan bids he warm adieu,
who prays their friendship may be long and true.

4 He prayeth, eke, that Hythe shall ever be
   the place where all the Fleets may rest and bait;
   for nothing better now desireth he,
   than for such Barons to quit reign and state:
   Eke, that ere light of Life his body flee
   he will on opportunity await
   his days to peril and his crown to waive,
   for King so kingly and for Braves so brave.

5 Response in sim'ilar speech to such discourse
   the Captain gave, and loosing canvas sailèd,
   straight for Auroran regions shaping course,
   where his long seeking still so scant availèd.
   No more his Guide and Pilot had recourse
   to fraud and falsehood, nay, he never failèd
   in his sure seamanship; so sped they o'er
   securer seas than those they sail'd before.

6 They fought the restless floods that front the Morn
   now ent'ering Indic Ocean, and descried
   Sol's chambers, where the burning God is born;
   and ev'ery wish was wellnigh satisfied.
   But now that ill Thyoneus' soul of scorn,
   mourning the mighty meeds of power and pride
   that Lusian valour wendeth dight to win,
   burns and blasphemes with madding rage insane.

7 He saw the potent hosts of Heav'en prepare
   in Lisbon town a novel Rome t' instal:
   Nor aught can alter; such high fortunes are
   ruled by the dreadful Pow'er that ruleth all.
   In fine he flies Olympus in despair,
   to find on earth new mode remedial:
   He thrids the humid Reign and seeks his court
   who gained the Gov'ernance of the Seas by sort.

8 Deep in the lowest depths of the profound
and lofty Caves, where surges slumb'ering lie;
there, whence the billows sally furibund
when to fierce winds the fiercer waves reply
bides Neptune, and abide their Lord around
Ner'eids, and many a sea-born Deity
where fit for cities leave the waves a plain
dry for the Godheads governing the Main.

9 Discover th' undiscovered depths of sea
Courts strewn with gravels of fine silver hoar;
and lofty turrets crown that Ocean-lea
chrystalline masses of diaph'anous ore:
However near the curious eye may be,
so much its judgment shall be less secure
an it be chrystal or the diamant-stone
that doth such clearness and such radiance own.

10 The gates of purest gold, where lies inlaid
rich seed of pearl that in the sea-shell breedeth,
with rarest shapes of sculpture are portray'd
whereon hot Bacchus pleasèd glances feedeth:
There 'mid the foremost, limned in light and shade,
old Chaos' face confus'd the stranger readeth:
the fourfold El'ements eke he sees translate
each in his several office and estate.

11 There Fire sublimely held supremest height,
who by no grosser substance was sustainèd
lending to living things his life and light,
since by Prometheus stolen and detainèd.
Behind him, standing high 'yond mortal sight,
invis'ible Air a lower place maintainèd,—
Æther, which conquered ne by Heat ne Cold,
ne'er suff'ereth Earth a vacuous space t' enfold.

12 There deckt with mount and boscage Terra stood
   Yclad in grass, shrub, tree of blossom'd head;
   affording life, affording divers food
   to ev'ry breathing thing her surface bred:
   The glassy figure, eke, ensculptur'ed stood
   of Water, veining Earth and interspread,
   creating fishes in their varied norm,
   and by her humour holding all in form.

13 Carved on another panel showed the fight,
   waged by the Gods against the Giantry;
   Typhoeus lies 'neath Ætna's serried height,
   far flashing crepitant artillery:
   There sculptured cometh gravid Earth to smite
   Neptune, when taught the salvage Man t' apply
   his gift, the Courser, and to worlds first shown
   the peaceful Olive-tree Minerva's boon.

14 With scanty tardance vext Lyæus eyed
   these varied marvels: Soon he past the gate
   of Neptune's Palace, who had thither hied
   the God's expected visit to await:
   Him at the threshold greets he, 'companied
   by Nymphs, who marvel at the freak of Fate
   to see, attempting such unusèd road,
   the Wine-god seek the Water-god's abode.

15 "O Neptune!" crièd he, "Regard not strange,
   that Bacchus comes a guest within thy Reign;
   even we highest pow'rs who reck no change
   are prone to suffer Fortune's fell disdain:
   Summon, I pray, the Gods who Ocean range
   ere say I more, if more to hear thou deign;
   they shall behold what ills the Gods befall,—
   all hear what evils overhang us all."

16 Already Neptune, deeming worth his heed
   a case so novel, sends in hottest haste,
   Triton to call the cold Sea-gods with speed
   that govern Ocean's breadth from east to west:
   Triton,— that boasts him of the Sea-king's seed,
   who had the reverend nymph, Salatia, prest,—
   was a tall huge-limb'd Carle, young, swart of hue,
   his Father's trumpet and his courier too.

17 The feltred beard, and matted locks that fell
   adown his head and o'er his shoulders strown,
   were water-pregnant weeds, and seemed it well
   no soft'ening comb had e'er their tangles known:
   Nor lacketh jet-black fringe of mussel-shell,
   Pendente from points where mingled growths are grown:
   For cap and cowl upon his head he wore
   the crusty spoils erst a huge lobster bore.

18 Naked his body, and of cloth are clear
   his loins, to swim without impediment;
   yet pigmy sea-things clothe with sea-born gear
   his limbs, in hundred hundreds spread and sprent;
   with shrimps, and crabs, and many such small deer
   which from cool Phoebe take their incremente;
   oysters and moss-fouled mussels, while each rib
   glistens with periwinkles glazed and glib.

19 His Conch, that mighty writhèd shell, in hand
   he bore, and forceful blew with draughty throat;
   whose harsh canorous voice, at his command,
   heard ev'ry Ocean, ech'oing far the note:
   Now by his summons warned the god-like band
   straight for the Palace left their seats, and sought
   the Deity who reared Dardania's Wall,
   by Grecian fury doomed anon to fall.

20 Came Father Ocean, whom accompanied
   the sons and daughters gotten in the Main:
   Comes Nereus, who led Doris for a bride,
   she who replenisht with her Nymphs his Reign:
   And, eke, prophetick Proteus thither hied,
   leaving his herd to browse the bitter plain:
   He came, that wizard; yet right well knew he
   what Father Bacchus wanted to the Sea.

21 Came from another quarter Neptune's ferè,
   begot by Coelus, borne by Vesta's womb,
   of gesture grave yet gay, fair sans compeer,
   the wond'ring waves were blandisht by her bloom:
   A light Cymár of costly weft her wear,
   subtle as though 'twere wove in airy loom,
   that bared the chrystal charms to longing eyne,—
   charms ne'er create in jealous shade to pine:

22 And Amphitrité, bright as flow'ers in spring,
   in such conjucture could not stay away;
   bringing the Dolphin, who her heart did bring
   her kingly lover's wish and will t' obey;
   with glorious orbs that conquer ev'erything,
   and steal his splendours from the Lord of Day:
   Hand clasping hand the coupled Consorts trod
   the sister spouses of the two-wived God.

23 She, who from furious Athamas of yore
   a fugitive, uprose to god-degree,
   her son, a lovely youngling, with her bore,[133]
   fated to sit in Heaven's consistory:
   They linger sporting on the pebbly shore
   with pearly conchlets, which the briny sea
   aye breeds, and now he stays his sport, and rests
   pillow'd on Panope's delicious breasts.

169

24 And eke the God,[134] once made in mould of man,
   who by the magick simples' poten spell
   changèd to fish, and from such chance began
   thing of time 'mid timeless Gods to dwell,
   came still bewailing tricksy Fortune's ban,
   which the fair maid by Circe's spite befel,
   Scylla he lovèd as by her belovèd;
   for love pervert pure hate hath often provèd.

25 And now the Godheads all in Council meet
   amid the vasty Hall, superb, divine;
   Goddesses seated on rich dais seat
   Gods throned on tall estrados chrystalline;
   when rose their awful Host his guests to greet
   who by the Theban sat on level line:
   Fumeth the Palace with the rich sea-mass[135]
   Araby's odours never shall surpass.

26 At length, when tumult sinks to stilly rest,
   and when the De'ities all their greetings close,
   to them Thyóneus opes his hidden breast,
   and the sad secret of his torment shows:
   A shade of sadness marks his look and gest,
   as though deprest by sense of 'during woes,
   resolved with alien steel alone to slay
   right soon the Lusus men, he 'gan to say:—

27 "Prince! who by birthright holdest high command
   o'er the proud seas that sweep from Pole to Pole;
   thou who dost curb the den'izens of the land
   that none o'erpass his term and certain goal:
   And, Father Ocean! thou whose 'circling band
   around the globèd universe doth roll,
   permitting only by thy just decree
   each in due bounds to flourish, Earth and Sea:

28 "And, eke, ye Water-gods, who ne'er endure
aught of injurious in your vast domain,
sans meetest chastisement condign and sure,
dealt to the worms who overrun your reign:
Why dwell ye reckless thus, how rest secure?
Who to such softness had the power to train
your hearts, with reason harden to behold
this race of mortals weak withal so bold?

29 Ye saw the wondrous insolent extremes
that dared the heavenly heights in arms to scale:
Ye saw that wildest phantasy that dreams
of conquering Ocean-tide with oar and sail:
Ye saw, and every day we see, meseems,
such braves, such insults that, if these prevail,
full soon, I fear, of sea and sky to find
Mankind the godheads, Gods the humankind.

30 You see that now this weak ephemeral brood,
who from a Vassal mine hath taken name,
with sprite high-flown, and heart of proudest mood,
you, me and all the world would tempt and tame:
You see how freely they defy your Flood,
a doughtier deed than Rome's high race could claim:
You see they seek to 'spy your whole domain,
to break the very statutes of your Reign.

31 "I saw how 'gainst the Minyæ,[136] first to find
the path that passeth through your realm, the wave,
much-injured Boreas, with his brother-wind
Aquilo and their peers, did rage and rave.
If to th' adventurous mortals who design'd
such wrongs the Winds appaid the boast and brave,
ye, who have higher right these wrongs to pay,
what wait ye? Doom of justice why delay?

171

32 Nor will I, Gods! consent, so should you trow
pure love of you from Heaven hath brought me down;
not thus your suff'ering feel I and your woe,
what wrongs I now resent are all mine own;
since the high honours, as your Godships know,
I won on earth, when fell by me overthrown
Inde's wealthy Reign, of Morning-lond the grace,
I see abated by this little race:

33 "For our all-Sovran Sire and eke the Fates
who rule this nether world as best they wot,
resolve with Fame which ne'er on man awaits,
to make th' abysmal sea these Baron's lot:
Hence shall you view, O Gods! their human hates
teach god to work god wrong: Ah! see ye not
of note and worth we have the smallest boast
whose value Reason valueth the most.

34 "Wherefore Olympus' height I now have fled,
to seek heart-salving balm for sore despair;
eke would I find, if rank thus forfeitèd
in Heav'en, your Waters still to honour care."
More would he say, but nothing more he said,
for tears, already trickling pair by pair,
leapt from his brimming lids, and as they came
the Gods of Water felt their sprites aflame.

35 The rage which sudden fired their hearts divine,
and roused to such display each vengeful soul,
suffered not counsel to contain design,
nor discount brookèd, nor endured control:
Now to great Æolus they send a sign,
as 'twere from Neptune, bidding him enroll
contrary Winds of wildest phrenesy,
and of all vent'urous sails sweep clean the sea.

36 Proteus the first and foremost there desirèd
    to speak his feelings as he felt him bound;
    the general Conclave deeming him inspirèd,
    by some myst'erious prophesy profound:
    yet was that Company divine so firèd
    by sudden tumult; brake such storm of sound
    that Tethys rising cries indignantly,
    "Well kens King Neptune what commanded he."

37 Now there superb Hippotades[137] gave vent
    to furious Winds erst pent in prison-hold;
    the while his wilful words fresh fury lent,
    against the Lusian Barons brave and bold.
    Sudden the summer-vault with clouds was sprent,
    for Winds, still growing fierce with rage untold,
    gather as on they go fresh might and main,
    house, tow'er, and hillock strewing o'er the plain.

38 While thus in Council met the Gods' array
    beneath the Seas, before soft breezes float
    our joyous weary Ships, and hold their way
    o'er tranquil Ocean on the long new route.
    The hour was that when hangs the Lamp of Day
    from hemisphere Eoan most remote:
    They of night's early watch[138] lay down to sleep,
    while others waked the second ward to keep.

39 Drows'iness mastered, all half-numbed and chill
    shivered with many a yawn the huddling Crew
    beneath the bulging main-sail, clothèd ill
    to bear the nightly breath that keenly blew;
    their eyes, kept open sore against their will,
    they rubbed, and stretcht their torpid limbs anew:
    To seek a waking-draught the men devise,
    spin stories, tell a thousand histories.

40 One 'gan to say, "Wherewith may better we
   spur tardy Time who lags so sore and slow,
   save with some pretty tale of joyance gay
   that heavy slumber trouble us no mo?"
   Replied Le'onardo, truest lover he,
   whose firm and constant thought was aye aglow:
   "What tale our tardy breasts may better move
   and kill old Time than some fair Lay of Love?"

41 "'Twere not, methinks," Velloso said, "thing meet
   on theme so soft in hours so hard to dwell;
   the rough Sea-labours, which do fag the fleet,
   Love's delicatest fancies rudely quell:
   Rather of fervid fight and battle-feat
   be now our story, for I see full well,
   life is all hardship, and good sooth I wis
   more trouble cometh; something tells me this."

42 All with his words consenting joint assail
   Velloso to recount whatever he knew.
   "I will recount," quoth he, "nor shall you rail
   at aught that seemeth fabulous or new:
   And that my hearers learn from this my tale
   high proofs of forceful deed to dare and do,
   e'en of my countrymen I'll say my say;—
   the Twelve of England shall adorn my lay.

43 "When of our Reign the curbing rein so light
   John, son of Pedro, held with mod'erate hand;
   and when his Realm had 'scaped the bane and blight
   oft dealt by hate of hostile neighbour-land;
   there in great England, where the rain falls white
   from Boreal snow-drift, fierce Erinnys plan'd
   to sow the dil'igent tares of wanton strife,
   and make our Lusitania lustre-rife.

174

44 "Betwixt the gentle Dames of th' English Court,
   and high-boru Courtier-crowd, one day it came
   that horrid Discord showed her dreadful port;
   of self-will sprung, or faith in common fame.
   The Courtier-throng that lightly loves in sport
   and careless mood to bruit the gravest shame,
   sware Honour they disproved, and Honesty
   in certain Dames, who boasted Dames to be.

45 Nay, more, if any Knight uphold as true,
   and with his brand and lance the cause defend,
   in lists or rasèd field, the same should rue
   foul infamy, or come to cruel end:
   The woman-weakness which but little knew,
   if e'er, such foul reproach, and yet which ken'd
   its want of nat'ural force could only crave
   their friends to succour and their kin to save.

46 "But as their sland'erers great and puissant were
   throughout the kingdom, none the cause would heed;
   nor kith, nor friends, nor fervid lovers dare
   support the Dames in darkest hour of need:
   Tempting with delicate tear and doleful air
   the very Gods to rise in arms, and aid
   from Heav'en, for sake of alabaster brows,
   to ducal Lancaster[139] the Bevy goes.

47 "This lord was English and in doughty fight
   against Castile for Portugale made war,
   wherein he proved the noble force and sprite
   of his companions, and their fav'ouring star:
   Nor less within our realm he saw the might
   of Love, whose am'orous feats as forceful are,
   when his fair daughter so the heart did win
   of our stout King that chose her for his Queen.

48 "He who in person succour must withhold,
     lest fire of civil discord thus be fan'd,
     replied:— 'When I my rights upheld of old
     to Spanish kingdom in th' Iberian land,
     I saw in Lusia's sons a soul so bold,
     such primacy of heart, such open hand,
     that they, and only they, I deem, shall dare
     with brand and firebrand for your case to care.

49 "'And, if, aggrievèd Dames! ye hold it meet
     I'll send my Heralds speaking in your name,
     while let your letters, courteous and discieet,
     declare your insult, and bewail your shame.
     Eke on your side, with pretty phrases sweet,
     and soft caresses, let each injured Dame
     temper her tears, and venture I to say
     you shall strong succour see and steadfast stay.'

50 "Thus doth the Duke experienced speak his mind,
     and of his bravest friends twelve names he quotes:
     That suit'able Champion be to each assign'd,
     he wills the namèd Knights be chose by lots;
     because the Dames be twelve; and when they find
     which Brave to which Belle-dame his life devotes,
     each unto each shall write and claim her rights,
     all to their King, the Duke to all the Knights.

51 "The mess'enger now in Lusia-lond arriveth;
     the Court rejoiceth at such novelty:
     Our King sublime to 'list the foremost striveth,
     but suffereth not the kingly dignity:
     No courtier but whose valiant sprite aspireth
     to volunteer with fervid volunty,
     and only he high favour'd is proclaimèd
     whom for such noble feat the Duke hath namèd.

52 "There in the loyal City whence ('tis said
    by olden Fame), arose the name eternal
    of Portugalia, a nimble barque he bade
    be 'quipt, who holds the helm of rule internal.
    The Twelve in briefest season ready made
    arms and accoutrements of use hodiernal;
    helms, crests, and mottoes of choice mode they choose
    horse, selle, and harness of a thousand hues.

53 "Now, when dismissèd by their King had been,
    sail from the Douro regions famed afar,
    the luck-loved Twelve, who did th' approval win
    of England's Duke experienced in war.
    Amid the dozen was no diff'erence seen
    in chivalry, while skill and strength were par;
    then one, Magriço[140] hight, and only he
    this way addrest the doughty company:—

54 "'Valiantest comrades! longings manifold
    I nurst for many a year the world t' explore,
    Rivers by Tagus nor by Douro roll'd,
    various nations, laws, and varied lore:
    And now that matters fit in certain mould
    (since Earth of marvels hath extended store),
    I would, an leave ye give, alone go round
    by land, and meet you upon English ground.

55 "'And, should I haply 'counter let or stay,
    from Him who holds of things the ultime line,
    and fail to find you on our trysting day,
    scant fault to you shall bring default of mine.
    You all shall do my duty in the fray;
    but, an my prescient sprite the Truth divine,
    ne stream, ne mount, ne jealous Fate hath pow'er
    to nill I hail you at th' appointed hour.'

177

56 "Thus spake Magriço and, his friends embracèd,
   he fareth forwards when their leave was tane:
   In Leon and Castile's old realms he tracèd
   sites patrial Mars had granted us to gain:
   Navarre and all the dang'erous heads he facèd
   of Pyrenee departing Gaul from Spain;
   and, seen of France the highest scenes and best,
   in Flanders' grand emporium [141] took his rest.

57 "There halting, or by chance or whim's command,
   for days he tarried, making much delay:
   Meanwhile the stout Elev'en, a glorious band,
   plow northern waters scatt'ering freezy spray.
   Arrived on stranger England's distant strand,
   at once to London-town all took the way:
   The Duke receives them in his festive hall,
   the Dames do service, greeting one and all.

58 "Now Time and Tide are ready for the fight
   with th' English Twelve who first afield are shown,
   chose by their King, right sure of every Knight:
   Helms, crests, greaves, coats, and harnesses they don:
   The Dames already deem the fulgent might
   of Portugalia's Mavors all their own:
   In golden owche and rainbow-silks yclad
   and thousand jewels, sit they gay and glad.

59 "But she, who claimèd by the chance of lot,
   missing Magriço, drest in mourning dyes
   sits sad; for she and only she hath not
   a knightly champion in this high emprize:
   Though our Elev'en proclaimèd on the spot,
   to England's Court, of battle such assize,
   that mote the Dames their cause victorious call,
   though of their champions two or three may fall.

60 "Now in the lofty publick Lists convene,
   the King of England and his suite and Court:
   In threes by threes, and fours by fours are seen
   spectators rangèd by the rule of sort.
   From Tage to Bactrus[142] ne'er did Sol, I ween,
   flame on such force and fierceness, power and port,
   as on those English Twelve, who leave their walls
   to front Eleven of our Portingalls.

61 "Champing their golden bits, fleckt spumy white,
   the chargers cast fierce fiery looks askance:
   On arms and armour Phoebus danceth bright
   as on dure adamant or chrystal glance:
   Not less on either side astound the sight
   numbers unequal, a quaint dissonance,
   to twelve eleven matched: Begins the crowd
   to vent its general joyaunce long and loud.

62 "All turn their faces curious to see
   where loudest bruit and hottest bate arise:
   When lo! a horseman, armèd cap-à-pie,
   pricks o'er the plain to claim of war the prize:
   Saluting King and Dames, straight rideth he
   to his Eleven: 'Tis the great Magriçe:
   With warmest accolade his friends he haileth,
   whom in the battle, certès, ne'er he faileth.

63 "The Ladye, hearing that the man was there,
   who would in combat guard her name and fame,
   wends glad the fleece of Helle's beast to wear,
   which more than Virtue vulgar hearts doth claim:
   They cry, 'Let go!' and now the trump's shrill blare
   fireth the warrior-heart with fiercer flame:
   All prick at once the spur, all slack the bit,
   all couch the lances; earth by fire is lit.

64 "The tramp of destr'iers riseth with a noise
as though some quake of earth rolled 'neath their tread:
Heart-strings in bosoms flutter; gazing eyes
are fixt in mingled sense of joy and dread:
This, from his charger not dismounting flies;
that groaneth falling with his falling steed;
this hath his snow-white mail with vermeil dyed;
that, with his helm-plume flogs his courser's side.

65 "Some sleep to wake no more, in lasting swoon
passing from life to death with hasty course:
Horses sans riders here o'er tilt-yard run,
and there the rider runs without the horse:
Now falleth English pride from off her throne;
for two or three depart the Pale parforce,
while they the battle-brand who came to wield,
find more than harness holds, or mail, or shield.

66 "To waste long words and War's extremes to show
of slashing cuts, and thrusts of cruel pain,
were work of wastrel-men who, well we trow,
of leisure lavish, vainest dream'ery feign:
Let it in fine suffice that all ye know
how with the fame of high finesse, remain
Victory's palms with us; and ev'ry Dame
a glorious victress, did retrieve her fame.

67 "The Duke our conqu'ering Twelve forthwith invites
where ring his halls with feast and wassail gay:
Hunters and kitcheners to toil incites
of the Twelve Dames that goodly company;
who glad had lavisht on their saviour Knights
a thousand banquets ev'ry hour o' the day,
long as on English-land they list to roam,
before returning to the dear-loved home.

68 "Withal, the great Magriço, men declare,
   wishing the Wonders of the World to view,
   abroad remainèd and performèd there
   for Flanders' Countess not'able service true:
   And be'ing no carpet-knight, but prompt to dare
   what exploits, Mars! thou biddest man to do
   He slew a Frank in field; and thus had he
   Torquatus' and Corvinus' destiny.

69 "Of the stout Twelve another cast his lot
   in Almayne, where him fiercely challengèd
   a wily German, who had planned such plot
   his life depended from a single thread."
   Velloso ceasing here, his mates besought
   he would not leave the glorious tale unsaid
   anent Magriço, and the meed he met,
   nor e'en the caitiff German Knight forget.

70 But at this passage when each prickt his ear,
   behold! the Master conning sky and cloud,
   pipeth his whistle; waken as they hear
   starboard and larboard all the startled crowd:
   And, as the breeze blew fresh'ening shrill and sheer,
   he bade them take in topsails shouting loud
   "Yarely, my lads! look out, the wind increases
   from yon black thunder-cloud before our faces."

71 Scarce were the foresails hurr'iedly taken in,
   when sharp and sudden bursts the roaring gale:
   "Furl!" cried the Master with as loud a din,
   "Furl!" cried he, "Furl for life the mainmast-sail!"
   The furious gusts wait not till they begin
   furling the canvas; but conjoint assail
   and tear it with such crash to shreds and tatters
   as though a ruined world the Storm-wind shatters.

72 Meanwhile the Crew with cries the welkin tore,
   in panick fear and gen'eral disaccord;
   for as the canvas split, the hull heel'd o'er,
   broad sheets of water shipping by the board.
   "Heave!" roared the Master with a mighty roar,
   "Heave overboard your all, tog'ether 's the word!
   Others go work the pumps, and with a will:
   The pumps! and sharp, look sharp, before she fill!"

73 Hurrieth to ply the pumps the soldier-host,
   but ere they reachèd them, the rolling sea
   and tem'erous waves the ship so pitch't and tost,
   all lost their footing falling to the lee.
   Three stalwart sailors who best thews could boast,
   sufficèd not to make the helm work free;
   tackles to starboard, yokes to port they lashèd,
   yet all their pow'er and practice stood abashèd.

74 Such were the gale-gusts, never Tempest blew
   with more of cruel will, of feller stowre,
   as though its mission were t' uproot and strew
   on plain of Babel, Babel's tallest tow'er:
   'Mid the great washing waves that greater grew,
   dwindled the puissant Ship to stature lower
   than her own cock; and 'twas a thing of fear,
   seeing her in such surges swim and steer.

75 The sturdy craft that Paul da Gama bears,
   beareth her mainmast broken clean in twain
   and well-nigh water-logged: The crew in prayers,
   calls upon Him who came to ransom men.
   Nor less vain clamours to the empty airs
   Coelho's vessel casts by fear o'ertane;
   though there the Master had more caution shown,
   furling his canvas ere the storm came down.

76 In air the Ships are thrown with ev'ry throw
   of furious Neptune's crests that kissed the cloud:
   Anon appeared the keels to settle low
   where horrid Glooms the deep sea-bowels shroud.
   While Notus, Auster, Boreas, Aquilo
   the world-machine to wreck and ruin crowd:
   Gleamèd and glarèd pitchy hideous night
   with Leven burning all the polar height.

77 The Halcyon birds their melancholy wail
   piped, as they cowered on the salvage shore;
   remembering aye the wrongful long-past tale
   of woes the waters wrought to them of yore:
   Meanwhile th'enamoured Dolphins fled the gale
   to shelt'ering grottos in the deep-sea floor,
   although the mighty winds and mightier waves
   threatenèd danger in their deepest caves.

78 Ne'er forged such lightning-bolts of living fire
   against the Giants' haught rebellious band,
   the great toil-sordid Blacksmith, in desire
   to grace with radiant arms his stepson's hand.
   Never was known the mighty Thunderer's ire
   to rain such fulm'inant fulgor o'er the land
   in the great Deluge, which alone withstood
   the pair that changèd stones to tiesh and blood.

79 How many mountains levelled with the lea
   those Waves that burst and brake with awful might!
   How many a gnarlèd trunk of ancient tree
   the Winds uptore with wild and wilful spite!
   Ne'er reckt those bulky cable-roots to see
   their heels upturned to meet the heav'enly light;
   nor thought the deep-laid sands that floods could flow
   so fierce, and raise aloft what lay below.

80 Da Gama, seeing that so near the scope
    of his long voyage, ev'ry chance had failèd;
    seeing the seas to depths infernal ope,
    then with redoubled rage the Lift assailèd:
    By nat'ural Fear confused, and sans a hope
    of Life, where nought of heart or art availèd,
    to that high Puissance, and that certain Aid
    which makes th' imposs'ible possible, thus pray'd:—

81 "Celestial Guard! divine, angelical
    of Skies and Earth and Sea sole Suzerain;
    Thou, who didst lead Thy people Israel
    thro' Erythrean waters cleft in twain:
    Thou, who didst fain defend thy servant Paul
    from sandy Syrtes and the monstrous Main,
    Who deign'edst the second Sire and children save
    to fill the regions emptied by the Wave:

82 "If through new perilous paths a way I wore
    through other Scyllas and Charybdes came,
    Saw other Syrtes reef the sandy floor,
    other Acroceraunian rocks infame:
    Why, when such labours are wellnigh no more,
    why are we thus abandoned, left to shame,
    if by our travails Thou be not offended
    Nay, if Thy greater glory be intended?

83 "Oh happy they whose hap it was to die
    on grided points of lances African;
    to fall, while striving still to bear on high
    our Holy Faith in regions Mauritan!
    Whose feats illustrious live in ear and eye,
    whose mem'ories aye shall haunt the heart of man;
    whose Lives by ending life win living name,
    whose Deaths are sweeten'd by a deathless Fame!"

84 Thus he, while battling Winds still fiercer clashèd,
   like raging Bulls indomitably wood;
   to greater rage the raging gale was lashèd,
   hissing and howling through the twiney shroud:
   The lightnings' dreadful night-light brighter flashèd,
   and fearful thunders rolled and rent the cloud,
   as though the Heavens to Earth unaxled fell,
   and the four Elements in battle mell.

85 But now the lovely Star[143] with sparkling ray,
   led forth clear Sol in Eastern hemisphere;
   Day's lovely Herald hasting to display
   her gladdening brow, and Earth and Sea to cheer:
   The Goddess-ruler of its skyey way,
   whom faulchion-girt Orion flies in fear
   when seen the billows and her dear-loved Fleet
   with equal anger and with fear was smit.

86 "Here, certès, Bacchus' handwork I descry,"
   quoth she "but Fortune ne'er shall him gain
   his wicked object, nor shall 'scape mine eye
   the damn'd intention which he plans in vain:"
   Thus she; and slipping instant from the sky
   lightly she 'lighteth on the spacious Main,
   bidding her Nymphs to wear as on she sped
   a rosy garland on each golden head.

87 Garlands she bade them wear of varied hue,
   on blondest tresses of the purest shine:
   Who had not said the ruddy florets grew
   on nat'ural gold, which Love had loved to 'twine?
   To tame and blandish by the charming view
   the noisome crew of Winds, she doth design
   her galaxy of Nymphs, a train as fair
   as Planets dancing on the plains of air.

185

88 And thus it was: For when in Beauty's pride
   showed the fair Bevy, faded straight away
   the force wherewith each windy Warrior vied,
   and all surrender'd happy to obey:
   It seemed their mighty feet and hands were tied
   by hanks of hair that dimmed the leven-ray;
   meanwhile her Boreas, she who ruled his breast,
   loveliest Orithyia, thus addrest:—

89 "Think not, fere Boreas! e'er 'twas thought of mine
   that thou hast lovèd me with constant love;
   for gentle ways be Love's securest sign;
   wrath has no power the lover's heart to move:
   See, an thou bridle not that rage indign,
   expect no grace of me, whom 'twill behove
   henceforth to murther Love by deadly Fear;
   for Love is terror when Fear draweth near."

90 Bespake fair Galatéa in such strain
   her furious Notus; for she wots right well
   long in her presence pleasure he had tane,
   and now she feeleth he must feel her spell.
   The Salvage scarcely can his joy contain,
   nor will his heart within his bosom dwell;
   o'erjoyed to view his Dame vouchsafe command,
   he deems 'tis little to wax soft and bland.

91 Thus eke had others equal pow'er to tame
   those other lovers who their hests obey'd;
   yielding to Venus every Wind became
   tranquil of semblance by new softness sway'd:
   She promised, seen their loves her aidance claim,
   in Love's sweet wars her sempiternal aid;
   and took their homage on her beauteous hands,
   to bear, while sail the Ships, her dear commands.

92 Now splendid Morning tipt the hills with red
whence rolls the Gange his sacred sounding tide,
when seamen percht upon the topmast head
Highlands far rising o'er the prows descried: [144]
Now, 'scaped the tempest and the first sea-dread,
fled from each bosom terrors vain, and cried
the Melindanian Pilot in delight,
"Calecut-land, if aught I see aright!"

93 "This is, pardie, the very Land of Inde,
what realms you seek behold! ahead appear;
and if no farther Earth ye long to find,
your long-drawn travail finds its limit here."
No more the Gama could compose his mind
for joy to see that Inde is known and near;
wich knees on deck and hands to Heav'en uprais̀ed
the God who gave such gift of grace he prais̀ed:

94 Praise to his God he gave, and rightly gave,
for he not only to that Bourne was brought
wherefore such perils he and his did brave,
wherefore with toil and moil so sore he fought;
but more, because so barely 'scaped the grave
when raging Ocean death for him had wrought
by the dure fervid Winds' terrifick might,
he was like one who wakes from dream of fright.

95 Amid such fierce extremes of Fear and Pain,
such grievous labours, perils lacking name,
whoso fair Honour wooeth aye shall gain,
Man's true nobility, immortal Fame:
Not those who ever lean on antient strain,
imping on noble trunk a barren claim,
not those reclining on the golden beds,
where Moscow's Zebelin downy softness spreads:

96 Not with the novel viands exquisite,
   not with the languid wanton promenade,
   not with the pleasures varied infinite,
   which gen'erous souls effeminate, degrade:
   Not with the never-conquer'd appetite,
   by Fortune pamper'd as by Fortune made,
   that suffers none to change and seek the meed
   of Valour, daring some heroick Deed:

97 But by the doughty arm and sword that chase
   Honour which man may proudly hail his own;
   in weary vigil, in the steely case,
   'mid wrathsome winds and bitter billows thrown,
   suff'ering the frigid rigours in th' embrace
   of South, and regions lorn, and lere, and lone;
   swall'owing the tainted rations' scanty dole,
   salted with toil of body, moil of soul:

98 The face enforcing when the cheek would pale
   to wear assurèd aspect glad and fain;
   and meet the red-hot balls, whose whistling hail
   spreads comrades' arms and legs on battle-plain.
   Thus honour'd hardness shall the heart prevail,
   to scoff at honours and vile gold disdain,
   the gold, the honours often forged by Chance,
   no Valour gained, no Virtue shall enhance.

99 Thus wax our mortal wits immortal bright
   by long Experience led, Man's truest guide;
   and thus the soul shall see, from heavenly height,
   the maze of human pettiness and pride:
   Whoso shall rule his life by Reason-light
   which feeble Passion ne'er hath power to hide,
   shall rise (as rise he ought) to HONOUR true,
   maugre his will that ne'er hath stoop'd to sue.

CANTO VII

1   And now th' Armada near'd the Morning-land,
    many so much desirèd to have seen,
    Reigns by those Indic currents moated, and
    by Gange who dwelleth in the sky terrene.
    Up Braves! and at them, an your valiant hand,
    to snatch victorious Palms determined bene
    Here ends your warfare; here before you lies
    the realm of riches and your rightful prize.

2   To you, O race from Lusus sprung! I say,
    to whom such puny part of Earth is dole'd
    nay, what say I of Earth, but of His sway
    who ruleth all the rounded skies enfold?
    You, whom ne dangers dure ne dire dismay
    from conqu'ering brutal Heathenesse withhold,
    but eke no greed of gain may wean from love
    of Mother-essence[145] throned the Heavens above.

3   Ye, Portingalls! as forceful as ye're few,
    who e'er disdain to weigh your weakly weight;
    ye, who at cost of various deaths be true
    the Laws of Life Eternal to dilate
    Cast by the heav'enly lots your lot ye drew,
    however poor or mean your mundane state,
    great deeds for Holy Christendom to show:
    So high, O Christ! exaltest Thou the low!

4 See them, those Germans,[146] stiff-neckt, herd-like horde
who browse the pastures of such wide extent,
to him rebellious who hath Peter's ward,
choose a new Shepherd, a new Sect invent:
See them absorbed in ugly wars abhor'd
(nor yet with blinded errant ways contente!)
fight, not the haught tyrannick Othoman,
but th' apostolick yoke they fain unspam.

5 See the hard Englander[146] proclaim his right
of that old Sacred City King to be,
where reigns and rules the base-born Ishmælite
(Honour of Truth so nude who e'er did see!);
'mid Boreal snows he taketh sad delight
to mould new mode of old Christianity:
For those of Christ he bares the ready brand,
not to rethrone Lord Christ in Holy Land.

6 Holds for himself meanwhile a faithless Roy,[147]
Jerus'alem City, the terrestrial;
who holds not holy law, but dares defy
Jerus'alem City, the celestial.
Then what of thee, vile Gaul![148] what need say I?
who wouldst thy vaunting self "Most Christian" call,
not that such title wouldest ward and guard,
but that the name thro' thee be smircht and mar'd!

7 Thy claim to conquer Christian lands beseems
one who so much and such fair land doth claim?
why seek not Cinyps[149] and the Nilus, streams
which ever hate that ántique Holy Name?
There should they feel of steel the hard extremes,
who would the Church's truthful song defame:
Of Charles, of Louis,[150] name thou didst inherit
and lands;— why not of justest wars the merit?

8 What shall I say of those who 'mid delights,
 which vilest Idlesse bare for manhood's bane,
 spend life and love to waste the gold that blights,
 and clean forget their antient valiant strain?
 Tyrannick hest to hostile act incites,
 which virile races view as foulest stain:
 To thee I speak, O It'aly! sunk by curse
 of thousand sins, who dost thyself adverse.

9 Ah, wretched Christians, who such cross incur,
 be you perchance the teeth by Cadmus sown,
 that waste of brother-blood ye thus prefer
 when all by self-same mother-womb are grown?
 How durst you see yon Holy Sepulture
 owned by the bandogs who such feuds disown,
 who come to hold and have your antient ground,
 their warlike prowess making them renown'd?

10 Ye know 'tis now their usance and decree,
 whereof they are observantistis entire,
 to levy restless hosts of Heathenry,
 and harm the hearts that dear Christ's love desire:
 While fierce Alecto 'mid your chivalry
 for ever soweth tares of wrath and ire:
 Look! an your eyes to risks like these ye close,
 How they and you to you be deadliest foes.

11 If lust of lucre and of lordship led
 your course to conquer far and foreign lands,
 see you not Hermus and Pactólus shed
 adown their fertile valleys aureate sands?
 Assyria, Lydia, spin the golden thread,
 lurk veins of sheeny ore in Africk strand
 Let these rich treasures sluggish sprites arouse
 since rouse you not the rights of Holy House.

12   Those fierce projectiles, of our days the work,
     murtherous engines, dire artilleries,
     against Byzantine walls, where dwells the Turk,
     should long before have belcht their batteries.
     Oh, hurl it back in forest-caves to lurk
     where Caspian crests and steppes of Scythia freeze,
     that Turkish ogre-prog'eny multiplied
     by op'ulent Europe's policy and pride.[151]

13   Georgians, Armenians, Grecians, hapless Thrace
     cry on your name to quell th' unspeakable horde
     that dooms parforce their darlings to embrace
     Alcoran's precepts (tax of blood abhord!):
     Prove, when you punish yon inhuman race,
     the Sage's spirit and the Soldier's sword;
     nor covet arr'ogant praise and vainest boast
     of vaunting valour o'er a brother-host.

14   But while ye blindly thirst to drink the blood
     of your own veins, Oh hapless Race insane!
     never hath failèd Christian hardihood
     in this our little household Lusitane:
     Her seats are set by Africk's salty flood;
     she holds in Asian realms the largest Reign;
     She sows and ears o'er all the Fourth new-found;
     and there would hasten had but Earth more ground.

15   Meanshile behold we what new chance befel
     the seld-seen Voyagers who Fame would earn,
     Since gentle Venus deigned the gale to quell,
     and futile furies of fierce winds to spurn;
     when they the large-spread Land's appearance hail,
     of stubborn obst'inate toil the bound and bourne,
     and where the Saviour's seed they wend to sow,
     enthrone new lords, new lights, new laws bestow.

16 Soon as along the stranger-shores they lay,
   a fragile fleet that fishing people bare
   they found, and by such guidance learnt the way
   to Calecut, whose denizens they were:
   Thither inclined the Prores without delay;
   for 'twas the City fairest 'mid the fair
   in land of Malabar and where abode
   the King, whose orders all that Region owe'd.

17 Outside of Indus, inside Ganges, lies
   a wide-spread country famed enough of yore;
   northward the peaks of caved Emeódus[152] rise,
   and southward Ocean doth confine the shore:
   She bears the yoke of various sovranties
   And various eke her creeds: While these adore
   vicious Mafóma, those to stock and stone
   bow down, and eke to brutes among them grown.

18 There, deep i' the mighty Range, that doth divide
   the land, and cutteth Asian continent,
   whose crests are known by names diversified,
   of ev'ry country where its trend is bent;
   outburst the fountains, which commingling glide
   in pow'erful streams that die when travel-spent
   in Indic Ocean, and the arms of these
   convert the country to a Chersonèse:

19 Twixt either river from this breadth of base
   puts forth the spacious land a long thin horn,
   quasi-pyramidal, which in th' embrace
   of Ocean lies with Isle Ceylón toforn:
   And, near the source that shows the natal place
   of Gange, if olden Fame of Truth be born,
   the happy Peoples of th' adjacent bowers,
   feed on the fragrance of the finest flowers;

20 But now of many usance, mode and name
   are all the tribes who have and hold the ground;
   Pathans and Delhis urge the proudest claim
   to land and numbers, for they most abound:
   Deccanis, Oriás, who both misclaim
   salvation in the sounding flood is found
   by Ganges rolled; and here the land Bengal
   is rich in sort her wealth exceedeth all.

21 The sovranty of bellicose Cambay,
   (men say 'twas puissant Porus' olden reign);
   Narsinga's Kingdom, with her rich display
   of gold and gems but poor in martial vein:
   Here seen yonside where wavy waters play
   a range of mountains skirts the murmuring Main,
   serving the Malabar for mighty mure,
   who thus from him of Canará dwells secure.

22 The country-people call this range the Ghaut,
   and from its foot-hills scanty breadth there be
   whose seaward-sloping coast-plain long hath fought
   'gainst Ocean's natural ferocity:
   Here o'er her neighbour Cities, sans a doubt
   Calecut claimeth highest dignity,
   crown of the Kingdom fair and flourishing
   Here he entitled "Samorim" [153] is King.

23 Arrived the Squadron off that wealthy land,
   she sent a Portingall to make report,
   so mote the Géntoo monarch understand
   who hath arrivèd in his distant port:
   A stream the Herald struck which, leaving land
   entereth Ocean; and his novel sort,
   his hue, his strange attire, his stranger-ways
   made all the lieges gather round to gaze.

24 Amid the swarming rout that thronged to view,
   cometh a Moslem, who was born and bred
   in distant Barb'ary 'mid her barbarous crew,
   there, where in antient day Antæus sway'd:
   Right well the Lusitanian realm he knew,
   or by the scanty distance thither led,
   or 'signèd by the Sword and Fortune's brand,
   to long-drawn exile in a foreign land.

25 With jocund mien our Messenger to sound,
   for-that he speaketh well the speech of Spain,
   he thus:— "Who brought thee to this new world's bound,
   far from thy Fatherland, the Lusitan?"
   "Op'ening," respondeth he, "the seas profound
   which never openèd the race of man;
   for Indus' mighty flood we hither bore,
   to win for Holy Faith one triumph more."

26 By the long voyage sore astonied stood
   the Moor Monsaydé, thus his name was known;
   when told the Lusian how the terr'ible flood
   had all the temper of a tyrant shown:
   But, as that errand's drift, he understood,
   concern'd the Ruler of the Land alone,
   he tells the stranger how the Monarch lay
   outside the city at a little way:

27 And that while travelled to the royal ear
   news of that advent strange, if judged he meet,
   repairing to his humble dwelling near,
   'twere well refreshment of the land to eat;
   whence by short rest restorèd and good cheer,
   the twain together might regain the Fleet;
   for life has nothing like the joy and glee
   wherewith near neighbours meet in far countrie.

28 The Portingall, accepting not ingrate
    what glad Monsaydé for his guest deviseth;
    as though their friendship were of olden date,
    eats, drinks, and does whate'er the host adviseth:
    Now from the City wend they, making straight
    towards the Squadron which the Moor agniseth;
    and scale the Flagship's flank, where all the crew
    with kindly glances Moor Monsaydé view.

29 Embraceth him our Chief, whom hugely please
    the well-remembered accents of Castile;
    seateth him near, and asketh him at ease
    anent the land and folk therein that dwell.
    Even as flockt on Rhodopé the trees,
    to hear the Lover of the Damosel
    Eurydice, his lyre of gold resound,
    the Folk to hearken flockt the Moor around.

30 Then he: "O Nation! who by Nature's hand
    was 'stablished neighbour to my natal nide,
    what mighty Chance, what Destiny's command
    upon such voyage drave you far and wide?
    Not causeless, no; though darkly, deeply plan'd
    from unknown Minho, distant Tagus-tide,
    your course o'er Oceans aye by keel unplow'd
    to Reigns such distance and such dangers shroud.

31 "God bringeth you, pardie! for He intendeth
    some special service which your works await
    For this alone He guideth and defendeth
    from en'emies, Ocean and the winds' wild hate.
    Know, that ye look on Inde wherein extendeth
    a world of nations, rich and fortunate
    in lucent gold, and gems of princely price,
    and odorif'erous fumes and biting spice.

32 "This Province, in whose Port your ships have tane
    refuge, the Malabar by name is known;
    its ántique rite adoreth idols vain
    Idol-religion being broadest sown
    Of divers Kings it is; but 'twas the Reign,
    as olden legend saith, of only one
    hight the last King was Sarmá Perimal,[154]
    who 'neath one sceptre held the Kingdom all.

33 "But as this region there and then was sought
    by other races from the Arab Bight,
    who Mahometic worship with them brought,
    the same my parents planted in my sprite,
    it hapt their wisdom and their pray'ers so wrought
    upon the Perimal; and lit such light
    that to the Faith convert with fervour high,
    he only hoped a Saint in it to die.

34 "He mans his ships and loads with merchandise
    and many an offering curious, rare and rich,
    and there religious life to lead he hies
    where lies our Prophet who our Law did preach
    But ere abandon'd home, his satrapies,
    that lackèd lawful heir, he parts to each,
    and all he lovèd: Hence his intimates he
    from want made wealthy, and from serfdom free.

35 "To this Cochim, to that falls Cananor
    one hath Chalé, another th' Isle Piment,
    a third Coulam, a fourth takes Cranganor,
    the rest is theirs with whom he rests content.
    Only one Youth, for whom warm love he bore,
    when all was parted, did himself presente:
    Nothing save Calecut for him remainèd,
    which, by her traffick, wealth and rank had gainèd.

197

36 "On him the title par'amount he bestows
   of Emperor, with sway o'er ev'ery state;
   and, made this partage, there he dil'igent goes,
   where, after Santon-life he met his fate:
   Thus 'twas the name of Samorim arose,—
   of all this region proudest potentate,—
   borne by the Youth, and by his heirs from whom
   this who now wields imperial pow'er is come.

37 "The Law that holds the people, high and low,
   is fraught with false phantastick tales long past:
   they go unclothèd, but a wrap they throw
   for decent purpose round the loins and waist:
   Two modes of men are known; the nobles know
   the name of Nayrs, who call the lower caste
   Poléas, whom their haughty laws contain
   from intermingling with the higher strain:

38 "For men who aye had office in one guise
   with mates of other office ne'er may wive;
   nor may the son the calling exercise
   save sire's and foresires' long as he shall live.
   These Nayrs as sin and shame, forsooth, despise
   the touch of outcasts, and they fain believe
   that, peradventure, if the touch occur,
   a thousand rites must wash their bodies pure.

39 "In sim'ilar form the Júdæan folk of old
   touch'd not the people s of Samaria-reign:
   But strangenesses far stranger than I've told
   of varied usages shall meet your eyne.
   None save the Nayrs affront the manifold
   chances of war, who like stone-wall sustain
   their King from enemies, arms aye in hand,
   in left the target, and in right the brand.

40 "Entitled Brahmins are their ghostly race,
    time-honour'd title of high eminence:
    His far-famed precepts, eke, they still embrace
    who first to Science lent a modest sense:[155]
    A living thing to kill they hold as base,
    such be from ev'ry flesh their abstinence.
    Only in joys venereal their delight
    hath more of licence and a laxer rite.

41 "Common the women are, although confin'd
    to those belonging to their husbands' blood:
    Happy condition! happy humankind,
    who over jealous wrongs may never brood!
    These and more customs various shall ye find
    among the Mal'abar men still holding good:
    Great is the country, rich in ev'ry style
    of goods from China sent by sea to Nyle."

42 Thus spake the Moorman: Now on vagueing wing
    about the city Rumour wildly flew
    with bruit of foreign comers; when the King
    sent out his servants seeking tidings true:
    Then through the streets begirt by mighty ring
    of ev'ry age and sex that flockt to View,
    came the Grandees who by the King were bade
    to bring the Captain of the strange Armade.

43 But he by royal leave allow'd for land
    to change his floating home, accompanied
    by his stout Portingalls, a chosen band
    in richest robes to meet the Monarch hied
    The beauteous contrasts of the hues command
    the crowd's approval, who with wonder eyed:
    Smiteth the cadence'd oar with cooly gleam
    now the salt ocean, then the frore fresh stream.

199

44 There stood a Regent of the Realm ashore,
 a chief, in native parlance "Cat'ual"[156] hight,
 by noble Nayrs surrounded, waiting for
 illustrious Gama, with a strange delight:
 Now to the land our Chief in arms he bore,
 and a rich-cushion'd couch in litter light
 he proff'ereth as a coach (an usage old),
 which bearer-people on their shoulders hold.

45 Thus he of Lusus, he of Malabar,
 wend whither sitteth 'wating them the King:
 Follow the Portingalls in form of War
 for foot-troops marching fierce and threatening:
 The people, buzzing with confusèd jar
 to see the strangers, fain of questioning
 gather'd, but in the cent'uries long gone by
 the Babel-tower did such hope deny.

46 Now with the Cat'ual Gama speech exchangèd
 on things th' occasion and the moment chose
 Interpreteth the tongues so far estrangèd
 Monsaydé, for the twain right well he knows.
 Thus the procession through the City rangèd,
 whither a noble, splendid pile arose;
 and, reached the precincts of a sumptuous Fane,
 through the tall portals paced on equal plane.

47 Here frightful forms of men's idolatries
 stand carved in lifeless stock and death-cold stone,
 varied in gestores, various of dyes,
 e'en as by feigning Fiend to man made known:
 Abominable forms the sight surprise
 with mingled members like Chimæra shown
 The Christians, wont to see their God-in-Man,
 these hybrid monsters with blank wonder scan.

48 One bore two horns insculpture'd on his brow
    like Jove called Ammon in the Libyan wold;
    this, double faces on one form did show,
    like two-faced Janus limned in church of old;
    that had of arms a long divided row
    mocking Briareus' members manifold;
    that thing a canine front external bore,
    such as th' Anubis Memphians did adore.

49 The barb'arous Géntoo in his Gods' abode
    a superstitious adoration paid;
    then both went straight, ne'er straying from the road,
    where the vain people's King his sojourn made:
    The stream of starers fuller still o'erflow'd,
    for all to sight the stranger Chief essay'd;
    while to the roofs and casements gazing came
    greybeard and stripling, damosel and dame.

50 Now near they, marching with no shorten'd stride,
    fair fragrant gardens and perfumèd bowers,
    wherein the royal palace-buildings hide,
    a structure sumptu'ous though not tall in towers
    The chiefs and nobles choose to build and 'bide
    where cooly bosquets teem with fruits and flowers
    Thus dwell the rulers of the race, delighting
    in seats the City and the Camp uniting.

51 The precinct-portals by their work betray
    subtleties telling of the daedal hand,
    in forms whose noble presences display
    the hoar antiquities of India-land:
    The marvel-stories of her antient day,
    with such a living art enfigured stand,
    that whoso reads them with a lore exact,
    knows from the Fiction what hath been the Fact.

52 There puissant armies show and proudly tread
  that Orient region which Hydasped laves;
  a smooth brow'd Capitayne is at the head,
  and with his leafy Thyrsus leads his Braves.
  By him was Nysa-city 'stablishèd
  hard by the margin of the murm'urous waves;
  so proper was the God e'en Semelé
  her son beholding would have said, "'Tis he!"

53 And there yon arrowy river draining dry
  th' Assyrian peoples multitud'inous bear
  a queenly sceptre, fem'inine seigniory,
  of fair the fairest and as foul as fair.[157]
  Fast by her side with fury flaming high
  her sculptured genet proudly paweth air,
  in whom her son a rival lover fand
  Oh vile incont'inence! Oh amour nefand!

54 At farther distance trembled in their pride
  the flags and banners of the glorious Greek,
  of Monarchies the Third, and conqu'ering hied
  far as the bill'owy Gange his sea doth seek:
  That youthful Captain's semblance is their guide,
  whom Vict'ory's wreathèd palms of valour deck,
  who claims a seat among the Gods above
  no longer Philip's son, but son of Jove.

55 While on these mem'ories dwelt the Portughuese,
  thus did the Cat'ual to the Captain say:—
  "Soon dawns the day when other victories
  shall these thou seest, dim and disarray:
  Here shall indited be new histories,
  made by the Wand'erers who shall wend this way:
  Thus Fate was found by wise and wizard men,
  inspirèd Magians who the future ken.

56 "And eke inspireth them the magick sense,
   that nought availeth to defend such Ill,
   of all that mortals bring to their defence;
   for earthly Wits must bend to heav'enly Will:
   It also saith the Stranger's excellence
   in Arts of Peace, as in his bellic skill,
   shall be so puissant, all the world shall know
   the Conq'ueror's measure by his conquered Foe."

57 Discoursing thus they reached the levée-hall,
   wherein that great and glorious Emperor
   sat on a cushion'd couch which, though 'twas small,
   for work and worth was never seen before:
   Showed his reclining gest imperial
   a potent, grave, and prosperous Signior:
   Golden his loin-cloth, and the diadem
   that crowns his brow doth blaze with many a gem.

58 Hard by his side an old man reverent,
   knelt on the floor, and now and then a few
   green leaves of pungent pepper did present,
   in wonted usage for the Sire to chew.
   A Brahmin, personage pre-eminent,
   with gliding gait beside the Gama drew,
   and led him up the potent King to greet,
   who with a nod designed a facing seat.

59 When near that splendid couch took place the guest,
   and others farther off, prompt glance and keen
   the Samo'rim cast on folk whose garb and gest
   were like to nothing he had ever seen:
   Then, speaking gravely from his stately breast,
   adding authority to noble mien,
   and gaining credence of the King and crowd,
   his royal message spake our Chief aloud:—

60 "A mighty King there thronèd, whither roll
    voluble Heavens in eternal round,
    where Earth by Earth conceals the rays of Sol,
    tingeing the world he left with gloom profound;
    hearing the rumours which from distant goal
    respond to Echo, how on Indie ground
    thine is the sole imperial Majesty,
    the knot of Friendship lief would knit with thee.

61 "And by long devious courses his command
    sent me to say, that all things mercantile,
    which go by ocean or which go by land,
    supplied by realms betwixt the Tage and Nyle;
    from foggy Zealand's frore Pole-fronting strand,
    to the far lands where Sol ne'er changeth style
    of days, that splendid shine on Æthiop shore,
    all these his kingdom holds in mighty store.

62 "And if thou wilt, with pacts and firmest ties
    of naked, sacred Peace and Friendship rare,
    allow exchange of superfluities
    his earth and thine with like abundance bear;
    making the rents and rev'enues richer rise
    (wherefore men toil and travail, sweat and fare)
    for both the countries, certès, shall pertain
    to him great glory and to thee great gain.

63 "And when thus knitted Friendship's steadfast knot
    which aye you mighty monarchs twain shall bind,
    prompt will he be against all adverse lot,
    by chance of warfare to thy reign design'd,
    with soldiers, arms, and ships; so men shall wot
    thy friend and brother they in him shall find:
    He hopeth eke that when thy course is tracèd
    by sure response to see my mission gracèd."

64 Such royal message spake our Chief before
   the Géntoo King, who thus vouchsafed reply,
   that to receive such fair Ambassador
   from land so far he holdeth honour high:
   But that his final will fain standeth o'er
   till tane the counsel of his ministry,
   who shall make certain, after long debate,
   what King he speaketh of, what race, what state.

65 Meanwhile from labours past the Chief may wend
   where rest awaits him, and in brief delay
   to the despatch he will due care extend,
   whereby their King shall greet their homeward way.
   This said, brought sombre Night the wonted end
   to human labours of the livelong Day,
   soothing the weary limbs with balmy swoon,
   and tirèd eyne with sweet Oblivion's boon.

66 The Gama, with his Portingalls remainèd,
   whom, upon hospitable thought intent,
   the noble Indian Regent entertainèd
   with feast and joy and general content.
   The Cat'ual, to his monarch's service trainèd,
   sought surest tidings; 'twas his regiment
   to learn how, when, and whence the Folk had come,
   what laws were theirs, what customs, and what home.

67 Soon as he saw the Delian Car of fire
   the fair Youth drives, come forth and light restore,
   he summoneth Monsaydé for desire
   to know the strangers new to th' Indian shore.
   Ready and curious now he 'gins enquire
   if certain signs, pure proofs, the Moorman bore
   anent these foreigners, as men had said
   hard by his country they were born and bred:

68 That punct'ual proof partic'ular he must bring
with general information; as 'twould be
notable service done to tell the King
all that could guide him in such novelty.
Rejoins Monsaydé:— "Alb'eit ev'erything
I lief recount, yet count it not from me:
I only ken they bide in distant Spain,
where bathe my nest and Phoebus in the Main.

69 "They hold a Prophet's Law who was begot
sinless, nor stained with carnal detriment
His Virgin-Mother; Him the Breath[158] they wot
of God who holdeth Earth in government.
But what my sires ancestral ne'er forgot,
of them, is Valour fierce, sanguinolent
in arms, that on their arm resplendent gloweth,
as many a Geste with our forefathers showeth.

70 "For they, with brav'ery better than of man,
outdrave our grandsires from the fertile leas
where fresh Guadiána and rich Tagus ran,
with famed and memorable instances:
Still seeking triumphs, in far African
parts, spurning perils of the stormy seas
our plans of safety and of peace they foil,
they break our lofty walls, our towns they spoil.

71 "Nor less of force and fraud they showed, whene'er
kindled were other wars by Fate's decree,
or when Spain's warlike sons to fight would fare,
or there, when others poured down Pyrenee:
And thus, in fine, to thrust of foreign spear
ne'er bowed they, owning alien mastery
ne'er yet was known, I swear no man can tell us
to Hannibals like these e'er came Marcellus.

72 "And if my tidings faulty seem and few,
    what thou requirest that to ask them send;
    ask of themselves, for they be proud and true
    and falsehoods most annoy them and offend:
    Go see their fleet and arms, their manner view
    of moulded metal, ready all to shend:
    Wend thou and note the Lusians' various art
    in Peace and War, the sight shall glad thy heart."

73 Flamed with desire the Idol-servant's mind
    to sight the marvels told him by the Moor:
    He bade the boats be manned, and straight incline'd
    to view the vessels which the Gama bore:
    Both leave the foreshore, and their boat behind
    came Nayran hosts, till Ocean curdled o'er:
    They scale the Flagship's gunwales strong and tal;
    and, reacht the main-deck, are received by Paul.

74 Her purple awnings and her banners shine
    with the rich tissue which the worm hath made;
    whereon appear portray'd with rare design
    the warlike actions of the mighty Dead:
    Here show fierce accidents of 'battled line,
    and there fere single-fights, a scene of dread,
    wherefrom the Géntoo seeking all to 'spy
    may not withdraw the pleasure of his eye.

75 He asks of all he sees: But Gama pray'd
    he first be seated, and in cool retreat
    be pleased to taste the food before him spread,
    which Epicurus' sect holds highest treat.
    The spumy vases gen'erous liquors shed
    which first did Noah make the world to weet:
    Yet nills the Géntoo-man to break his fast,
    as 'twas forbidden by the laws of Caste.

76 The blaring Trumpet, which in Peace the thought
    of Warfare im'ages, rends the lift like thunder:
    The diabolick instruments fire-fraught
    wake slumb'ering echoes there, the sea-depths under.
    Noted the Géntoo all: But most he sought
    to read th' intention and the works of wonder
    done by the Heroes which in scanty space
    Picture, mute Poesy, had power to trace.

77 He riseth, Gama rising by his side,
    and there Coelho with the Mauritan:
    With curious eyne a warlike form they eye'd,
    an old white Sire of aspect sovereign,
    whose name and honours in our hearts shall 'bide,
    long as the World shall know the name of man:
    In garb of Grecian usage stands he dight,
    bearing device of leaf-branch in his right.

78 His right a leaf-branch bore: — But oh! how blind
    I madly rush to 'tempt without your stay,
    ye Nymphs of Tagus and Mondego kind,
    a path so varied, long and ard'uous way!
    Lend me your favour while my way shall wind
    o'er the deep Ocean 'mid the Storm's affray;
    for sore I fear me an ye leave the helm
    the waves my fragile barque shall overwhelm.

79 See how my Lay so long to sing hath striven
    your Tagus and the Lusians dear to you,
    how oft this exile Fate from home hath driven,
    new labours ever suff'ering, losses new:
    Now tempting Ocean, then all helpless driven
    the dread Mavortian risks and wrongs to rue;
    self-doomed as Canacé to death abhor'd,
    in this hand aye the Pen, in that the Sword:

80 Now sunk by hateful scornèd Penury
to chew the bitter bit of beggar-bread:
Then mockt by Hope already brought so nigh
to be anew and more than e'er misled:
Then with bare life in hand condemned to fly
where life depended from so fine a thread;
only a greater miracle could save,
than what to Judah's King[159] new life-lease gave.

81 And still, my Nymphs! 'twas not enough of pain
such sorrow-clouds around my life should close;
but they, for whom I sang the patriot-strain,
with sad return must pay my toils, my throes:
In place of Peace and Rest I hoped to gain,
in lieu of Bay-wreaths bound around my brows,
troubles by men unseen they must invent,
when ills of every kind my soul torment.

82 Behold, ye Nymphs! what high-bred Lords and wise
breedeth your Tagus, what a gen'erous race,
who in such fashion with such favours prize
the Bard whose boon hath lent their lordships grace!
For coming writers what examples rise
to raise Man's genius to its Pride of Place,
to shrine memorious in the Poet's story
Deeds that deserve to gain eternal glory!

83 But since such hosts of ills around me lie,
let not my Fancy of your favour fail
here chiefest wanted as the goal draws nigh,
that mighty feats wax mightier by my tale:
Aid me you only, long indeed sware I
no grace to grant where good doth not prevail,
and none to flatter whatso their degrees,
on pain of losing all my pow'er to please.

84 Think not, ah no, my Nymphs! I would enfame
the man who dares his country and his King
forget for private int'erest's pit'iful claim,
by law of God and Man a felon thing.
Nor poor ambition, whose degraded aim
is to win office, shall my Song e'er sing,
whose only object in th' ignoble prize
is larger range of Vice and Infamies.

85 None, who misusing pow'ers on him confer'd,
makes them the panders of his ugly greed;
none, who to court and cringe before the herd
in change of figure Proteus shall exceed.
From me, Camenæ, fear no fav'ouring word
for him who comes, in grave and honest weed,
in new-born rank his King contenting more,
to fleece and flay the miserable poor.

86 Nor him who, holding 'tis but just and right,
his King's severest orders to fulfil,
holds it not Justice fitly to requite
the servile brows that weary sweat distil:
Nor him whose bosom, lacking pract'ical light,
seeketh for causes, and by prudent skill
taxeth with niggard heart and hand unfair,
the toils of aliens which he doth not share.

87 Only of men I'll sing the glorious name
who riskèd darling life for God, for King;
when losing life they lengthened life by fame,
and well deserved the best that Bard can sing.
Apollo and the Nine, who with me came,
redoubled fury to my song shall bring
when rest and breathing from my travail tane
I to my toil refresht shall come again.

CANTO VIII

1 Tarried the Cat'ual, standing mute before
the first of painted forms that stood in sight;
who for Device in hand a leaf-branch bore,
with meteor-beard, long-flowing, flossy-white.
"Whose counterfeit presentment this; wherefor
the strange device he holdeth in his right?"
When Paul, with sober accents answering said,
while the wise Moor for both interprètèd:

2 "All of these figures which to thee are shown
so bold in bearing, dreadful to behold,
and bolder, dreader far, the men were known
in mouth of Fame, for words and works of old:
Antients yet moderns are, still brighter grown
with names in Genius' highest rank enrol'd:
This first in sight is Lusus, from whose fame
our 'Lusitania' gained her royal name.

3 "He was the Theban's son or comrade tried,
the God who divers regions overran;
it seems he came to hold our Spanish nide,
pursuing conquests which his youth began:
Douro's and Guadiana's plains of pride,
of yore 'Elysian Fields,' his fancy wan
so much, he there would give his weary bones
the Tomb eterne, the term our country owns.

211

4 "The branch-Device, thou see'st him bear in hand,
   is the green Thyrsus Bacchus wont to wield,
   which to our cent'ury doth belief command
   he was a comrade or belovèd child.
   See'st thou yon other treading Tagus-land,
   the Plow'er who long hath plow'd the wild Sea-field,
   where the perpetual walls he reared on high,
   and fane of Pallas for all memory?

5 "Ulysses 'tis who builds that sacred fane
   to her, whose favour tongue facund supplies;
   if there he fired tall Troy on Asian plain
   here made he mighty Lisbon's walls arise."
   "Whom, here, who cumbers with the slain
   the field, whose furious presence frights the eyes?
   He drives great armies to disgraceful rout,
   and on his banners painted eagles float."

6 The Géntoo thus, and Gama's answer came:—
   "Thou see'st a Herdsman who his flock forsook;
   we know that Viriátus was his name,
   who aye preferred the Lance before the Crook:
   He shook and shattered Roman pride and fame;
   from this unvanquisht victor ne'er she took
   Ah, no! nor ever could her power take
   the primacy which Pyrrhus failed to break.

7 "Not force but fraud she used, and underhand
   she filch't his life that cowed her coward sprite;
   for mighty straits make men of honest brand
   break the magnan'imous laws of Honour bright.
   This other here, against his angry land
   with us forgatherèd, an exiled wight:
   Right well chose he the men wherewith to rise,
   and of immortal lustre snatch the prize.

212

8   "Thou see'st with us he beats the Flags that bear
     Jove's valiant birds, victorious, sovereign;
     e'en in those days no Braves so brave but wear
     our yoke, subjected to our might and main:
     See his so subtle arts, his wily care
     the people by his deep design to gain;
     that Prophet-Hind aye dealing wise advice:
     Sertorius he; the Doe is his Device.

9   "See now this other painted flag upon,
     of our first Kings the great progenitor:
     Our Hist'ory makes him to be Hung'ary's son,
     but strangers say Lorraine the hero bore.
     When with the chivalry of proud Leon
     and the Gallego he lay low the Moor,
     unto Sanct Sep'ulchre saintly Henry hied
     that might his kingly trunk be sanctified."

10   "Say, prithee, who be this that frights my sight?"
     (asketh th' astonied man of Malabar)
     "who all these squadrons, all these men of might
     with his thin legions thus can rout and mar?
     Who breaks such bulwarks proud in breadth and height,
     who gives such battle, never tired of war,
     who comes so many crowns in many parts
     to trample under foot, and estandarts?"

11   "The First Afonso 'tis," the Gama spake,
     "by whom the Moor all Portugalia lost
     for whom Fame sware her oath by Stygian Lake
     no more of noble Roman name to boast:
     The Zealot he whom God would ne'er forsake
     by whose brave arm He tames the Moorish host,
     for whom their wallèd reign He lays so low
     no more is left for future days to do.

12 "Had Caesar, or King Alexander led
    a power so puny, men-at-arms so few,
    against the multitudes unnumberèd
    this excellent Commander overthrew;
    deem not their names had earth thus overspread,
    nor could their deathless glories death subdue:
    But leave we such inexplicable Deeds
    and see what worth of vassal-men he leads.

13 "This whom thou seest sight with kindling eye
    his broken pupil, fierce in high disdain
    bidding him rally flying hosts, and try
    once more the desp'erate fortunes of the plain:
    Returneth Youth with Age to do or die,
    and turns the vanquisht Vanquisher again:
    Egas Moníz, the gallant vet'eran hight,
    is Knighthood's mirror to each loyal knight.

14 "See' him here self-yielded with his sons he goes,
    naked of silk and cloth with neck in cord,
    because the Youth to break the promise chose
    which to Castile he gave with plighted word:
    He lured by specious promises the foes
    to raise the siege when sov'ereign waged the sword:
    To life's last pains he dooms his sons and wife
    and self-condemnèd saves his Liege's life.

15 "Less did the Consul[160] whom the hosts surround
    when to the Caudine Forks he careless came,
    and there his head to bow and pass was bound
    'neath the triumphant Samnites' yoke of shame:
    This, blamed at home, an inborn firmness found
    to yield him singly, true to constant aim;
    this other yieldeth self and innocent seed
    and wife,—more glorious and more grievous deed.

16 "See'st thou the Brave who, left his ambuscade,
   falls on the King besieging yon tall town,
   the town unsieging and the King waylaid:
   Illustrious action Mars might call his own!
   See him, here wends he, limned in yon Armade,
   till eke at sea the Moormen slain or flown
   lost all their galleys; while he claims the prize
   that heads our host of mar'itime victories:

17 "Fuás Roupinho 'tis; o'er wave and land
   his name shall aye resplend with equal light,
   reflecting flames that lit his daring hand
   in Moorman galleys under Ab'yla's height.
   See how at just and saintly War's command
   happy he loses life in holy fight:
   Enters by Moorish hands the heavenly calm
   his Soul, triumphant with the well-won Palm.

18 "See'st not this Gath'ering in strange garb that came
   swarming from out yon Navy new and brave,
   who holp our first of Kings the foe to tame
   and 'leaguing Lisbon saintly proof they gave?
   Behold Henrique,[161] Knight of peerless fame,
   and eke the Palm that grew beside his grave:
   Thro' them His marvels God to man hath shown:—
   Germans be they the martyrs Christ shall own.

19 "Behold a Churchman brandishing his skeyne
   against Arronches which he takes, the chance
   of Leiría 'venging lately tane
   by men who couch for Mafamed the lance.
   'Tis Theotonio, Prior.[162] See again
   besiegèd Sant'arem, and shalt see the glance
   assured that figures on the mure and first
   wave o'er the walls the Quinal Banner durst:

20 "See here he hies, where low our Sancho layeth
    the Vandal Moor who in fierce fight atones;
    pierceth th' opponent host, his Antient slayeth,
    and trails th' Hispalic pendon o'er the stones:
    Mem Moniz he, who in his life portrayeth
    the valour buried with his Father's bones;
    digne of these Banners, since his force ne'er failèd
    to raise his own, to rout whate'er assailèd.

21 "Behold that other, sliding down his spear,—
    bearing two head of sentinels he slew,—
    better to hide his ambush; now appear
    his Braves whose might and sleight the town o'er-threw:
    And now her 'scutcheon shows the Cavalier
    proper who holds in hand the coupèd two
    cold ghastly heads. A deed ne'er done indeed!
    Giraldo Sem-pavor[163] the stout name read.

22 "See'st not a Spaniard[164] who, dissatisfied
    with our ninth King Afonso, by old hate
    of Lara movèd, with the Moor abide
    in friendship hostile to our Port'ugal state?
    Abrantes town he takes accompanied
    by the hard Infidel, his Moorish mate:
    But see a Portingall with pow'r so spare
    rout him, and stoutly lead him prisoner:

23 "Martim Lopés the Knight by name is known
    who from the traitors palms and laurels took.
    But here behold the Bishop Mil'itant shown,
    who changed for steely Lance his golden Crook:
    See him, 'mid faithless faithful found alone,
    fight to refuse refusing, shake and shock
    the cruel Moorman: See in shining skies
    the sign whereby his few he multiplies.

24 "See, fly the Kings of Cord'oba and Sevile
    routed, with other twain in shortest tale:
    Routed! nay, rather, ruined. Miracle
    God-wrought, not worked by arm of mortal frail!
    See Alcacer low bend her haughty will;
    ne tow'ers of flesh, ne walls of steel avail
    'gainst Lisbon's Bishop, Dom Matheus: See!
    crowned with the palmy crown there standeth he.

25 "Behold a Master of Castilian line,[165]
    a Portingall by right of birth, o'errun
    Algarves Kingdom till she shows no sign
    of men-at-arms his force hath not undone:
    By guile, and might and main, and star benign
    towns, castles, cities, all are stormed and won.
    Soon 'spite her townsmen Tavila-town he breaks,
    and for the Se'ven slain Hunters vengeance takes.

26 "See him with bellic arts from Moormen gain
    Sylves, they gainèd with enormous host:
    Paio Corrêa 'tis, whose might and main
    and cunning purpose men aye envy most.
    Nor pass the fighting three[166] in France and Spain
    who won a name that never shall be lost
    for tournay, challenges and joustings gay;
    winning of publick trophies proud display:

27 "See'st them? how clept 'Adventurers,' they came
    Castileward, whence alone the prize and pride
    they bore, the winnings of Bellona's game
    as to their loss all found a fall who tried:
    See them strike down the Knights of proudest fame
    who of the three the principal defied,
    'tis Gónçalo Ribéiro, name so brave
    hath nought to fear from Lethe's whelmy wave.

217

28 "To one attend, whose Fame so far extendeth,
   that with no fame of old she rests content,
   who, when his country on a thread dependeth
   lends stalwart shoulders to the burthen bent;
   See'st not how anger-flusht he reprehendeth
   the cowèd throng's suspicions cold and lent;
   and makes the wretches hail the gentle rein
   of home-born King, not foreign Suzerain?

29 "See him, with daring and advice replete
   God-guarded only and by Holy Star,
   make possible th' impossible, and defeat
   one-handed, proud Castilia's pow'er of war.
   See how by valour aided, might and wit,
   in second slaughter vict'ory similar
   he gains o'er those who, fierce as infinite, dwell
   betwixt Tartessus and Guadiàna's vale?

30 "See'st not already all but overthrown
   our Lusitanian pow'er, when left his line
   the Capitayne devout, who wends alone
   t' invoke that Essence, the Most Highest Trine?
   Now see him summoned hast'ily by his own,
   who plead that Fortune must parforce incline
   to whelming force, and pray his presence cheer
   the soldiers, and enforce their feeble fear.

31 "Yet see the careless holy confidence,
   wherewith ''Tis not yet time,' he answerèd
   as one in God reposing trust immense
   of human vict'ory won by heav'enly aid:
   E'en so Pompilius, hearing the offence
   of en'emies urging o'er his land the raid,
   to him who brought the heavy news replies,
   'But I, you see, am offering sacrifice!'

218

32 "If one whose Brave'ry rests his God upon,
perchance thou wouldest know how named and known,
'Portugale's Scipio' is the name he won,
but 'Nuno Alvares' claims more renown.
Happy the Land that bare her such a son!
or, rather sire: For long as Suns look down
on Earth where Ceres and joint Neptune reign
for such a Scion she shall sigh in vain.

33 "In the same Warfare see what prizes gaineth
this other Captain of a slender band;
driving commanders he the drove regaineth
which they had lifted with audacious hand:
See how the lance again in gore he staineth
only to free, at Friendship's firm command,
his thrallèd friend whom Honour made a thrall:—
Pero Rodrigues 'tis of Landroal.

34 "Look on this Treachetour[167] and how he payeth
his caitiff trick'ery and his perj'ury fell;
Gil Fernandes of Elvas 'tis that slayeth
the wretch, and sends him to his proper Hell:
Harrying Xeres-plain the crops he layeth
with floods of blood that raineth proud Castile:
But see how Rúy Pereira's face and front
enshield the galleys, bearing battle-brunt.

35 "See yon sev'enteen to Lusus who belong
upon this hillock standing, life defend
against the Spaniards who four hundred strong,
to take them captive in their rear extend:
But to their sorrow these shall find ere long
the stout defenders also can offend:
Feat digne to last till Earth succumb to Time;—
in the far Past, in Present day sublime!

219

36 "How the three hundred Braves, 'twas known of old,
   did with a thousand Romans battle wage,
   in the good times when virile deeds and bold
   which Viriátus did, illumed his age:
   He snatcht memorious triumphs from their hold,
   bequeathing this our noblest heritage,
   the Brave tho' few shall ne'er the Many fear,
   as sithence thousand times we proved full clear.

37 "Pedro and Henry view, those Infants twain
   of kingly John the gen'erous progeny:
   That gars his fame illustrious to remain
   in German-land and doometh Death to die:
   This Prince inspired by Heaven claimed the Main
   as her Explorer; and lay bare the lie
   of tumid Moor's vain boast in Ceita's wall,
   and, forced the gateway, entered first of all.

38 "See'st Country Pedro,[168] daring to support
   two sieges laid by Barb'ary's might entire;
   and see'st yon other Count[169] who shows the port
   of earthly Mars in martial force and fire:
   Sufficeth not to fence Alcacer-fort
   From swarming hosts; his spirit flieth higher,
   his King's beloved life the Brave defends
   us stone-wall standing till his own he ends.

39 "And here the Painters who in Art prevail,
   pardie, had many painted and portray'd;
   but fail their pencils and their colours, fail
   prize, praise, and premium, of Art's life the bread.
   Fault of the vices flowing from th' entail
   of men degen'erate, who so far have stray'd
   from valour's paths where trod their lustrous sires,
   deep mired in vanities and low desires.

40 "Those high illustr'ious Fathers who gave birth
    to generations on their grace depending,
    fought for fair honour, sternly strove on Earth
    to found a fam'ily that could bear descending:
    Blind! if paternal toils of priceless worth,
    won name, fame, claim so far and wide extending,
    they leave their lesser sons but more obscure,
    when left in crap'ulous vice to live impure.

41 "Als there be others, sons of wealth and might,
    who to no lordly tree by birth belong:
    Fault of the Kings, who oft some favourite
    prefer to thousands, wise and true and strong:
    For these the painted Past hath poor delight,
    feeling vain colours work them present wrong;
    and aye as nat'ural foe in hate they bear
    the speaking pictures which their semblance wear.

42 "Gainsay I not, that some of high descent
    from wealthy houses, men of gen'erous strain,
    still with their noble lives and excellent
    'herited titles worthily sustain:
    And if the light which ancestry hath lent
    no novel glory by their doings gain,
    at least it faileth not, nor dim it groweth:—
    But ah! few men like these the Painter knoweth."

43 Thus Gama's el'oquence told the mighty deeds,
    disclosed by various tints to stranger view,
    where Art to sing'ular Artist-hand concedes
    depainting Nature with her nat'ural hue.
    The Cat'ual's ready glance distinctly reads
    the surd-mute story and the tale so true:
    A thousand times he askt, a thousand heard
    each tasteful battle which his eyne prefer'd.

44 And now the light a doubtful lustre showèd,
when veiled the mighty Lamp its lucent ray
beneath the sky's round rim, and lum'inous glowèd
on our Antipodes the smile of Day:
The gen'erous crowd of Nayrs and Géntoos rowèd
off from the stalwart ship on homeward way,
seeking repose and sleep's delicious swoon,
to weary beings Night-tide's gentle boon.

45 Meanwhile those Augurs who most fame affy
in false opinion, that by sacrifice
forecast of future things which dubious lie,
thro' diabolick sign and show they wis;
by royal mandate hied Black Arts to ply,
and various offices 'gan exercise,
to find what projects brought across the Main
unheard of foreigners from unknown Spain.

46 By Demon-aidance truthful sign they learn,
how doth this novel visitor portend
a yoke perpet'ual, servitude eterne,
the Race's ruin and its valour's end.
Th' amazèd Augur, whom the proofs constern,
wends to the King and tells (e'en as he ken'd)
the fearful symptoms that had met his sight
by victim'd bowels brought anon to light.

47 These signs confirming, to a Priest devout,
a man of mark in Mafamedé's creed,
from preconceivèd hatred not remote
'gainst Holy Faith, that doth all faiths exceed,
in the False Prophet's form of evil note,
who drew his being from slave Hagar's seed,
Bacchus the hateful in a dream appears,
whose hate is doubled by redoubled fears.

48 "Guard ye, my children, guard ye,"—thus he spoke,
   "from snares and perils laid by deadly foes
   who o'er the tumid waters hither flock,
   before the danger more immediate grows."
   The Moorman, startled by these words, awoke
   in visionary fear: But soon arose
   the thought that vulgar dream his brain opprest,
   and thus returned he tranquil to his rest.

49 When Bacchus thus returneth:—"Know'est thou not
   the mighty Maker, who the Law devisèd
   for thy forefathers, he whose will ye wot
   and lacking whom had many been baptizèd?
   I wake for thee, for me dost sleep, thou sot?
   Then by the Future soon shalt be advisèd
   how these new-comers come with bane and ban
   to break the laws I taught to seely man.

50 "Until this feeble folk full force hath won,
   contrive resistance in all manner o' ways;
   for, easy 'tis upon the rising Sun
   firm eyne to fix sans fear of blinding rays:
   But, when to zenith hath his race been run
   the strongest eye-sight that would dare to gaze
   remaineth dazed, and so shall ye remain
   unless ye let them ere the root be tane."

51 Then with the Dreamer's sleep away he speedeth:
   Trembling remains th' astonisht Hagarene;
   springing from couch his slaves bring light he biddeth,
   the fervid venom fest'ering in his spleen.
   As the pale dawn-light, which the sun precedeth,
   display'd her angel-cheek and brow serene,
   convoked the Doctors of the turpid sect,
   he of his vision renders 'count direct.

52 Divers opinions couchèd contrary
   are told and heard as each best understood:
   Astute waylayings, argute treachery,
   were workt and woven in their vengeful mood:
   But shirking treason which may danger dree,
   they sought the spilling of the Strangers' blood
   with plots and projects of the subtlest school,
   by bribes the Rulers of the Land to rule.

53 With golden bribe, rich fee, and secret gift,
   they strive the country-principals to please;
   showing with proofs discreet of not'able drift,
   how shall perdition all the people seize;
   "These be," they say, "a folk of scanty thrift,
   rovers who run from occidental seas,
   pyratick rapine is their sole design,
   sans Roy, sans Loy, or human or divine."

54 Ah! how behooves the King, who rules aright,
   to choose his counc'illors or his friends belovèd,
   by rule of conscience. Virtue's inner light,
   whose sprites sincere affection long have provèd!
   The man exalted to that dizzy height,
   the kingly throne, of things from note removèd
   can gain no notice sure, no knowledge clear,
   save what th' adviser's tongue will teach his ear.

55 Much less I counsel Kings to rest secure
   in the clear conscience of the men who show
   of humble pauper cloak the form of lure;
   Ambition haply lurketh rags below:
   And men in all things pious, just, and pure,
   often of worldly knowledge little know;
   for ill shall trustful Innocence take part
   in mundane matters, when God holds the heart.

56 But each and ev'ry Cat'ual gross in greed,
   the puissant rulers of the Gentile herd,
   gained by the glozings of the hellish breed,
   unto the Portingalls dispatch defer'd.
   Whereon the Gama,—whose one only heed
   despite the mischief by the Moormen stir'd,
   was at the kingly feet sure sign to lay
   of the discover'd World left far away:—

57 Worketh for this alone, as well he knew
   that, when sure tidings and clear proofs appear,
   arms, armour, ships, and men would send anew
   Mano'el, the King who rules the Realm sans peer;
   that to his yoke and law he would subdue
   the globèd earth, and e'en the wat'ery sphere;
   himself was nothing but the dil'igent hand
   that pioneer'd the road to Orient-land.

58 The Géntoo Monarch forth he fares to find,
   that with dismissal he may wend his ways;
   seeing already how the Moor's black mind
   would baulk his heart's desire by long delays.
   The King, who if by tales of forgèd kind
   amazèd were, 'twould not so much amaze,
   confiding fully in his Augurs' troth,
   confirmèd too by Moormen's wordy froth:

59 Feels Fear a-freezing his ignoble breast:
   Burneth on other hand a base desire,
   which ever held his spirit in arrest,
   flaming with Lucre-lust's unquench'able Fire:
   The richest profit sees he manifest
   appear in future, if with truth entire,
   he make just contract and its cons'equent gain,
   for long years offered by our Lusian Reign.

60 Hereon the counc'illors whom the King most prizèd
different counsels and opinions dealt;
for those whereby he wont to be advisèd
money's almighty magick might had felt.
To call our valiant Captain he devisèd,
and him when come thus spake:—"Now, an thou wilt
here in my presence own the nude clean truth,
thy felon actions still shall claim my ruth:

61 "The message, say they and I understand,
thy King hath sent me, is a falsehood vain;
no King doth own thee, ownest thou no land,
but leadest vaguing life upon the Main:
Say! who from ultimate Hispanian strand,
or King or Lord past hope of cure insane
would send his navies or one ship to stray
over such distant Ocean's dubious way?

62 "And if great wealthy kingdoms doth thy King
sway, as thou say'est with kingly majesty,
what rich rare presents do I see thee bring
earnests of doubtful unknown verity?
The splendid robe, the costly offering
betwixt high King and King link amity:
I hold no valid sign, no certain pledge,
the pleas a vagrant seaman may allege."

63 "If as hath hapt to many a high-born Brave,
perchance in exile be your lot to roam,
my land shall lend you refuge and shall save;
for ev'ry country is the strong man's home:
If ye be Pyrats housed upon the wave,
own it me, fear nor infamy nor doom;
for in all ages life to save must be
the primal law of life's necessity."

64 He thus: The Gama, who divin'd the game
   perfidious, with a cunning treason play'd
   by jealous Mahometick hearts, whence came
   the foul suspicions which the King misled:
   With high-soul'd confidence, as did beseem,
   commanding credence which he merited,
   bowing to Venus Acidalia's hest
   proffered this answer from his prudent breast:—

65 "If man's orig'inal Sin in hoary Time,
   whereby sore fall became our hapless fate,
   had never caused the cup of deadly crime,—
   that cruel scourge of every Christian state,—
   with enmity to brim in every clime
   for Adam's sons with falsity innate
   (O King sublime!) of that foul turpid sect,
   ne'er hadst thou held me of such deed suspect.

66 "But, sithence nought is won or good or high
   sans stumbling-blocks, and sees each nobler deed
   on fair Hope's footstep Fear aye following nigh,
   which on its bosom-sweat delights to feed;
   meseems thou deignest little to rely
   on this my very truth, nor takest heed
   of other reasons, which regard thou must
   didst thou not trust to men unworthy trust.

67 "For, an I be a Robber rapine-fed,
   undivagous, far banisht from mine own,
   how can I, thinkest thou, so far have sped
   to seek these seats unseen, these realms unknown?
   By what false Hope, what love of profit led
   should I 'mid angry seas my lot have thrown,
   Antarctick rigours and the fires of air,
   which they who dwell beneath the Ram must bear?

227

68   "If thou demand that gifts of high degree
     must the good credit of my words maintain,
     I came but stranger climes and skies to see
     where Nature chose to set thine antient reign:
     But if my Fortune grant such good to me
     home to return and Fatherland regain,
     By rich and splendid presents thou shalt learn
     the 'assurèd tidings of my glad return.

69   "If this my visit Chance inop'inate seem,
     that King should send from far Hesperian strand,
     know that yon noble heart and bosom deem
     no geste, no poss'ible feat too great and grand.
     Well seems it fitting, that the thought supreme
     of Lusian spirit should at least command
     larger belief and faith of loft'ier flight,
     and hold it boundless in its height and might.

70   "Know that long ages passèd, since our old
     Kings with a settled purpose 'gan propose
     to conquer toils and travails manifold,
     which aye to noble plans their pow'er oppose.
     They opèd hostile seas that fain withhold
     from mortal man the boon of soft repose;
     they willed to trace their bounds, to track their shore,—
     the farthest margent where their billows roar.

71   "Conceit right worthy of his branch so blest
     that vent'urous King,[170] who plowed in primal rank
     the waves and drave from out his well-loved nest
     the last possessor of Mount Ab'yla's flank:
     He by rare Genius, toils that never rest,
     unto one plank conjoining other plank,
     disclosed the parts, where shine in clearest air
     Argo with Hydra, Ara with the Hare.[171]

72 "These early seeds abundant harvest bore,
   and waxt our bosoms braver till we came
   little by little stranger paths t' explore,
   devel'oping each an antecedent aim:
   The latest dwellers on the Blackmoor shore
   Austral, whose eyne ne'er saw the Sev'enfold Flame,[172]
   were seen by us when left behind in turn
   whatever peoples 'neath the Tropick burn.

73 "Thus with firm bosom, fixt resolve to win,
   we vanquisht Fortune and we snatcht the prize,
   till harbour'd this thy new-found kingdom in
   we taught the crowning Column here to rise:
   Cleaving perforce clean through the liquid tin,
   horrible Tempests' importunities,
   to thee we come, and only pray from thee
   some sign and signal which our King shall see.

74 "This, King, be truth: Nor deem that I would make,—
   for such uncertain good, such petty gain,
   which, b'eing my words untrue, mote be the stake,—
   such long proemium forgèd, false and vain.
   Liefer would I my rest unending take
   on the fierce restless bosom of the Main
   by mother Thetis rockt, a Pyrat dour
   who makes his wealth by making others poor.

75 "If then, Oh King! this honest truth of mine
   thou take for what it is, one-fold, sincere,
   aid us, to our despatch thy heart incline
   and gust of glad return to mar forbear.
   But an my tale appear some feigned design,
   heed thou my pleadings proved so fair and clear,
   as seen by Judgment-lights that never fail,
   for Truth is strong and Truth shall aye prevail."

76   Th' attentive Monarch felt assured content
     when thus Da Gama provèd his discourse:
     Conceives in him reliance confident,
     and the firm trust that lent his language force:
     He weighs of every word the full intent
     pond'ering the pleading from such trusty source;
     and 'gins to hold as men by self deceivèd
     those caitiff Cat'uals who had bribes receivèd.

77   Jointly his lucre-lust claims firm effect,
     which Lusian contract shall he hopes ensure;
     Hope bids him listen, and far more affect
     the Captain's honour than the crafty Moor:
     In fine he biddeth Gama hie direct
     aboard, and thence from hurt and harm secure
     the fittest stuffs for traffick shoreward send
     against his spicey stores to truck or vend.

78   The stuffs to send, in fine, he gives command,
     which in Gangetick realms the rarest be
     if aught of value brought he from the land,
     where ends the shore and where begins the sea.
     Now from the Royal presence venerand
     the Captain seeks the port to make his plea
     before the Cat'ual honored with his charge,
     for loan of boat as his were all at large.

79   For boat whereby to board his ship he pleadeth:
     Yet the bad Regent plotting novel snare
     wherein to 'trap the stranger, nought concedeth,
     but stay and hindrance straightway doth prepare;
     Then, faring from the quay, his Guest he leadeth
     far from the royal Palaces; and there,
     where kens the Monarch nought of such intent,
     would work the mischief which his malice meant.

230

80 When reached the distant site, he 'gan to say
    fitting conveyance should be soon supplied,
    or to the dawning of the crastine day
    the passage to defer he best decide.
    But now perceivèd from prolonged delay
    the Gama how the Géntoo was allied
    with the deep-plotting Moors' revengeful brood,
    a truth he had not hereto understood.

81 This Cat'ual also gifts and bribes had tane,
    tempted like others by the Moslem folk;
    eke was he chief who held the guiding rein
    of all the cities 'neath the Samo'rim's yoke:
    From him alone the Moormen looked to gain
    their base and wicked wills by hook or crook:
    He, who in concert vile with them conspires,
    despaireth not to glut their ill desires.

82 To him the Gama with much instance prays
    for passage shipward, but without avail;
    for thus had order given, as he says,
    the proud successor of the Perimal.
    "What cause of hindrance here, why these delays
    to land the stuffs and goods of Portugal?
    Subjects perforce obey what Kings command
    who dares their dreadful orders countermand?"

83 That bribed Cat'ual lent no heed as due
    to the high words; nay more he rackt his thought
    to find some subtle phantasy and new,
    some deep and devilish scheme, some monstr'ous plot;
    or how his brutal steel he might imbrue
    in that detested blood he ever sought;
    or how the vessels he might blast and burn
    that none and nought therein may home return.

84 That none to Fatherland return intendeth,
and nothing less, the Moslems' fiendish plan;
so ne'er shall ken how far and wide extendeth
Th' Eoan land our sovran Lusitan,
In fine goes not the Gama whom forfendeth
of those barbarian hordes the ruling man;
lacking whose permit none might leave the beach
as all the boats were borne beyond his reach.

85 To the Chiefs reasons and rough words replieth
that Idol-worshipper, he must command
to bring near shore the Fleet that distant lieth
so mote it easier be to board and land:
"Of foe or thief the tactick it implieth
when in far ofiing thus the vessels stand,"
quoth he, "for ne'er shall true and trusty friend
from those he loveth danger apprehend."

86 Shrewd Gama seeth in each wily word
the Cat'ual's drift, who fain would bring the Fleet
nearer, where dire assault of flame and sword
were ready made for wreaking mortal hate.
His thoughts he scatters better aid t' afford:
He seeks in Fancy's realm some cure discreet
some counterplot 'gainst evil plans preparèd;
in fine he fearèd all, for all he carèd.

87 As beam reflected by the burnisht bright
mirror of steel, or glass-plate chrystal-clear,
which sometime struck by ray of solar light
in other part re-strikes the dazzling glare;
and waved by wanton hand of curious Spright
about the house to sparkle here and there,
o'er walls and roofs the shimm'ering species plays,
nor rest its trem'ulous, fitful, quiv'ering rays.

232

88 So did his vaguing judgment fluctuate
   when captive Gama's mem'ory brought to mind
Coelho, lest he peradventure wait
   ashore with boats as by command design'd:
With message priv'ily sent he warned his mate
   fast for the Fleet his homeward way to find,
lest he fall lightly in the bitter lace
he feared, the fierce fell work of Moorish race.

89 Such should be he who would, by grace of Mart,
   follow th' illustrious and their fame outvie:
His nimble thought must fly to every part,
   see through, and 'scape the danger ere 'tis nigh.
His soldier-instinct rare, and subtle art
   must read, mark, learn his baffled enemy;
note all in fine; nor shall that Captain's lot
be praise of mine, who pleads I thought it not!

90 Insists the Malabar his guest remain
   pris'oner, till orders bring th' Armada near;
he constant, firèd with hot high disdain,
   hears eve'ry menace with unfrighten'd ear;
rather shall he the weight on self sustain
   which vilest malice born of hate and fear
machinates, than to shade of risk expose
his Liege's navy riding safe from foes.

91 That livelong night in durance vile he lies,
   and of next day a part, when he ordains
once more to see the King: But leave denies
   the Guard that not a few of men contains.
To tempt with other tricks the Géntoo tries,
   fearing his Monarch pay him for his pains,
when shown the malice which must soon be known,
if there a longer time the stranger wone.

92 He bids him order ev'ry stuff be brought
     straight shoreward, all he hath of vendible,
     that they might duly bartered be or bought;
     for who nills commerce war is wont to will.
     Though knows the Gama what felonious thought
     and damnable desires that bosom fill,
     yet he consenteth, for right well knows he
     with these same stuffs he buys his liberty.

93 Concert they now the Blackmoor shall prepare
     launches and lighters fit the wares to land;
     to trust his boats our Captain did not care,
     where fone might capture or might hold in hand.
     Put forth th' almádies for the beach to bear
     Hispanian stuffs, the best he mote command:
     He writes his brother fearing all delay
     to send the bales that shall his blackmail pay.

94 The merchandise now landed is ashore,
     where by that greedy Catual 'tis tane:
     Alvaro and Diogo guard the store,
     with leave to truck or vend as best they can.
     That more than duty, than obedience more,
     Gain rules th' ignoble breast of lawless man
     well doth that Pagan to the worldling show;
     for gained the goods he let the Gama go:

95 He lets him go, for in the goods he thought
     to hold sufficient pledge and pawn that may
     a better penny to his purse be brought,
     than if for longer time our Chief he stay:
     The Gama, certain that no more he ought
     to land, and haply 'counter fresh delay,
     and to his vessels being now restor'd,
     resolves with tranquil mind to bide aboard.

96 Aboard the ships he bides with mind at ease
    till seen what circumstance the days shall show;
    for now his spirit no reliance sees
    upon that bribèd Regent vile and low.
    Here let the Casuist who riddle rees,
    see how the wealthy as the wantful too,
    are ruled by lucre and the noxious thirst
    of gain that gars us dare and do the worst.

97 By Thracia's Sovran Polydore is slain,
    only to have and hold his wealthy store;
    the guarded edifice may not contain
    Acrisius' daughter 'gainst the golden shower;
    so raged Tarpeia's avarice insane
    that she in truck for shining yellow ore,
    the lofty towers to the foe betrayeth,
    and stifled, crusht, the price of treason payeth.

98 This opes of warded Fort the valvarte-wall,
    maketh the felon friend his faith forego:
    This changeth noblest Thane to vilest Thrall
    and yieldeth Captains to the luring foe:
    This maketh purest maiden foully fall,
    and know no fear, no reck of Honour trow:
    This Art and Science shall at times deprave,
    blind sanest judgment, consciences enslave:

99 This loves to gloss with subtler sense than meant
    the Texts: This maketh Laws and Laws unmaketh:
    This tainteth subjects with a traitor-taint:
    This in the patriot King the tyrant waketh.
    E'en he, self-vowèd to th' Omnipotent,
    as proved by thousand instances, forsaketh
    God's way by Gold's enchanting Siren woo'd;
    yet haply showing still some tint of good.

CANTO IX

1 Within the City long remainèd pent
  nor found a purchaser our Factor-twain:
  The wily Infidels by foil and feint
  made every trader cease from trade and gain:
  For all they purposèd, and hoped, and meant,
  was there the stout Discov'erers to detain
  of India, till arrive th' expected Fleet
  of Mecan vessels and the foe defeat.

2 There, where the City crowns the Red Sea bight
  founded by Egypt's royal Ptolemy,
  and from his sister-spouse Arsin'oe hight,
  to Suez changèd in our modern day;
  the harbour lieth at a distance light
  from far-famed Meca, raised to high degree
  by the false superstition and profane,
  the Holy Water of the Moorish men.[173]

3 Gidà the hythe is 'titled, where the trade
  of all the Red Sea shore-lands flourish most,
  whereby was great and grateful gain convey'd
  unto the Sóldan,[174] who possest the coast:
  Hence to the Malabars, by contract made
  with th' Infidel, tall ships, a potent host,
  each year fares sailing over Indic seas
  stocking their teeming holds with spiceries.

4 Upon these ships firm hopes the Moors had set,
 e'en as their puissance was so much the higher,
 that these who sought their gains so grateful great,
 they might consume with crepitating fire:
 For the good succour all confiding wait,
 and from th' Explorers naught they now require,
 save to retard their sailing in such sort,
 that the famed Meca-fleet should make the port.

5 But He who rules the Heav'ens and human race,
 who for whatever willèd hath His will,
 the fittest causes from afar doth trace
 which shall His provident effects fulfil;
 pitiful accidents of ruth and grace
 dealt to Monsaydé, who, with guarded skill,
 devoted self Da Gama to advise,
 and gain his rightful guerdon,—Paradise.

6 He, whom the Moorish rout might not suspect,
 being like them a Moor, but firmly thought
 a villain member of the villain sect,
 unveiled the frauds with foulest treason fraught:
 The ships by distance from the shore protect,
 in stealth with pious heart full oft he sought,
 mourning the causeless evils that ordain
 malignant hate and vengeance Sarracen.

7 He warns the wary Gama that th' Armade
 due from Arabian Meca year by year,
 is that whereon his fellows' hope is laid,
 to be the deadly arm of certain snare:
 "They sail with armed hosts amain," he said,
 "and Vulcan's horrid thunderbolts they bear;
 So may ye read'ily fall an easy prey
 as you be poorly furnisht for the fray!"

237

8 And eke the Gama, now considering
   the time had come for him to quit the Port,
   and that no gladder tidings from the King
   he could expect who doth the Moors support;
   the Factors left ashore straight summoning,
   he bade them haste aboard: And, lest report
   of such a flitting might their flight impede,
   he bids them privily their steps to speed.

9 But in the shortest space had Rumour flown
   on res'onant wing, nor here as wont did lie,
   that both the Factors were in prison thrown,
   when found attempting from the town to fly.
   Without delay the true report was known
   to the shrewd Captain, who incont'inently
   reprisals dealt on certain who had sought
   the Fleet to traflick with the gems they brought.

10 Now those detained are merchants grave and old,
   richards of Calecut in good repute;
   and in their absence all their brethren hold
   the ships withhold them and full true the bruit.
   But in the Fleet our Mar'iners brave and bold
   the capstans man, and each in several suit
   is told to task; these haul the cables in,
   those with hard breasts to shove the bars[175] begin.

11 Others to yard-arms hanging on let go
   the sail that bellies with a bell'owing sound;
   yet the King heareth louder sounds which show
   that fast the Squadron fareth homeward-bound:
   The wives and children, dight to die of woe
   for their lost loved ones, crowd in tears around
   the Samorim, and piteously complain
   from these their fathers, mates from those are tane.

238

12 Forthwith the Lusian Factors he restoreth
   with stuffs in fullest tale and all-tax free,
   despite the rancorous Moor who all abhorreth,
   so might the prison'd lieges renderèd be:
   Pardon for his deceit the King imploreth.
   The Captain greeteth, far more glad to see
   Factors than phrases hear; sets loose some Blacks
   and, making sail, adown the coast he tacks.

13 Down coast he tacketh, for he comprehendeth
   that with the Gèntoo King 'twere labour vain
   to knit those peaceful bonds, which he intendeth
   should strengthen commerce and her object gain:
   But seeing how the glorious Realm that trendeth
   Aurora-ward, must aye well-known remain,
   with these glad news he seeks dear Fatherland,
   sure tokens taking of what things he fand.

14 He taketh eke some Malabars aboard
   parforce, the fellows by the Samorim sent
   when were the Factor-pris'oners restor'd:
   Of purchased stores he taketh hot piment:
   Nor is of Banda the dried flow'er[176] ignor'd,
   nutmeg and swarthy clove, which excellent
   makes new Malucan Isle,[177] with cinnamon
   the wealth, the boast, the beauty of Ceylon.

15 All this was gathered by the deft design
   of true Monsaydé, borne aboard the Fleet:
   who thus of Angel-influences digne
   is register'd in Christ His roll-call writ:
   Blest African! whom clemency divine
   in prison-gloom with Gospel-light hath lit,
   who thus couldst find, from country forced to roam,
   the way to mortal man's true heav'enly home!

239

16 Then turning from that coast of torrid heat
the vent'urous Prores their southing courses bend,
where Nature pleased to place her farthest mete,
the Good Hope Cape, where Austrine shorelands end;
bearing the joyful news, and hopes to greet
their Lisbon homes from Morning-land they wend,
again resigned to snares of terror spread
by seas uncertain, glad, withal in dread:

17 The joy one's own dear Land once more to view,
sweet home and kith and kin to sight again,
with whom old voyage-feats we face anew,
and tell of climates strange and stranger men;
to taste the honey'd draught of praises due
by long mischances, toil, and ill and pain,
each hath of pleasure such a perfect store,
the shallow vessel of man's heart brims o'er.

18 Natheless the Cyprian goddess, who ordainèd
had been her Lusitanian sons to guard;
and by the Sire Eterne had been constrainèd,
through rolling years to lend them watch and ward;
the Glory gallant toils and travails gainèd
the weals that nobly suffered ills reward,
for them ordaining was, who did intend
all their sea-sorrows in sea-joys should end.

19 In thought revolving for a season brief
how they had faced the might'iest Sea that flows;
and thinking how the God sore gall and grief
worked, who in Amphionean Thebæ rose;
she had already planned right glad relief
a prize outweighing all their passing woes,
to find them rare delight and gentle rest
deep in the liquid chrystal's tranquil breast:

20 Something, in fine, of that repose so sweet,
    refocillating bodies weary-wan,
    for these her wanderers, and pay interest meet
    of toil, that short'eneth life of short-lived Man.
    Then to secure the ear it seemèd fit
    of her Son-god, whose might of Gram'arye can
    degrade the high Divine to low terrene,
    and raise our human clay to Heav'en serene.

21 And, duly pond'ering, all her thoughts incline
    there to bespread upon their wat'ery way,
    'mid waves of Ocean-stream, some Isle divine
    with bloom enamel'd and with green'ery gay;
    for she hath many, where her realms confine
    with the First Mother[178] girt by 'bosoming bay,
    besides those Gardens of the Midland Seas,
    within the portals oped by Hercules.

22 There 'tis her will, the watery Damosels
    await the coming of her hero-train,
    the Nymphs who worth'ily bear the name of belles,
    for eyne a pleasure and for hearts a pain;
    with choirs and dances, and by potent spells
    bring secret hoards of Love their love to gain,
    that all should labour with the best of will
    the Youths they love with lover-joys to thrill.

23 Erst so she schemèd for the son she bare
    to her Anchises, that he welcome found
    in the fair country, where by subtle snare
    a single ox-hide spanned the spacious ground:
    She seeks his aidance whom she may not spare,
    fierce Cupid, in whose force her force is bound;
    that e'en as in her olden enterprize
    he aided, aid he now to pluck the prize.

24 Yoked to her chariot are the Birds whose song
   doth exequies of Death in life's own tide,
   and they whose figure took in syne gone long,
   Peristera[179] who pluckt the daisies pied.
   Behind the hasting Goddess troop the throng,
   all through the lift with billing kisses glide:
   Where'er on windy wings the Goddess flies
   with gracious movement she serenes the skies.

25 Now o'er th' Idalian mounts her car impendeth,
   where for her coming waits her Archer-son,
   who mustering potent host with it intendeth
   to fare on famous expedition,
   and rebel worlds debel till he amendeth
   those direful errors long by mortals done,
   who love goods given by the Gods above
   for man to use and not for man to love.

26 He saw Actaeon, hunter so austere,
   so blindly bent on snatching brutal prize,
   that to pursue some ugly beast and fere,
   far from the human form divine he flies:
   The Boy for vengeance sweet as 'tis severe
   charms with chaste Dian's shape his hungry eyes;
   then let the for'ester take him careful heed
   lest his loved Hounds upon their Hunter feed.

27 He sees the wide world o'er how evry Lord,
   for public welfare naught doth reck nor feel;
   he sees that none the boon of love afford,
   save where Philautia[180] counsels selfish weal:
   He sees how men who sit at royal board
   for words of wisdom aye prefer to deal
   in sale of flatt'eries vile, which ne'er permit
   the tares be weeded from the fair young wheat.

28 He sees that men, to poverty who owe
   duty of Holy Love and Charity,
   live only pow'er to gain and wealth to show,
   pretending Justice and Integrity:
   Of ugly Tyr'anny breeding asp'erous woe
   they coin a right with vain severity:
   Laws they devise in favour of the King;
   Laws which the lieges favour down they fling,

29 He sees, in fine, none love as all should love,
   save that which dealeth only ill delight:
   Nor for a longer time doth it behove
   to waive a punishment as dire as right.
   He bids his summoned Ministers to move
   armaments, fitted for that mortal fight
   he lists engage with yon misgovern'd crowd,
   that hath till now allegiance disavow'd.

30 Of these small wingèd Impes a band is set
   to varied labours in their several crafts;
   these on the grindstone piercing piles to whet,
   and those to shave and thin the caney shafts:
   Soothes ev'ery labour love-sweet canzonet,
   wedding strange chances to the song that wafts
   sonorous melodies and roundels gay;
   suave is the song, angelical the lay.

31 Th' immortal Furnaces wherein they forgèd
   for their swift arrows points that penetrate,
   with fiery Hearts by way of fu'el are gorgèd,
   and Vitals vital still that palpitate:
   The temp'ering waves wherein the tips were mergèd,
   are lovers' Tears in love unfortunate:
   The live bright light and never-failing fire
   is ever burning ne'er outburnt Desire.

32 Some hied their dext'erous hands to exercise
    on the rude Vulgus' hard unfeeling hearts:
    Re-echo'd through the welkin frequent sighs
    of victims smitten by the shaft that smarts:
    Fair be the Nymphs who deal the remedies
    dear to the hurts they deal, and such their arts,
    the sorely hurt not only they revive,
    but boon of life to life unborn they give.

33 Beauteous the many, while the few are plain,
    consonant with the qual'ity of the wound;
    for to heal venom spread through ev'ery vein
    the bitter'est Theriacks oft the best are found.
    Many are doomèd aye to wear the chain
    by subtle bond of weirdest witch'ery bound:
    thus haps it mostly, when the darts acerb
    are armed and tinctured with the poyson-herb.

34 And from such wilful shots discharged sans aim,
    wherewith those awkward Impes aye joy to play,
    arise a thousand loves that mar and maim
    the victims wounded in such wretched way:
    E'en of the Heroes boasting highest fame
    a thousand impious loves the sight dismay;
    Such was May Byblis, such the Cinyrsean:[181]
    This Youth Assyrian born, and that Judaean.[182]

35 Ye too, my Lordlings! oft have seen the hour
    when love of Shepherd-lass your souls hath smit;
    and ye, my Ladies! oft the couthless boor
    hath meshed your Ladyships in Vulcan-net.
    These waiting nocturns to the tryst fain scour,
    those scale the casements and o'er pantiles flit:
    Yet hold I mainly that such loves indign
    are more the Mother's than the Son's design.

244

36 Now the light char'iot on the green depose
   he pure white Cygnets, slowly softly wending;
   and Dionæa, who conjoinèd shows
   roses in waste of snows, is seen descending.
   Her Bowyer-son who dareth Heav'en oppose,
   to greet her hasteth with douce smile unbending;
   while of the little Cupid lads a band
   crowdeth to kiss the Queen of Beauty's hand.

37 She, to save precious time from vanities,
   whispers the Boy embosom'd in her arms
   confident thus:— "Dear Son whose hand supplies
   the firmest footing of my chiefest charms;
   Son! on whose pow'ers my power aye relies;
   thou, holding cheap Typhoeus' dread alarms,
   her force by thine t' enforce, an urgent case
   bringeth thy mother to bespeak thy grace."

38 "The Lusitanick toils well hast thou ken'd,
   whom I for ages watch with tenderest guise.
   Since sware the Parcæ unto me, their friend,
   they shall adore my name, my favour prize;
   and, as their feats of armèd prowess shend
   all feats of rival Rome, I lief devise
   some mode of aidance in what things I may,
   far as our force o'er man extendeth sway.

39 "And, seen how hateful Bacchus hath beguile'd,
   with mortal plots, their course on Indic plain,
   and how by wavy Ocean's injuries foil'd
   rather than tirèd they were lost or slain:
   I will that in this sea to them so wild,
   'mid ever restless waves their rest be tane:
   Here shall they gather guerdon sweet and glorious
   of toils that make the names of men memorious.

Luís de Camões

40 "Wherefore I pray thee, Son! forthwith go fire
the Nereus-maidens on their deep-sea ground;
burn they with Lusian love, bring warm desire
to these Explorers of a world new found,
all in an Islet joined in glorious choir,
an Isle unknown in Ocean-depths profound
embowel'd, I will haste on high to raise
where lovely Flora with her Zephyr plays:

41 "There with a thousand sherbets, odorous wine,
delicious viands, perfumed breath of roses,
in sing'ular scenes of palace chrystalline,
fair couches, fairer what on couch reposes;
with thousand joys unvulgar shall, in fine,
each Nymph await the Brave her fancy chooses
and all love-smitten, longing to bestow
what Hope can figure, or what eyes can show.

42 "'Tis my good will that in the Neptune-reign,
my place of birth, a fair brave race be born,
which a shrewd proof shall be to worlds malign,
and to the rebels who thine empire scorn;
that nought shall save, ne mure adamantine
ne triste Hypocrisy, these men forsworn:
Ne'er shall these earth-things hope their selves to save
when burn imortal Love-fires 'neath the wave."

43 Thus willeth Venus and her wilful Boy
obeys, and flies to see her will be done;
he bids them bring his bow of ivory,
with golden-headed arrows many a one:
The Cyprian with glad gest of wanton joy
within her chariot receives her son;
and slacks the bridles for the Birds whose song
the Phætonian death wailed loud and long.

246

44 But Cupid warneth that still wants their scheme
a famous Go-between of high degree
who, though a thousand times she baulked his aim,
a thousand times firm friend prefer'd to be.
Gigantia was the Goddess, daring dame,
vain-glorious, boastful, false and true was she
who sees with hundred eyne, flies every where
and that she sees a thousand tongues declare.

45 They wend to seek and send her on in state,
to blow her trumpet of the clearest strain;
and so the wandering Braves to celebrate,
as never mortals could such praises gain:
Now Fame, with murm'uring sounds that penetrate,
flies through the deepest grottos of the Main:
and scatt'ereth Truth believèd true to be;
for Fame's own gossip is Credulity.

46 These goodly lauds, and rumours excellent
the hearts of God and Goddess, whilom firèd
by Bacchus and to harm the Heroes bent,
changed and with something likest love inspirèd.
The fem'inine bosom, ever diligent
in shifting will, of settled will soon tirèd,
now crieth cru'elty, shame and over zeal
for such high valour evil will to feel.

47 Meanwhile the lither Lad had loosed his bow
shaft urging shaft; loud groans from Ocean rise:
They pierce point-blank the waves that restless flow
these straight, those whirling in a spiral guise:
The fair Nymphs fall and breathe the secret throe,
the 'bosomed burthen of their burning sighs;
each falls ere seen the face that makes her die,
for oft the ear hath loved before the eye.

48 Now of his iv'ory Lune the cusps drew near,
   with might and main th' indomitable Boy,
   who fired at Tethys more than any fair,
   for-that was she to love the coyest coy.
   Now of its arrows is the quiver bare,
   nor lives in sea-plain Nymph her life to 'joy;
   and, if the wounded breathe a living breath
   'tis but to savour that they strive with Death.

49 Give way, ye tall cerulean waves, give way!
   for look ye, Venus brings her medicine,
   showing the snow-white belly'ing sails that stray
   o'er swelling crests of billows Neptunine:
   That thou reciprocal response convey,
   Oh ardent Love! to longings feminine,
   an honest modesty must ne'er withstand
   whatever Venus deigneth to command.

50 Now the fair Nereid-choir itself enrol'd;
   and side by side the gentle bevy sped
   with tripping dances, usance known of old,
   straight for that Island whither Venus led:
   And there the Goddess 'gan to all unfold
   her thousand feats of loving hardihed:
   They, to be victims of sweet Love preparèd,
   each trick would try and dare whate'er she darèd.

51 Cutting the broad highway the vessels ride
   o'er ample Ocean seeking Home's dear shore,
   wishing but cool sweet water to provide
   for their long voyage briny waters o'er:
   When all attonce with start of joy descried
   Love's Isle rise lovely stretched their eyes before,
   as bursting radiant through the morning air
   rose Memnon's Mother delicately fair.

248

52 The bien and bonny Isle afar they hail,
   by Venus wafted through the wavy flood,
   (e'en as the Zephyrs waft the snow-white sail)
   whither the sturdy Fleet fast sailing stood;
   and lest unheeding pass the crews, and fail
   there to take harbour as she willed they should,
   right on their courses threw her lovely bower
   that Acidalian of omnip'otent power.

53 Firm and immobile she disposed it where
   she saw the seamen seek and shape their way;
   so fixt stood Delos when Latona bare
   Phoebus and her who joys in forestry.
   Thither the hurrying Prores thro' Ocean tare
   where bends the seaboard in a little bay
   quiet and curved, upon whose snow-white sand
   her rosy shells strewed Cytherdéa's hand.

54 Three fairy hillocks threefold headlets showèd
   swelling superbly gracious to the sight,
   whose greeny clothing grass-enamel'd glowèd,
   in that fair joyous Island of Delight:
   While glassy-clear three limpid fountains flowèd
   from peaks with gleaming verdure deckt and dight;
   and from the milk-white rocks derivèd flow
   fugitive wavelets, prattling as they go.

55 Down a sweet dale that dints the hillocks, glide
   the sparkling waters to their trysting-place,
   and make a table of so fair a tide;
   never could Fancy such a landskip trace:
   O'erhang it graceful groves on ev'ry side
   like one who bendeth pranking form and face,
   and in the chrystal mirror joys to view
   his proper semblance and resemblance true.

56 Skywards a thousand trees rise tall and straight,
    apple'd with od'orous fruitage passing rare:
    Here th' Orange painteth on her dainty freight
    the hues that burnt in Daphné's burnisht hair:
    Droops low crusht earthwards by her juicy weight,
    the Citron glowing with her saffron gear:
    Lemons with scented spherelets deckt and drest
    mock budding honours of the maiden's breast.

57 The forest-growths that clothe the hillocks trine
    with frondent ringlets fronts and heads array;
    Alcides' Poplars with the Laurels twine
    loved by the laurel'd fair-faxt Lord of Day:
    and Cythersea's Myrtles with the Pine
    of Cybelé, to strange amour a prey:
    The spiring Cypress pointeth to the skies,
    where man hath built his air-based Paradise.

58 Pomona's choicest gifts spontaneous grow,
    and all in diff'erent taste and gust abound;
    no want of cult'uring hand these arbours know,
    withouten culture better fares the ground:
    Cherries with Tyrian tincture purpled glow;
    and Morus eke that mimicks Amor's sound;
    while from her patrial Persia-land the Pome[183]
    flourisheth fairer in her foreign home.

59 Gapes the Granado tints incarnadine
    whereby, O Ruby! shent is all thy sheen;
    'braced by her husband-Elm the happy Vine
    beareth her berrièd birth, here red, there green.
    And ye, O Pears! if long your boughs design
    with luscious pyramids to deck the scene,
    busk ye to 'dure what hurt and harm may wreak
    to your soft flanks the Bird's injurious beak.

60 The gorgeous tapestry, rare colours blending
    and robing rustick earth with rainbow dye,
    makes Achæmenia's[184] webs the less resplending,
    yet softer shades on sombre vales to lie.
    Here the Cephisian fiow'er[185] his head low bending
    eyeth the lakelet lucid as the sky:
    There Cínyras' grandson-son[186] still bleeds in bloom,
    and, Paphian goddess! still thou wail'st his doom.

61 'Twere hard, in sooth, to judge which case be true,
    where sim'ilar splendours mantle earth and air,
    if fair Aurora lend the flow'ers her hue,
    or if the flowers lend her hues so fair.
    There Zephyr aided Flora to bestrew
    Vi'olet with colours Love-wan lovers wear;
    with Iris red and freshest blooth of Rose,
    which on the Damsel's cheek all beauteous glows:

62 The snow-white Lily with the rory tear
    of Dawntide dripping, and the Mangerona:[187]
    Letters on hyacinthine leaves appear,
    Hyacinth loved by son of lone Latona:
    Each fruit and flow'ering Daisy shows full clear,
    that fain would Chloris rival with Pomona.
    Then, if the Birds disport on airy wing
    Earth has a joyaunce for each four-foot thing.

63 Along the streamlet sings the snowy Swan,
    percht on her spraylet answereth Philomel:
    Startled Actæon stands no more to scan
    his horny forehead where the waters well;
    Here the fast lev'ret flies the hunter-man
    from densest thicket, or the shy gazelle:
    There hurrying homewards to her darling brood
    the light-wing'd Birdie bears the grateful food.

64 'Mid such a freshness swift-foot sprang aground
   our second Argonauts, far-left the Fleet,
   where in the wood-depths willing to be found
   strolled the fair Nymphs as though no fear they weet;
   These waked the Zitter's soft pathetic sound,
   those made the Harp and Flute sing song as sweet;
   and bearing golden bows appeared a few
   the prey pursuing they did not pursue.

65 Thus taught their Tut'oress in such teaching wise,
   to scatter careless o'er the hill and plain;
   so might the Barons see'ing a doubtful prize,
   first burn with hot desire the prize to gain.
   Some maids whose nat'ural charms the veil despise,
   in pride of soveran Beauty justly vain,
   casting all Art's adulteries aside,
   bathe their puré bodies in the pearly tide.

66 But the stout seamen when their feet were set
   ashore, all hastenèd to greet the strand;
   nor was there any who his ship had quit
   sans hopes of finding game upon the land:
   None think such game that needs ne springe ne net
   on those fair hillocks thus would come to hand;—
   so bien, so bonny, so benign a prey
   by Venus cast love-wounded in their way.

67 Some with the spingard armed and arbalest,
   hoping to slay the horny hart or hind,
   in sombre bosques and valleys hotly prest,
   determined Vert and Venerie to find:
   Others in shadows that high noon arrest
   from scorching verdant turf, to walk incline'd
   along the gentle riv'ulet's grassy reach,
   o'er the white pebbles purling to the beach.

68 Begin with sudden start the Youths to 'spy
   variegate colours glance through greeny boughs;
   colours that catch the judgment of man's eye
   as not of nat'ural bloom, ne flow'er, ne rose;
   but fleecy laine and silk of diff'erent dye,
   Dress, that with double force Desire endows,
   wherein the human Rose herself enshrines,
   and, Art enhancing Nature, brighter shines.

69 Loud cries Velloso, marv'elling at the sight:
   "My masters! wondrous game," quoth he, "is this;
   if yet endure that olden Pagan rite,
   the Grove be sacred to the Goddesses:
   Here meet we more than what the human Sprite
   ever desirèd; and right well we wis
   excellent wonders and great things here lie
   by Nature veiled from Man's imprudent eye.

70 "Follow we fast these Goddesses, and speer
   an they be Fantasm or divine indeed!"
   Thus he; and, fleeter than the fleet-foot deer,
   all follow coursing o'er the riv'erine mead.
   Between the branches flying Nymphs appear,
   haply with more of hurry than of speed;
   and, slack'ening pace with shrieks and laughter gay,
   each yields her graces as her greyhound's prey.

71 From this the breezes golden tresses blow,
   from that the robe's frail hem is reft aside:
   High burns Desire, enkindled by the snow
   of living loveliness so sudden 'spied.
   One falls apurpose, and her fall doth show
   by loving languor more than plaint or pride,
   she wills her foll'ower stumble, falling o'er
   the lovely quarry on the pebbly shore.

72 Others seek other places where the stream
   reveals of bathing Nymphs the secret charms:
   who startled 'gin to fly with shriek and scream,
   as though surprized by rude assault of arms.
   While others feigning to feel less esteem
   for fear and shame than force, veil false alarms,
   plunge in the brake and give to greedy eyes
   denied to grasping hands the goodly prize.

73 That, who in hurry to resume contrives
   the modesty that marks the Hunter-maid
   hides in the wave her limbs; another strives
   to snatch the garment on the stream-bank laid.
   Youngling there is who in the river dives
   all clad and booted (lest too long delay'd
   by dofling garments he should miss the game),
   to quench in water Love's consuming flame.

74 As Hound of Hunter, crafty beast and ware,
   taught cripples to retrieve from brook or tarn,
   seeing the steely tube upraised in air;
   cov'ering the well-known quarry, duck or hern;
   ere heard the crack, uneath the sight to bear
   he plungeth, certain praise and prize to earn,
   and swimmeth barking: Thus the Brave made free
   to seize the Fair,—no Phoebus' sister she!

75 Le'onard, a soldier whom good gifts adorn,
   a knightly Belamour and delicate,
   who was not once the prey of Cupid's scorn,
   but ever dree'd Love's life-long spite and hate;
   he, who so long believed he was not born
   to Love-luck being e'er unfortunate,
   not that he held all Hope beyond his range
   when Destiny shall deign his doom to change:

254

76 Here willed his Fortune, he should wing his way
   chasing the fairest Daughter of the Wave,
   Ephyre, lief to make him dearly pay
   that which for giving Nature to her gave.
   Spent by the race he stayed his steps to say:—
   "O thou too beauteous cruelty to crave,
   when of my life the palm to thee is dight,
   ah! wait this body since thou hast its sprite!"

77 "All rest of running weary, Nymph divine!
   Each yields her wishes to her en'emy's will;
   Why to the wood alone fly only mine?
   Who told thee I am I, who chase thee still?
   If told thee so mine angry doom malign,
   which allwheres dogs me always to mine ill,
   believe it not, e'en I when I believèd,
   each hour a thousand times my heart deceivèd.

78 "Tire not thyself, to tire me; for if I
   must chase those flying charms and chase in vain,
   such is my Fortune an thou wait and try
   her will perverse shall never gar me gain.
   Wait! if thou will I would again descry,
   what subtle mode of 'scape for thee remain,
   and thou in fine shalt note, and fain confess so,
   Tra la spiga e la man qual muro è messo.[188]

79 "Ah, fly me not! E'en so may Time foot-fleet
   ne'er from thy youthful beauties urge his flight!
   For only stay the twinkling of thy feet
   and thou shalt vanquish Fortune's dure despight.
   What Emp'eror, nay what mighty Host dare meet
   the force array'd by Chance's furious might,
   which in whate'er I wished still hounds my way,
   this canst thou do, thou only, an thou stay?

80 "Wouldst in my roll of foes thyself enrol?
To back the stronger is not bravely done!
Wouldst steal my lib'eral heart that was so whole?
Loose it me then, the faster thou shalt run!
Burthens thee not this Soul, my mesquin Soul,
which in those threads of glancing gold bespun,
tangled thou bearest? or thus won the prize,
hast lightened Fortune which so heavy lies?

81 "In this sole Esp'erance thee, my Fair, I chase;
that or thou weary her sad load to bear;
or haply shall thy Beauty's magick grace
have power to change her sour malignant Star:
And if thus change she, cease this useless race,
for Love shall smite thee, gentle Ladye fair:
And thou shalt wait when Love shall smite thee sore;
And if thou wait that wait I, want I more?"

82 No longer fled the lovely Nymph, to play
her sad pursuer's heart, her pow'er to try;
as still to revel in the lovely lay
which told the soldier's loving agony:
Bending her brow that beamed a holy ray,
all bathed with sweetest smiles of gentle joy,
she falls a victim at the victor's feet,
melted with purest love by dear defeat.

83 Ah me! what hungry kissings wake the wood!
What choirs in suavest unison acclaim!
What pretty pettings! What coy pettish mood
which pleasant laughter presently became!
What Morn and Noontide saw and understood,
as Venus joyed her lovers' joys to 'flame,
were better far t' experience not to judge,
yet judge it he whose Fate such boon shall grudge.

84 This way in fine conform the fair and bright
   Nymphs, and each Bride with love her Groom endowers,
   all heads are crowned with chaplets of delight,
   of bays and gold and amaranthine flowers:
   Their soft white palms they prest in wedded plight:
   With formal phrase and stipulating powers
   that pledge for endless time their mutual Faith,
   honour and joyaunce, till life end in Death.

85 One, chiefest She, whose mandate proudly led
   the Nymphs, obedient vassals of her throne,
   Coelus and Vesta's progeny 'twas said,
   as by her queenly bearing might be known;
   who over Earth and Ocean glamour shed,
   he noble Captain, digne such boon to own,
   with honest princely pomp comes forth to greet
   as for such great egregious Ladye meet:

86 And, told the station and the name of her,
   in high exordium with high grace ornate,
   her cause of coming 'gan to him prefer,
   by the high influ'ence of immobile Fate;
   and ope before his eyne the gen'eral sphere
   of vasty regions, seas unnavigate,
   the secret knowledge couched in prophecy,
   which he and his alone deserved to see:

87 Taking his hand in hers she guides her guest
   straight to a tow'ering head of Hill divine,
   whereof a splendid Pleasaunce is the crest,
   plated with purest gold and chrystal shine.
   Therein the greater part of day they rest
   where loving play and lasting pleasures reign:
   The Queen enjoys her loves in palace-bowers,
   the Nymphs in sylvan shades amid the flowers.

88 Thus Fair and Brave in fittest union meet,
    while minute by the merry hours of light;
    and taste the genial gladness rare as sweet
    which their long labours and dark days turn bright:
    Man's high heroick deed, and daring feat
    of famous force, the World shall aye requite
    with guerdon merited, and boon sublime,—
    a Name and Fame that stand the test of Time.

89 For, all our Ocean-maids so fair, so sprightful,
    Tethys, and eke her Isle of angel-ground,
    None other thing be they, but the delightful
    Honours that make our human life renown'd:
    That high pre-em'inence and that glory rightful
    are but the Triumphs, and the brows becrown'd
    with Palms and Bay-wreaths, wond'ring gaze and praise:
    Such the delights my fabled Isle displays;

90 These Immortalities,— in young world feignèd
    by men who cherisht toils of noble aim,
    there on Olympus' star-lit heights, attainèd
    on inclyt wings that soar to deathless Fame,
    whose Deeds of Derring-do the guerdon gainèd,
    by dint of endless toil and moil we name
    the Path of Virtue, stony, steep t' ascend,
    but joyous-glad, delicious-sweet at end:

91 Were nought but prizes brother-men impart
    in change for Feats immortal, sovereign,
    to that baronial Host, whose Arm and Art
    made to be Gods that had been only men:
    Jupiter, Phoebus, Mercury, and Mart,
    Æneas, Rom'ulus, and the Theban twain,
    Ceres, Diana, Juno, Pallas, were
    but human flesh to human weakness heir.

92 Yet Fame, that trumpet of Man's high emprize,
    on Earth bestowed them names of strange estate,
    Godheads, and deathless Semi-deities,
    Indigetes and Heroes, "Grand" and "Great."
    Wherefore, oh, ye! who Fame's fair guerdon prize,
    if in the World with these ye lief would mate,
    awake from Slumber, shake off Sloth ignave
    that sinks Man's freeborn soul to soul of slave.

93 And bridle Av'arice-sin with iron bit,
    rein that Ambition which o'er-reigns your race
    in thousand fashions, and the base conceit
    of vicious Tyr'anny breeding vile disgrace:
    Such tinkling honours, gold so counterfeit,
    to true and honest worth ne'er raised the base:
    Better to merit and the meed to miss,
    than, lacking merit, every meed possess.

94 Or give us Peace, and Laws impartial deal,
    that baulk the rich from plund'ering poorer men;
    or cloak your forms in coats of flashing steel,
    and crush the law of hostile Saracen:
    Thus shall your valour raise the Commonweal
    all gaining ampler, none a smaller gain;
    deservèd riches shall to you be rife
    with Honours, alt-relief of human life.

95 Thus shall ye serve the King ye love so dear
    now with your proffer'd counsels sagely bold
    then by the Sword, that shall your names uprear
    to dizzy heights where trod your sires of old:
    To 'tempt impossibilities forbear;
    who wills aye finds a way; and thus enrol'd,
    your names shall rival this heroick band,
    and gain fair greeting in Dame Venus' land.

CANTO X

1 Now had the glowing Amourist, who won
  fair faithless Larissæa's love, incline'd
  his steeds where lies, girt by the great Lagoon[189]
  Temistitam, the western world behind:
  Favonius' breath the brenning of the Sun
  cooleth, and o'er the nat'ural tanks his wind
  crisps the sea-mirror, and awakes the Lily
  slumb'ering with Jasmin through the noontide stilly:

2 When the fair Nymphs, who each her lover led,
  hand linkt in hand, conforming and content,
  trooped where the radiant Pleasaunce reared its head
  all gay with gold and metals lucident;
  when bade the Queen that tables there be spread
  with varied viands chosen, excellent
  for loved and loving vigour to restore,
  the pow'ers which Love from weary nature bore.

3 There on the radiant thrones, rich, chrystalline,
  sit the blithe couples, cavalier and dame;
  while on the golden dais in state recline
  the lovely Goddess, Gama loved by Fame:
  Delicious dainties, delicate, divine,
  that ántique Egypt's lux'ury sink to shame,
  heap the huge chargers of the tawny gold
  from far Atlantis-treas'ury hither roll'd.

4 The wines of fragrant scent not sole excel
   Falernus' vintage, proud Italia's boast,
   but e'en th' Ambrosia Jove esteems so well
   and eke esteems his sempiternal Host;
   in cups where steely file may not prevail,
   they spume crisp foam that glads man's innermost
   bosom, and warms his heart with sudden glow;
   and with ice-water temper'd, leap and flow.

5 Told were a thousand tales of joy and mirth;
   sweet smiles met subtle sayings warm with wit
   which to this course and that gave double worth,
   and sharpened edge to blunted appetite;
   Nor of the Harp harmonious was there dearth,
   (which in profoundest Pit the naked Sprite
   awhile can respite from eternal pain),
   sweeten'd by Siren-voice of Angel-strain.

6 Thus sang that Nymph, the fairest of her kind,—
   her descant ech'oing down the halls sublime,—
   with consonance of instrument combine'd
   and all conforming to one tone and time:
   A sudden silence husheth every Wind,
   and makes the Wavelet plash with softer chime,
   while salvage animals in nat'ural lair
   to slumber charmed, a dreamy musick hear.

7 Her voice of silver raiseth to the skies
   the coming race of Barons high renown'd,
   whose prototypes were shown to Proteus' eyes
   within the hollow Sphere's diaph'anous round;[190]
   Jove's goodly present and the choicest prize
   giv'en him in vision. To the Realm profound
   the tale prophetick told he, and the Maid
   in Mem'ory's depths the glorious hist'ory laid.

8   Subject of buskin 'tis, and not for sock,
     what in that vasty Lake the Nymph made known,
     things from Iópas hid and Demodoque;
     Phoeacian this, and that of Carthage-town.
     Thee, my Calliope! I now invoke
     in this mine éxtreme labour, thou alone
     canst for my writing to my sprite restore
     the gust of writing, which I 'joy no more.

9   My years glide downwards, and my Summer's pride
     mergeth in Autumn, passing, ah! how soon;
     Fortune my Genius chills, and loves to chide
     my Poet-soul no more my boast and boon:
     Hopes long deferrèd bear me to the tide
     of black Oblivion, and eternal Swoon:
     But deign to grant me thou, the Muses' Queen,
     to praise my People with my proper strain!

10   Sang the fair Goddess how the wide Seas o'er
     from Tagus bank, whence Gama cut his path,
     shall sail strong Navies, conq'uering ev'ry shore
     where Indie Ocean sucks his mighty breath:
     How all the Kings, who Géntoo gods adore,
     and dare our yoke reject shall rue the wrath
     of hard and hardy Arms, with steel and lowe,
     till low to Gama or to Death they bow: [191]

11   Of one she chaunted that in Malabar [192]
     held of the Priesthood highest dignity,
     who, lest be loosen'd with the singular
     Barons the knot of love and amity,
     shall see his towns, his cities in the war
     with fire and sword, and wrath and cruelty
     undone, which potent Samorim shall wage:
     Against the stranger such shall be his rage.

12 And eke she singeth how shall join the Fleet
    in Belem moor'd, to 'bate this deadly bane,
    when of his burthen nought could Ocean weet,
    our great Pacheco,[193] 'Achilles Lusitan:
    Lo! as he ent'ereth all his weight shall greet
    the curvèd timber and the fervid Main,
    as in the waters every keel that groaneth
    sits deeper swimming than its nature owneth.

13 But hardly landed on those Orient ends,
    and, leaving with the royal Unbeliever
    of Cochim-realm, some native troops where bends
    its salty branches Cochim's snakey river;
    the Nayrs' infernal bands he breaks and rends,
    in the Pass Cambalam,[194] whereat shall shiver
    with freezing fear the Orient's fiery glow,
    seeing so few so many men o'erthrow.

14 The Samorim shall summon fresh allies;
    Kings hurry'ing come from Bipur and Tanor,[195]
    and where Narsinga's serrièd crests arise
    vowing high valour to their Grand Seignior:
    Lo! at his bidding every Nayr-man hies,
    that dwells 'twixt Calecut and Cananor,
    two hostile peoples linkt at War's demand,
    by sea the Moormen come, Géntoos by land.

15 Again shall scatter all their strong array
    Pacheco grandly bold on shore and Main;
    the mighty Meiny he shall crush and slay,
    and be the Marvel of the Mal'abar plain:
    Again shall dare the Pagan sans delay
    to offer battle for his bitter bane;
    taunting his Host and off'ering vainest vows
    his deaf, and dumb, and heedless Gods to 'rouse.

16 No more the Passes only now defending,
   he shall with fire consume thorpe, fane and town:
   The Hound, waxt wood to see with toil unending
   his fencéd Cities on the plain bestrown,
   shall drive his soldiers, life so freely spending,
   against Pacheco, who with wings hath flown
   for double movement: But at single bout
   hither and thither all he puts to rout.

17 Shall come in person Sam'orim fight to dare,
   to cheer his forces and fresh force enjoin;
   but soon a bullet singing through the air
   shall stain him red in lofty palanquin.
   Naught now availeth him, ne wile ne snare
   ne force Pacheco deemeth like to win;
   he shall vain venoms deal, deal treasons base
   which aye gain less of gain by God's good grace.

18 "He[196] shall a seventh time," she sang, "aspire
   the brave beleaguer'd Lusian to assail,
   whom toil and travail lack the strength to tire;
   but save confusion nothing shall avail:
   Then shall he bring to battle dread and dire
   machines of timber, unknown, terrible,
   to sink the Carvels by the board assailèd,
   when force and fraud both tried alike have failèd.

19 "On water-plain upheaping fiery hill
   he now shall 'tempt the Lusian Fleet to 'flame:
   But soldier-science and the war-man's will
   the strength shall weaken wherewithal he came.
   Ne'er hath a Baron famed for martial skill,
   that starward soarèd on the wings of Fame,
   rivallèd this, who Palms from all hath won:—
   Illustrious Greece, or Rome, my words condone!

20 "For, such fierce battles in such manner gainèd
   by a poor hundred or few more, such fight,
   such feints, such strength, such stratagems sustainèd,
   so many hounds not heartless hurled to flight;
   such feats, I say, must seem as Fables feignèd,
   or that the Hosts of Heav'en invoked, alight
   earthward to aid him, shall to him impart
   daring and doing, heart and warrior art.

21 "Nor he who in the chámpaign Marathonian,
   Darius' mighty powers piecemeal rendeth;
   nor with four thousand men Lacedæmonian
   he who the Pass Thermopylæ defendeth;
   nor youthful Cocles of the strain Ausonian,
   who with the whole Etrurian host contendeth
   the Bridge to hold, nor Quintus Fabius e'er
   like this in war showed strength and savoir-faire."

22 But here the Nymph's triumphant measure dies,
   shifting to sadden'd murmur low and slow,
   she sings 'mid tears and ill-suppressèd sighs
   the mighty Gestes that did no grat'itude know.
   "Oh, Behsarius! thou who aye shalt rise
   in ninefold Choir, and ever nobler grow,
   if Mars dishonour'd didst behold in thee
   one to console thee here thy Shade shall see!

23 "Thou hast a Rival, not alone in deed
   but in his dolence and his guerdon dour:
   In thee and him two breasts of noblest breed
   we see degraded to low state obscure:
   To die in 'spital, on the bed of need,
   who King and Law like wall of i'ron secure!
   Thus do capricious Kings, whose will demandeth
   more than what Justice or what Truth commandeth:

24 "Thus do the Kings who, drunk with flatt'ery, feel
    the charm of show that gains their hearts' contente;
    the doles of Ajax' arm the due they deal
    to tongue of vain Ulysses fraudulent:
    But,—oh Revenge!—these goods of little weal,
    wasted on those who ghosts of Good present,
    if brave and gentle Knights miss all their grants,
    such grants but glut their greedy sycophants.

25 "Yet thou! who paidest in such sorry ways,
    such liege, oh King! unjust in this alone,
    if ne'er 'twas thine to give him grade and praise,
    'twas his to give his King a golden throne.
    Long as Apollo bathes with blessèd rays
    this ball of Earth, I swear, shall aye be known
    amid the Great and Good his name and fame,
    and thine for Av'arice aye shall bear the blame!

26 "See now!" she sang, "another[197] comes in pride
    of the Blood Royal, and he brings from home
    the Son, whose name shall sound o'er Ocean-tide,
    high as the Roman's in best days of Rome.
    The two with warrior arms to hearts affied,
    shall deal to fertile Quiloa dreadful doom,
    and crown a gentler King of loyal strain,
    who ends the Tyrant's fell perfidious reign.

27 "Mombasah-city, with her brave array
    of sumptuous palace, proudest edifice,
    defaced, deformed by fire and steel shall pay
    in kind the tale of byegone malefice.
    Thence on those Indian shores which proud display
    their hostile fleets, and warlike artifice
    'gainst the Lusians, with his sail and oar
    shall young Lourenço work th' extremes of war.

28 "What mighty vessels Sam'orim's orders own
covering Ocean, with his iron hail
poured from hot copper-tube in thunder-tone
all shall he shatter, rudder, mast and sail;
then with his grapples boldly, deftly thrown,
the hostile Ammiral he shall assail,
board her, and only with the lance and sword
shall slay four hecatombs of Moors abhor'd.

29 "But God's prevision 'scaping human sight,
alone who knows what good best serves His end,
shall place the Hero where ne toil ne might
his lost young life availeth to forfend.
In Chául-bay, where fierce and furious fight
with fire and steel shall fervid seas offend,
th' Infidel so shall deal that end his days
where Egypt's navy doth conjoin Cambay's.

30 "There shall the pow'er of man'ifold enemies,—
for only stronger force strong force can tire,—
and Winds defaulting and fierce injuries
of Ocean, 'gainst a single life conspire:
Here let all olden men from death arise
to see his Valour, catch his noble fire:
A second Scaeva[198] see who, hackt and torn,
laughs at surrender, quarter holds in scorn.

31 "With the fierce torture of a mangled thigh,
torn off by bullet which at random past,
his stalwart arms he ceaseth not to ply,
that fiery Spirit flaming to the last:
Until another ball clean cuts the tie
so frail that linkèd Soul and Body fast;—
the Soul which loosèd from her prison fleets
whither the prize eterne such Conq'ueror greets.

32   "Go, Soul! to Peace from Warfare turbulent
     wherein thou meritedst sweet Peace serene!
     for those torn tortured limbs, that life so rent
     who gave thee life prepareth vengeance keen:
     I hear e'en now the furious storm ferment,
     threating the terrible eternal teen,
     of Chamber, Basilisco, Saker-fire,
     to Mameluke cruel and Cambayan dire.

33   "See with stupendous heart the war to wage,
     driven by rage and grief the Father flies,
     paternal fondness urging battle-gage,
     fire in his heart and water in his eyes:
     Promise the sire's distress, the soldier's rage,
     a bloody deluge o'er the knees shall rise
     on ev'ry hostile deck: This Nyle shall fear,
     Indus shall sight it, and the Gange shall hear.

34   "As when some lusty Bull would train and teach
     his limbs for cruel fight, with horns he playeth
     on trunk of builder-oak, or mast-like beech,
     and wounding empty air his might essayeth:
     Thus ere his keels Cambaya's Gulf can reach
     Francisco, fierce with vengeful ardour preyeth
     on Dabul,[199] op'ulent harbour, whets his brand
     and 'bates the tumid bragging of the land:

35   "And soon shall scatter, sailing up the Bight,
     of Diu[200] enfamed for siege and battle dread,
     Calecut's strong Armada weak of fight,
     that trusts to paddles steely mail instead:
     She of Melique Yáz, who boasts her might
     of balls by thee, O Vulcan! scatterèd,
     shall see her Carvels to the frore deep sent
     where hidden sleeps the humid element.

268

36 "While she of Mir Hosem[201] which, linkèd fast
with grapples waits th' Avenger side by side,
shall sight the lopt-off arms and legs float past,
sans owner-bodies, o'er the shifting tide:
Like flamey bolt on Earth by thunder cast
in blinding mist of blood the Braves shall ride:
There naught shall strike the shrinking ear and eye
save fire and steel-flash, shout and slogan-cry.

37 "But, ah! that homeward from such wars victorious,
bound for the Tagus of his Fatherland,
he nigh should forfeit meeds so great and glorious,
by sad black chance I see in Fortune's hand!
The Cape of Storms that guards his name memorious
shall guard his bones, nor blush shall stain its strand,
that noble spirit from the world to tear,
Egyptian strength ne'er tore nor Indian snare.

38 "There salvage Caffres shall have pow'er to do
what ne'er could do the pow'er of dext'erous foe;
and the rude fire-charred club and staff subdue
whom ne'er subduèd ball nor artful bow.
Forsooth His judgments hide from human view!
Vain fools who vainly judge what none may know,
call a misfortune, term a fate malign,
what is but Prov'idence pure, all-wise, divine.

39 "But, oh! what lustrous Light illumes mine eyes,"
resumed the Nymph, as rose again her tone,
"there where Melinde's blood-dyed Ocean lies
from Lamo, Oja, Brava-town, o'erthrown
by hand of Cunha, such a deed ne'er dies,
o'er farthest seas his name shall aye be known
that lave those Austral Islands, and the shore
Saint Lawrence[202] hight and ring the wide world o'er.

40 "This Light is glance and glare of lucent arm
wherewith your Albuquerque's hand shall tame
the Hormuz Parsi's heart which be his harm,
refusing gentle rule as yoke of shame.
There shall he see of shafts the strident swarm,
in air revolving with recurvèd aim
upon his archer, for our God shall aid,
who holy faith of Mother Church would spread."

41 "There the Salt Mountains[203] never shall defend
corruption from remains of men that met
War's doom, and o'er the seas and shores extend
of Gerum Isle,[204] Maskat and Calayat:
Till by pure force of arms they learn to bend
the subject neck, and pay the scot of Fate:
Compulsion sore this wicked Reign shall vex
and tithe of pearl that Barem's oyster decks.

42 "What wreaths of glorious Palms I see them weave
wherewith by Victory's hand his head is crown'd;
when he sans shade of fear or shame shall reave
illustrious Goa's Island world-renown'd.
See, forced by Need's hard law his prize to leave,
he seeks new favouring chance; and, soon as found,
the taken he retakes; such Arm and Art
shall conquer Fortune and the self of Mart.

43 "Lo! he returns and bursts what dares oppose,
thro' bullet, lance-plump, steel, fire, strongest hold;
breaks with his brand the squadded host of foes,
the serried Moor, the Géntoo manifold.
His inclyt sold'iery more of fury shows
than rampant Bulls, or Lyons hunger-bold,
that Day[205] for ever celebrate and digne
of Egypt's Martyr-maid, Saint Catherine.

44 "Nor shalt thou 'scape the fate to fall his prize,
    albeit so wealthy, and so strong thy site
    there on Aurora's bosom, whence thy rise,
    thou Home of Opulence, Malacca hight!
    The poysoned arrows which thine art supplies
    the Kríses[206] thirsting, as I see, for light,
    th' enamoured Malay-men, the Javan braves,
    all of the Lusian shall become the slaves."

45 She had more stanzas sung in Siren-strain,
    lauding her Albuquerque's high renown,
    when she recalled the pass'ionate deed, the stain
    on his white fame that o'er the world hath shone.
    The mighty Captain whom the Fates ordain
    to view his toils win Glory's lasting Crown,
    should ever 'prove him kind and loved compeer
    of his own men, not cruel judge severe.

46 In days of hunger and of dire distress, sickness,
    bolts, arrows, thunder, lightning-glint,
    when the sore seasons and sad sites oppress
    his soldiers, rendering services sans stint;
    it seemeth salvage act of wild excess,
    of heart inhuman, bosom insolent,
    to make last penalty of Laws atone
    for sins our frailty and our love condone.

47 Abominable incest shall not be
    his sin, nor ruffian rape of virgin pure,[207]
    not e'en dishonour of adultery,
    but lapse with wanton slave-girl, vile, obscure:
    If urged by jealous sting, or modesty,
    or used to cruelty and harshness dour,
    Man from his men mad anger curbeth not,
    his Fame's white shield shall bear black ugly blot.

271

48 Learnt Alexander that Apelles lovèd
and his Campaspe gave with glad consent,
though was the Painter not his Soldier provèd,
nor in hard urgent siege his force was pent.
Felt Cyrus, eke, Panthéa deeply movèd
Araspas, by the fire of Passion brent,
though he had tane her charge, and pledged his oath
dishonest love should never break his troth:

49 But see'ing the noble Persian 'slaved and sway'd
by pow'er of Passion, sans in fine defence,
he gives light pardon, and thus gained his aid'
in gravest case, the fittest recompense.
Himself perforce the mate of Judith made
Baldwin hight "Bras-de-fer," but his offence
her father, Charles, for troublous times condone'd,
and gave him life the Flanders' reign to found.

50 Again the Lyre its soul of musick sheds,
and sings the Nymph how shall Soáres fly
air-winn'owing flags whose terror far o'erspreads
the ruddy coasted lands of Araby:
Th' abominable town, Medina, dreads
as Meca dreads and Gidá, and where lie
Abassia's ultime shores: while Barbora fears
the fate that floodeth Zeyla-mart with tears.

51 "And, eke, the noble Island Taproban,
whose ancient name ne'er fail'd to give her note,
as still she reigns superb and sovereign
by boon of fragrant tree-bark, biting-hot:
Toll of her treasure to the Lusitan
ensign shall pay, when proud and high shall float
your breezy banners from the lofty tower,
and all Columbo fear your castled power.

52 "Sequeira,[208] too, far sailing for the shore,
   of Erythras, new way shall open wide
   to thee, Great Empire! who canst vaunt of yore
   to be Candáce's and the Sheban's nide:
   Masuá[209] that hoards in tanks her watery store,
   he shall behold by Port Arquico's side;
   and send explorers to each distant isle,
   till novel wonder all the world beguile.

53 "Succeeds Menézes;[210] less enfamed his sword
   shall be in Asia than in Africk-land:
   he shall chastise high Hormuz' erring horde
   and twofold tribute claim with conq'uering hand.
   Thou also, Gama! shalt have rich reward
   for ban of exile, when to high command
   entitled, 'County' thou shalt be restorèd
   to the fair region this thy Feat explorèd.

54 "But soon that fatal Debt all flesh must pay,
   wherefrom our Nature no exception knows,
   while deckt with proudest Royalty's array,
   from Life shall reave thee and Life's toils and woes:
   Other Menézes[211] cometh sans delay,
   who few of years but much of prudence shows
   in rule; right happy this Henrique's lot
   by human story ne'er to be forgot.

55 "Conquer he shall not only Malabar,
   destroy Panáné and Coulété waste,
   hurling the bombards, which through hurtled air
   deal horrid havock on th' opposing breast;
   but, dower'd with virtues truly singular,
   he deals to seven-fold Spirit-foes his hest:
   Covetise with Incont'inence he shall spurn,—
   the highest conquest in the years that burn.

56 "Him, when his presence shall the stars invite
O Mascarenhas brave![212] thou shalt succeed;
and if injurious men shall rob thy right
eternal Fame I promise for thy meed!
That ev'ry hostile tongue confess thy might
and lofty valour, Fate for thee decreed
far more of Palm-wreaths shall thy glory crown,
than the Good Fortune due to thy renown.

57 "Where Bintam's[213] reign her baleful head uprears,
Maláca humbling with her harmful hate,
in one short day the thousand tyrannous years
with bravest bosoms shalt avenge and 'bate:
Inhuman travails, perils without peers,
a thousand iron reefs, and dangerous strait,
stockade and bulwark, lances, arr'owy sleet,
all shalt thou break, I swear, all shalt submit.

58 "But Inde's Ambition, and her Lucre-lust,
for ever flaunting bold and brazen face
in front of God and Justice, shall disgust
thy heart, but do thine honour no disgrace.
Who works vile inj'ury with unreas'oning trust
in force, and footing lent by rank and place,
conquereth nothing, the true Conq'ueror he
who dares do naked Justice fair and free.

59 "Yet to Sampaio[214] will I not gainsay
a noble valour shown by shrewdest blows,
that shall o'er Ocean flash like thunder-ray,
curded with thousand corpses of his foes.
He shall in Bacanor make fierce assay
on Malabar, till owns in terror-throes
Cutiále,[215] beaten with his battered Fleet
the dreadful ruin of a rout complete.

60 Nor less of Diu the fierce and fere Armàde,
the dread of Cháúl, daring, proudly man'd,
with single glance shall fall, till all have fled
our Hector da Sylveira's heavy hand:
Our Hector Portingall, of whom 'tis said,
that o'er yon ever armed Cambayan strand,
such wrath on Guzerats 'tis his to wreak
as Trojan Hector wreakèd on the Greek.

61 "Then shall succeed to fierce Sampaio's powers
Cunha,[216] and hold the helm for many a year;
building of Chálé-town the lofty towers,
while quakes illustrious Diu his name to hear:
Bassein to him her sturdy standard lowers,
yet not sans bloodshed, for with groan and tear
Melíque[217] se'eth his proudest estocade
storm'd not by firebrand but by sway of blade.

62 "Next comes Noronha,[218] whose auspicious sway
Diu from the barbarous Rumé-warman rends;
Diu, which beleaguer'd in his warrior way
Antonio da Sylveira well defends:
Soon must Noronha doom of death obey,
when branch of thine,[219] O Gama! aidance lends
to govern empire, and his fiery zeal
Fear's pallid hue to Red Sea waves shall deal.

63 "From thine Estevam's hands shall take the rein,
one raised already to a high degree
by his Brazilian wars, and trophies tane
from the French Pyrat[220] homed upon the sea:
Then dubbèd Amm'irall of our Indian Main,
Damán's proud Valverte in her panoply
he scales, the first that open gate to thread
by flames and thousand fletchers coverèd.

275

64 "To him Cambaya's King, that haughtest Moor,
    shall yield in wealthy Diu the famous fort,
    that he may gain against the Grand Mógor
    'spite his stupendous pow'er, your firm support:
    Thence shall he wend, most valiant conqueror,
    to hem the Géntoo King, in Cal'ecut port
    so let and hinder'd, he and all who hied
    with him, retirèd in their blood red dyed.

65 "Low shall he lay the city Repelim
    her Monarch forcing with his men to run;
    then well-nigh reached the Cape 'clept Comorim,
    another wreath of Fame by him is won;
    the strongest squadron of the Samorim
    who doubted not to see the world undone,
    he shall destroy with rage of fire and steel:
    Be'adálá's self his martial yoke shall feel.

66 "Then from all Indus-land thus swept the foes,
    the Conqu'eror, coming scepter'd state to claim,
    finds no resistance where none dare oppose,
    for nations tremble at his terrible name.
    Alone shall risk of War the scourging woes
    Baticalá²²¹ and dree Be'adálá's shame:
    Here blood and corpses shall defile the land
    deformed by thund'erous gun and fiery brand.

67 "This shall be Martin, who the name of Mart
    beareth and eke the deeds the name that gave:
    As much esteemed for arms in every part,
    as wise in stratagem, in counsel grave
    Castro²²² succeeds, who Lusia's estandart
    shall bear for ever in the front to wave;
    Successor the Succeeded's work who endeth;
    that buildeth Diu, this buildèd Diu defendeth.

68 "The fightful Perse, th' Abassian, and the Rume
who hath revived the name of Rome, their liege,
of varied customs, various in costume,
fell tribes a thousand flocking to the siege;
on Earth against the Heav'ens shall vainly fume
that gars such handful so their lands abridge:
In blood of Portingalls this Paynimry
voweth its crookt and curved moustache to dye.

69 "Dread Basiliscos, Lyons' fiery flare,
fierce Catapults, and mines that hidden spring,
shall Mascarenhas[223] and his Barons dare,
and to th' assurèd Death glad mien shall bring:
Till, when all Hope is fled and reigns Despair,
Castro, the saviour, cometh offering
his sons' young lives, and wills their names survive
God's sacrifices aye in Death to live.

70 "One son, Fernando, sci'on of tree so high,
where violentest flames with loudest roar
blow shatter'd ramparts to the smoky sky,
there, stricken down on Earth, shall Heav'enward soar:
Alvaro, when mankind dread Winter fly
and shift from humid path for arid shore,
opens the waters 'spite what risks oppose,
and fighteth winds and waves to fight the foes.

71 "When, see! the Father cuts the wavy waste,
leading what resteth of the Lusitan;
with warman's arm and arts which e'er be best
he offers battle's rem'edy sovereign:
These scale the remparts and at gateways jest,
those cut broad gates through squads with rage insane:
Deeds they shall do so digne memorious glory,
song shall not suit nor Hist'ory hold the story.

277

72 "He shall once more upon the field appear
a strong intrepid victor, where his sight
Cambaya's puissant King[224] shall strike with fear,
and hideous hosts of quadrupeds[225] affright:
Nor less shall fail his puissant reign t' uprear
the Hydalcham,[226] when mighty arms shall smite
chastisèd Dábul, mistress of the coast,
nor shall spare Pondà's distant inland post.

73 "Barons like these, with peers from various parts,
all worthy marvel and all mastering Fame,
raisèd to rank of Mart by martial arts,
shall come the pleasures of this Isle to claim:
Their hands shall wave triumphant estandarts
wherever keel-edge cutteth Ocean-stream:
Such men these Nymphs these banquets aye shall find,
Honours and Glories to high Gestes assign'd."

74 Thus sang the Siren, while her sister-choir
with their sonorous plaudits filled the hall;
wherewith to hail the hour of glad desire
crowning the happy marriage-festival.
"However Fortune's wheel shall turn its tire,"
with one harmonious accent chaunted all,
"renownèd People! rest your souls secure
of Honour, Valour, Fame, while worlds endure!"

75 When man's corporeal necessity
was with the noble viands satisfied,
and when in sweet melodious suavity,
all had their lofty future feats descried;
Tethys, with grace adorned and gravity,
that with a higher pomp and double pride
be crowned the revels of this joyous day,
to glad and happy Gama thus 'gan say:—

76 "To thee Supremest Wisdom guerdon gave,
Baron! who hast beheld with fleshly eyne
what things the Future hath the pow'er to save
from Mortals' petty pride and science vain.
Follow me firmly, prudent as thou'rt brave,
to yonder craggy brake with all thy train!"
Thus she, and straightway through a long wood led
arduous, gloomy, fere for foot to tread.

77 Nor far they steppèd when on culm'inant height
where stretcht a gem-enamel'd mead they stood;
Smaragd and Ruby-strewn, so rich the sight
presumed 'twas Paradisial floor they trod:
Here swimmeth air a Globe,[227] through which the light
of purest radiance piercèd in such mode
that as its polisht surface clearest clear,
so doth its centre and its core appear.

78 What mote its matter be escapes their eyes,
yet 'scapes them not it holdeth in embrace
var'ious Orbs, by wand of Him All-wise
disposed to circle round one central place:
Rolling it sinks and then returns to rise,
And yet ne sinks ne rises; while one face
is shown to all and every part, each part
begins in fine and ends with heav'enly art:

79 Uniform, perfect, and self-poised it be,
like th' Archetype who drew the grand design.
Stood Gama overwhelmed this globe to see
with joy, and hope its nature to divine:
When thus the Goddess:—"Here th' Epitome,
in little volume, to those eyes of thine
I give the gen'eral World, so shalt thou view
where goest thou, shalt go, and what shalt do.

80 "Here see the mighty World-machine appear,
    ethereal where the fourfold el'ements blend,
    made by His deep design, His lofty lere,
    who lacks beginning and who has no end.
    He who surrounding holds this shapely sphere,
    this globe in filèd surface packt and pen'd,
    is God: But what God is th' intelligence
    of mortal genius ne'er shall dare pretence.

81 "This primal Orb, that rolling doth enclose
    the lesser circles in its lines confin'd;
    this Sphere, whose flood of clearest radiance flows
    blinding man's vision and his vulgar mind
    is hight th' Empyrean:²²⁸ Here the Blest repose,
    here perfect Spirits bliss eternal find,
    inéffable joys which He alone may ken
    Who hath no likeness in the World of Men.

82 "Only to this Imperial Sphere belong
    the Gods of Truth; for Saturn, Janus, I,
    Jove and his Juno are a fabled throng,
    a mortal figment, a blind phantasy:
    Only to deck the Poet's sprightly song
    we servèd; and, if more humanity
    we gained of man, 'twas that his wit hath given
    our names and natures to the stars of Heaven:

83 "And, eke, because that Holy Providence,—
    the Jupiter of mythologick strain,—
    by thousand Spirits wise in perfect sense,
    ruleth all mundane things it doth sustain.
    Prophetick Science doth this Truth dispense,
    a Truth so many instances maintain:
    Sprites that be good aye guide and favour man,
    the bad his course impede whene'er they can.²²⁹

84 "Here willèd Picture, lief with change to play
pleasing and teaching, mixing gay and grave,
to give them titles which your olden lay
to fabled Gods in poet-fables gave:
For even th' Angels of th' eternal day
as Gods enrollèd were in sacred stave;
which e'en denies not such exalted name
sometimes to sinner though with falsest claim.

85 "In fine the God Supreme who works His will
by second worldly causes, all commands:
Return we now the works profound to tell
of His divine and venerated Hands.
Beneath this circle, where all blissful dwell
pure godly Sprites, which fixt for ever stands,
another rolleth, and so swift none see
its course: This is the Primum Mobilé:[230]

86 "And with its rapt[231] and rapid whirl it drags
all lesser spherelets which its womb containeth:
By work of this the Sun who never flags
with alien courses Day and Night sustaineth:
'Neath this swift orb another orb slow lags,[232]
so slow, so hard a curb its ardour reineth,
while Phoebus makes, with ever splendid face,
two hundred rounds, this moves a single pace.

87 "Lower this other view,[233] enamel'd gay
with burnisht figures gleaming radiant bright;
which in it too hold constant ordered way,
orbs on their axes scintillant empight:
Thou seest well 'tis dight with brave array
of broad and golden Zone, the Zodiac hight,
wherein twelve starry forms of an'imals shine,
that Phoebus' mansions limit and define.

88 "Behold in other parts the portraiture,
   limned by the Stars that sparkling glances shed:
   Behold the Wain, attend the Cynosure,
   and, with her fierce Worm-father, Andromed:
   See Cassiopeia's beauty lovely pure,
   with turbulent Orion's gesture dread:
   Behold the Swan that doth in song expire,
   the Hare and Hounds, the Ship and dulcet Lyre.

89 "Beneath this firmamental canopy
   thou seest Saturn's sky, that Godhead old:
   With faster flight doth Jove below him fly,
   and Mars yet lower, bellick planet bold:
   In the fourth seat shines Heaven's radiant eye;
   then Venus leadeth all her Loves enrol'd;
   Mercury wends with eloquence divine;
   and 'neath him Dian showeth faces trine.

90 "In all these orbits motion different
   shalt see; in these 'tis swift, in those 'tis slow;
   now fly they farthest from the firmament,
   then sweep they nearest earth that lurks below;
   even so willed the Sire Omnipotent,
   who made the Fire and Air, the Wind and Snow:
   These lie more inward, as thou shalt be shown,
   and Earth with Ocean for their centre own.

91 "Within this centre, Inn[234] of humankind,
   whose reckless spirits not alone defy
   suff'erings and ills to stable Earth confine'd,
   but e'en the Sea's fierce instability;
   thou shalt see various Continents define'd
   by blindly raging tides, where parted lie
   the various Realms which various monarchs sway,
   whose varied Customs varied laws obey.

92 "See high, haught Europe that adores the Rood,
   for pow'er and polity o'er all renown'd:
   See Africk grudging ev'ery worldly good,
   yon rough, incult and monster-haunted ground;
   whose Stormy Cape till now your search withstood,
   by Nature 'stablished as her Austral bound:
   Behold this quarter where the Blackmoors dwell
   sans-loys, sans-foys, whose numbers none can tell.

93 "Behold the Ben'omotápa's puissant reign
   of salvage Negros, nude and noisome race,
   where shall for Holy Faith be foully slain
   martyr'd Gonçalo,²³⁵ suffering sore disgrace:
   This hidden Hemisphere to golden vein
   gives birth, which man must win by sweat of face
   See from yon Lake, whence Nilus rolls his tide,
   how springs Cuáma²³⁶ from the farther side.

94 "Behold those Blackmoors and their huts that stand
   sans doors, each castled in his natal nest,
   they trust of Royal Justice the command,
   and in the candour of the neighbour's breast:
   Behold how furious flies the bestial band
   like flock of dingy stares thick packt and prest;
   to fight Sofala's fortress they pretend
   which dext'erous Nhaia's arm and wits defend:

95 "See there the Lakes that cradle Father Nyle
   whose ultime sources men of old ne'er knew:
   See how he waters, 'gend'ering cockadrille,
   Abassia-lond whose sons to Christ be true:
   Behold how bare of bulwarks (novel style)
   they show a better front against the foe:
   See Meroe-island whilom known to fame,
   which now the wild inhabitants Nobá name.

96 "On distant Africk hills a son of thee
in Turkish wars shall win the fame of Brave;
hight Dom Christóvam shall the hero be,
but flesh from destined Death no skill shall save.
Here view the Coast where shelter from the sea
and glad relief to thee Melinde gave:
Note how yon Rhaptus-stream,[237] whose wide expanse
natives call Obi, ent'ereth in Quilmance.

97 "The Cape which Antients 'Aromatic' clepe
behold, yclept by Moderns Guardafú;
where opes the Red Sea mouth, so wide and deep,
the Sea whose ruddy bed lends blushing hue:
This as a bourne was far thrust out to keep
Asia distinct from Africk, and a few
of the best markets Negro seaboards claim
Arquico are, Masuá and Súanquem.

98 "View éxtreme Suez where, old Annals say,
once stood the city hight Hero'opolis;
by some Arsin'oe called, and in our day
she holdeth Egypt's fleets and argosies:
Behold the watery depths, where clove his way
Moses the mighty in past centuries:
Asia beginneth here her huge extent
in regions, kingdoms, empires opulent.

99 "See Sinai mountain,[238] with her boast and pride
the silver bier of saintly Catherine:
See Toro-port and Gidá, scant supplied
with fountain-water soft and crystalline:
Behold the Straits which end the southern side
of arid Aden-realms, that here confine
with tall Arzíran range, nude stone and live,
whence soft sweet rains of Heaven ne'er derive.

100 "See threefold Ar'aby, cov'ering so much ground,
    where tawny peoples vague o'er vasty space;
    whence come the Rabytes,[239] best for battle found,
    light-limbed, high-fettled, noble-blooded race.
    Behold the coast that trends to bind and bound
    yon other Persian Strait, where sight can trace
    the Headland proud the potent name to own
    of Fartak-city, erst to Fame well-known.

101 "Behold insign Dofar that doth command
    for Christian altars sweetest incense-store:
    But note, beginning now on further band
    of Rosalgáte's[240] ever greedy shore,
    yon Hormuz Kingdom strown along the strand,
    whose fame for riches still shall higher soar
    when the Turk's galleys, and his fierce Armade
    see Castel-Branco[241] bare his deadly blade.

102 "Behold of Asabón the Head, now hight
    Mosandam, by the men who plough the Main:
    Here lies the Gulf whose long and lake-like Bight
    parts Araby from fertile Persia's plain.
    Attend yon Barem Isle, with depths bedight
    by the rich pearly shell whose blushes feign
    Auroran tints; and view in Ocean brine
    Euphrate and Tygre in one bed conjoin.

103 "Great Persia's noble Empire here behold,
    ever on Destr'ier or in Camp of War,
    whose sons disdain the copper-tube to mould,
    and hands not horny with the Cymitar.
    But see yon Gerum Isle the tale unfold
    of mighty things which Time can make or mar;
    for of Armúza-town yon shore upon
    the name and glory this her rival won.

Luís de Camões

104 "Here Dom Philippe de Menézes view
approved a doughty valiant man-at-arms,
who with his Portughueze exceeding few
shall quell the Lára²⁴² Parsi's potent swarms:
Pedro de Sousa too shall make them rue
reversèd Fortunes, Warfare's deadliest harms,
who had his prowess in Ampáza²⁴³ shown,
and took the land by sweep of sword alone.

105 "But now the Narrows and their noted head
Cape Jask, Carpella called by those of yore,
quit we, the dry terrene scant favourèd
by Nature niggard of her normal store:
Whilere Carmánia 'twas intitulèd:
But view fair Indus-flood whose waters pour
adown his natal heights, and in the range
of neighbour-mountains see the source of Gange.

106 "Behold Ulcindé's most luxuriant land
and of Jaqueté-shore yon intime bay;
the monster Bore which roaring floods the strand,
and ebb which flieth with like force away.
See where Cambaya's rich feracious band
boundeth re-entering seas, the Gulf Cambay;
and thousand Cities which I leave untold,
here hoard their wealth for you to have and hold.²⁴⁴

107 "See, runs the cel'ebrate seaboard Hindostánian
southward till reached its point, Cape Comori,
erst 'Cori' called, where th' Island Taprobanian
('tis now Ceylon) encrowns the fronting sea:
Besides these waves thy people Lusitanian,
who with their doughty arms will follow thee,
by conq'uering wars shall lands and towns debel,
wherein your sons and sons of sons shall dwell.

286

108 "The regions lying 'twixt these Rivers twain,[245]
     thou see'st, with various tribes are infinite:
     Here rule the Moslems; there the Géntoos reign
     whose Holy Writ the Devil did indite:
     See where Narsinga's seigniories contain
     the saintly relicks blessing human sprite,
     Thomé's remains, the Miss'ioner sanctified
     who thrust his finger in Lord Jesu's side.

109 "Here rose the potent City, Meliapor
     naméd, in olden time rich, vast and grand:
     Her sons their olden idols did adore
     as still adoreth that iniquious band:
     In those past ages stood she far from shore,
     when to declare glad tidings o'er the land
     Thomé came preaching, after he had trod
     a thousand regions taught to know his God.

110 "Here came he preaching, and the while he gave
     health to the sick, revival to the dead;
     when Chance one day brought floating o'er the wave
     a forest-tree of size unmeasuréd:
     The King a Palace building lief would save
     the waif for timber, and determinéd
     the mighty bulk of trunk ashore to train
     by force of engines, elephants and men.

111 "Now was that lumber of such vasty size,
     no jot it moves, however hard they bear;
     when lo! th' Apostle of Christ's verities
     wastes in the business less of toil and care:
     His trailing waist-cord to the tree he ties,
     raises and sans an effort hales it where
     a sumptuous Temple he would rear sublime,
     a fixt exemple for all future time.

112 "Right well he knew how 'tis of Faith aver'd
'Faith moveth mountains' will or nill they move,
lending a listening ear to Holy Word:
As Christ had taught him, so 'twas his to prove:
By such a mir'acle much the mob was stir'd;
the Brahmins held it something from above;
for, seen his signs and seen his saintly life,
they fear the loss of old prerogative.

113 "These be the Sacerdotes of Géntoo-creed,
that of sore jealousy felt most the pain;
they seek ill-ways a thousand and take rede
Thomé to silence or to gar him slain:
The Principal who dons the three-twine thread,[246]
by a deed of horror makes the lesson plain,
there be no Hatred fell, and fere, and curst,
as by false Virtue for true Virtue nurst.

114 "One of his sons he slaughters, and accuses
Thomé of murther, who was innocent:
Bringing false witnesses, as there the use is,
him to the death they doom incontinent.
The Saint, assurèd that his best excuses
are his appeals to God Omnipotent,
prepares to work before the King and Court
a publick marvel of the major sort.

115 "He bids be brought the body of the slain
that it may live again, and be affied
to name its slayer, and its word be tane
as proof of testimony certified.
All saw the youth revive, arise again
in name of Jesu Christ the Crucified:
Thomé he thanks when raised to life anew
and names his father as the man who slew.

116 "So much of marvel did this Mir'acle claim,
straightway in Holy Water bathes the King
followed by many: These kiss Thomé's hem
while those the praises of his Godhead sing.
Such ire the Brahmans and such furies 'flame,
Envy so pricks them with her venom'd sting,
that rousing ruffian-rout to wrath condign
a second slaughter-plot the priests design.

117 "One day when preaching to the folk he stood
they feigned a quarrel 'mid the mob to 'rise:
Already Christ his Holy man endow'd
with saintly martyrdom that opes the skies.
Rainèd innumerable stones the crowd
upon the victim, sacred sacrifice,
and last a villain, hast'ier than the rest,
pierced with a cruel spear his godly breast.

118 "Wept Gange and Indus, true Thomé! thy fate,
wept thee whatever lands thy foot had trod;
yet weep thee more the souls in blissful state
thou led'st to don the robes of Holy Rood.
But Angels waiting at the Par'adise-gate
meet thee with smiling faces, hymning God.
We pray thee, pray that still vouchsafe thy Lord
unto thy Lusians His good aid afford.

119 "And you, ye others, who usurp the name
of God's Apostles, miss'ioners like Thomé,
say, an ye boast of apostolick claim
why fare not Holy Faith to preach and pray?
If ye be salt see how yourselves ye shame,
cleaving to home, where none the Prophet play;
how shall be salted in dark days as these
(Pagans I leave) such hosts of heresies?

120 "But now this per'ilous theme I pass beyond;
gain we again the limnèd shore and site.
Here with the City whereof Fame is fond,
bends the long bow-line of Gangetick Bight:
Runneth Narsinga rich and potent lond,
runneth Orissa vaunting tissues bright,
and at the bottom of the Bay's long line,
illustrious Ganges seeks his home, the brine:

121 "Ganges whose acc'olents bathe, and bathing die,
and die in lively faith withal secure
whatever sins upon their spirits lie,
the Holy Waters lave them sinless-pure.
See Cathigam,[247] amid the highest high
in Bengal-province, proud of varied store
abundant, but behold how placed the Post
where sweeps the shore-line t'wards the southing coast.

122 "Arracan-realm behold, behold the seat
of Pegu peopled by a monster-brood;
monsters that 'gendered meeting most unmeet
of whelp and woman in the lonely wood.
Here bells of sounding orichalc they fit
upon their bodies, by the craftihood
of subtle Queen, who such new custom plan'd
to 'bate th' accursèd Sin and Crime nefand.

123 "Behold Távái City,[248] whence begin
Siam's dominions, Reign of vast extent;
Tenassarí, Quedá of towns the Queen
that bear the burthen of the hot piment.
There farther forwards shall ye make, I ween,
Malaca's market grand and opulent,
whither each Province of the long seaboard
shall send of merchantry rich varied hoard.

124 "From this Peninsula, they say, the sea
parted with puissant waves, and ent'ering tore
Samátra's noble island, wont to be
joined to the Main as seen by men of yore.
'Twas callèd Chersonèse, and such degree
it gained by earth that yielded golden ore,
they gave a golden ep'ithet to the ground:
Some be who fancy Ophir here was found.

125 "But on her Lands-end throned see Cingapúr,
where the wide sea-road shrinks to narrow way:
Thence curves the coast to face the Cynosure,
and lastly trends Auroraward its lay:
See Pam, Patáne,[249] and in length obscure,
Siam, that ruleth all with royal sway;
behold Menam, who rolls his lordly tide
from Source Chiámái called, Lake long and wide.

126 "Thou see'st in spaces of such vast extent
nations of thousand names and yet unnamèd;
Láós in land and people prepotent,
Avás and Bramás[250] for vast ranges famèd.
See how in distant wilds and wolds lie pent
the self-styled Gueons,[251] salvage folk untamèd:
Man's flesh they eat: their own they paint and sear,
branding with burning iron,—usage fere!

127 "See Mecom river fret Cambodia's coast,
his name by 'Water-Captain' men explain;
in summer only when he swelleth most,
he leaves his bed to flood and feed the Plain:
As the frore Nyle he doth his freshets boast;
his peoples hold the fond belief and vain,
that pains and glories after death are 'signed
to brutes and soulless beasts of basest kind.

128 "This Stream with gentle, bland repose shall greet
in his embrace the Song,[252] that swam to land
from sad and piteous shipwreck dripping wet,
'scaped from the reefs and rocks that fang the strand;
from hunger-tortures and the perilous strait,
what time went forth the dour unjust command
on him, whose high sonorous lyre shall claim
such want of Fortune and such wealth of Fame.

129 "Here courseth, see, the callèd Champa[253] shore,
with woods of od'orous wood 'tis deckt and dight:
See Cauchichina still of note obscure,
and of Ainam[254] yon undiscoverèd Bight:
Here the proud Empire famed evermore
for wide-spread lands and wealth and matchles might,
of China runs, and boasts the whole her own
'twixt torrid Cancer and the frigid Zone.

130 "Behold yon wondrous and incred'ible Wall,
this and that other Region built to part;
most certain symbol this which shows to all,
Imperial Puissance proud in arm and art:
These their born Princes to the throne ne'er call,
Nor Son succeedeth Sire in subject heart;
the prop'erest man as Monarch they devise,
Some Knight for virtue famèd, brave and wise.

131 "Parforce hide other vasty lands from thee
until what time no land remain unfound:
But leave thou not those Islands of the Sea,[255]
where Nature rises to Fame's highest round:
This Realm half-shadowed, China's empery
afar reflecting, whither ships are bound,
is the Japan, whose virgin silver mine
shall shine still sheen'ier with the Law Divine.[256]

132 "Here see o'er Oriental seas bespread
    infinite island-groups and alwhere strewed:
    Tidore, Ternáte view, whose burning head
    lanceth the wavy flame and fiery flood:
    There see the groves the biting clove-bud shed,
    bought with the price of Portughueze's blood;
    here dwell the golden fowls, whose home is air
    and never earthward save in death may fare.

133 "See Banda's Islets, which enamelled glow
    various painted by the rosy fruits;
    variegate birds, that flit from bough to bough,
    take tithe and tribute of the greeny nuts:
    See Borneo's sea-girt shore where ever flow
    the perfumed liquor's thick and curded gouts,
    the tears of forest-trees men 'Camphor' clepe,
    wherefore that Island crop of Fame shall reap.

134 "Timor thence further sendeth forth her store
    of fragrant Saunders, wood medicinal:
    See Sunda's Isle,²⁵⁷ so stretch her farther shore
    that hideth Auster's regions of appall:
    The wand'ering men who inner wilds explore,
    tell of a stream whose marvels never pall;
    for, where its lone and single current floweth,
    dead wood that in it falls a live stone groweth.

135 "Behold yon land, made island of the sea²⁵⁸
    by Time, whose trembling flame in vapour swelleth,
    see Petroil-fountain, and the prodigy
    of od'orous juice the weeping tree distilleth;²⁵⁹
    sweeter than scent-tears shed in Araby
    by Cin'yras' daughter, where for aye she dwelleth;
    and see, how holding all that others hold,
    soft silk she hoardeth and the nugget-gold.

136 "See in Ceylon that Peak[260] so stark, so gaunt,
    shooting high o'er the clouds or mocking sight:
    The native peoples hold it sacrosanct
    for the famed Stone where print of foot is pight:
    O'er lone Maldivia's islets grows the plant,[261]
    beneath profoundest seas, of sov'reign might;
    whose pome of ev'ry Theriack is confest
    by cunning leech of antidotes the best.

137 "Eke shalt thou see toforn the Red Sea strait
    Socotra, famed for Aloe's bitter growth:
    I subject other sea-girt Isles to 'wait
    your steps where sandy Africk seaboard show'th:
    and yieldeth floating mass[262] rare, odorate,
    but whence it cometh none of mortals know'th:
    Of Sam Lourenço see yon famous Isle,
    which certain travellers Madagascar style.

138 "Here distant Orient's new-found climates see,
    climes on the world by this your Feat bestowèd
    that opened Ocean-portals patent-free,
    whose vasty plain with doughty hearts you plowèd.
    But in the Ponent als a reason be,
    a Lusian's noble exploit be avowèd,
    who being greatly by his King aggrieved,
    shall force a passage Fancy ne'er conceived.[263]

139 "See yon huge Region whose contin'uous lines
    course from Callisto to the contr'ary Pole;
    superb shall't be by boast of lucent mines
    whose veins Apollo's golden tincture stole.
    Castile, your ally, worthily designs
    to make its barb'arous neck her yoke to thole:
    In varied regions bide its various tribes,
    with different rites which different use prescribes.

140 "But here where Earth spreads wider, ye shall claim
     realms by the ruddy Dye-wood made renown'd:
     These of the 'Sacred Cross'²⁶⁴ shall win the name:
     By your first Navy shall that world be found.
     Along this seaboard, which your arm shall tame,
     shall wend him seeking Earth's extremest bound
     Magellan who, good sooth, by birth shall be
     a Portughueze in all save loyalty.

141 "And when his courses pass the midway place
     which from the Pole Antarctick parts the Line,
     he shall behold an all but Giant race²⁶⁵
     holding the countries which therewith confine:
     Still onwards lie the Straits that aye shall grace
     his name, which sea with sea through land conjoin;
     a sea and land where horrid Auster bideth,
     and 'neath his frozen wings their measure hideth.²⁶⁶

142 "Thus far, O Portingalls! to you was given
     the feats of future ages now to know;
     how o'er those Oceans which your keels have riven
     great-hearted Barons grandest deeds shall do:
     And hence, since all with mighty toils have striven,
     toils by whose Fame your favour aye shall grow
     with your eternal Spouses debonnair,
     who shall weave glorious crowns for you to wear:

143 "Ye can embark, for fav'ouring blows the Wind
     and to your well-loved home the seas be clear."
     Thus spake the Goddess, and the Braves incline'd
     from the glad Island of sweet Love to steer.
     They bear refreshment of the noblest kind,
     they bear the longed-for Comp'any, each his Fere,
     the Nymph that ever shall in heart abide,
     long as the sunshine warmeth land and tide.

144 So fared they, cutting through the Main serene
with favouring breezes that ne'er blew in ire,
till they had sighted that familiar scene
their Fatherland, and ever fond desire.
They past the Tagus-mouth, our stream amene,
and gave their Country and their dread loved Sire,
who willed their voyage, glory and renown
and added lustrous titles to his crown.

145 No more, my Muse![267] no more, for now my Lyre
untunèd lies, and hoarse my voice of Song;
not that of singing tire I, but I tire
singing for surd and horny-hearted throng.
Favours which Poet-fancy mostly fire
our Land gives not, ah, no! 'tis plunged too long
in lust of lucre, whelmed in rudest folly
of vile, austere and vulgar melancholy.

146 Nor ken I wherefore, by what Fate indign
she 'joys ne genial pride, ne gen'eral taste,
which strengthen mortal spirit and incline
to face all travail with a happy haste.
Wherefore, O King! thou whom the Will Divine
hath on the kingly throne for purpose place'd
look that thou be (and see the realms of Earth)
sole Lord of vassals peerless in their worth!

147 Look how they gladly wend by many a way,
with raging Bulls' or rampant Lyons' might,
self-doomed to sleepless night and foodless day,
to fire and steel, shaft-show'er and bullet-flight:
To torrid Tropicks, Arcticks frore and grey,
the Pagan's buffet and the Moor's despight;
to risks invis'ible threating human life,
to wrack, sea-monsters and the waves' wild strife.

148 All risks to serve thy cause they dare affront,
   to thee though distant yield they homage due,
   of ev'ry hard command they bear the brunt
   sans answer, ever prompt and ever true:
   On single look of favour could they count,
   infernal Demons, black with Hell's own hue,
   with thee they fain encounter, and they dare
   unconquer'd Conqueror their King declare.

149 Favour them alway, gladden every face
   with thy fair Presence, blithe Humanity;
   of rig'orous rule relieve them, deal the grace
   of milder law that leads to sanctity:
   impart to long Experience rank and place,
   an with Experience 'habit Honesty
   to work thy Sovran will; thus all shall trow
   what things befall them, Whence and When and How.

150 All favour thou in Duty's different way,
   as in each life the storèd talent lies:
   Let the Religious for thy gov'ernance pray,
   and beg a blessing on each high emprize;
   fast they and fash their flesh for those who stray
   in vulgar vices, and as wind despise
   Ambition, ne'er shall holy Priest mislead
   glare of vain-glory, nor of gain the greed.

151 Foster the Cavaliers with fair esteem,
   that oft their fearless, fiery blood have lent
   to spread not only Heaven's law supreme,
   but eke thy royal Rule pre-eminent.
   Such men who fare to face each fell extreme
   of climate in thy cause aye diligent,
   conquer a double foe; the fone that live,
   and (deadlier task) with dark, dumb danger strive.

152 So do, my Sire! that sons of famous lands
     Britons, Italians, Germans and the Gaul,
     ne'er vaunt that might of mortal man commands
     thy Portingalls, who should command them all.
     Take counsel only with experienced hands,
     men who long years, long moons, saw rise and fall:
     Many for gen'eral science fitness show,
     yet the partic'ulars none save experts know.

153 Elegant Phormion's philosophick store,
     see how the practised Hannibal deridèd,
     when lectured he with wealth of bellick lore
     and on big words and books himself he pridèd.
     Senhor! the Soldier's discipline is more
     than men may learn by mother-fancy guidèd
     Not musing, dreaming, reading what they write;
     'tis seeing, doing, fighting, teach to fight.

154 But I, what dare I say, rude, humble, low,
     to thee unknown, yes, even in thy dreams?
     Yet oft from lips of Babes and Sucklings flow,
     I trow, the words of wisdom man esteems:
     Right honest studies my career can show
     with long Experience blent as best beseems,
     and Genius here presentèd for thy view;—
     gifts, that conjoinèd appertain to few.

155 For serving thee an arm to Arms addrest;
     for singing thee a soul the Muses raise;
     nought lacks me save of thee to stand confest,
     whose duty 'tis the Good to prize and praise:
     If Heav'en concede me this, and if thy breast
     deign incept worthy of a Poet's lays;—
     as doth presage my spirit vaticine
     viewing thee pace the human path divine:—

156 Or do'ing such derring-do, that ne'er Meduse
    shall Atlas-mountain like thy glances shake,
    or battling on the plains of Ampeluse
    Marocco's mures[268] and Terodant to break;
    my now esteemèd and rejoicing Muse
    thy name o'er Earth, I swear, so famed shall make,
    an Alexander shall in Thee be shown
    who of Achilles envy ne'er shall own.

Translator's notes

[1] Ceylon.

[2] The "Tagides" are the Poet's Muses.

[3] Alluding to Eclogues, Pastorals, etc.

[4] Invocation to Dom Sebastiam.

[5] The Arms of Portugal (Canto III. 53, 54).

[6] The Ganges (not the Jordan).

[7] Ariosto, i. 2, etc.

[8] For the "Great Constable," Egas and Fuas, see Cantos IV. 23, and VIII. 13, 17.

[9] D. Joam III. and the Emperor Charles Quint.

[10] End of exordium: narrative begins.

[11] Sertorius.

[12] Madagascar.

[13] Here Cabo-das-Correntes.

[14] African daggers and short swords.

[15] Mohammed Rasúl Allah.

[16] Pronounced Kílwá.

[17] Palæologus, A.D. 1453.

[18] Arabic.

[19] The Parcæ.

[20] Camoens had studied the ground.

[21] Arab, for canoe.

[22] A perfect sketch.

[23] Moslems.

[24] The "puer æternus" "Deus bi-mater."

[25] The five zones of Parmenides.

[26] Low Lat. Cendalum = thin silk.

[27] Subaudi, "so hapless."

[28] Christianity

[29] Alluding to Da Gama's "sea-quake."

[30] Historical (?)

[31] Islet off the Cutch coast, pronounced Dyú

[32] Duarte Pacheco Pereira.

[33] Antony and Cleopatra.

[34] Magalhaens (Magellan), Canto X., 138.

[35] Melinde nearer the Line (S. Lat. 3° 9').

[36] Sol entering Taurus, Easter Sunday, April 15, 1498.

[37] *Escarlata*, a woollen cloth.

[38] The "dragoman", Fernam Martins.

[39] Our "assegai."

[40] Tangier.

[41] Tanais, the Don.

[42] Whence Adam ("red man").

[43] Borussians = Prussians.

[44] Ruthenians = Eastern Galicians.

[45] Harz and Erzgebridge.

[46] Amisius or Amisia (Ems).

[47] *Hod.* Vardari or Bradi.

[48] Padua.

[49] Seine and Garonne.

[50] Viriatus = vir, vires, virtus (*paronomasia*).

[51] De Bouillon, crowned first King of Jerusalem, A.D. 1099.

[52] The Favourite figure *correctio*.

[53] Valdevez, or Campo da Matança, A.D. 1128 (Canto IV. 16).

[54] i.e., of festal grab (Canto VIII. 14).

[55] Battle of Ourique, A.D. 1139.

[56] Isma'il = Ishmæl.

[57] i.e., disclose Thyself, show a sign.

[58] The conqueror's custom.

[59] St. Irene, Sanctarem, Santarem.

[60] Second Crusade, A.D. 1147.

[61] Giraldo Sem-Pavor, who took Evora.

[62] Burnt by the Moors.

[63] Synans.

[64] The Ararat of fiction.

[65] Cape St. Vincent.

[66] The Guadalquivir.

[67] African Ceuta, opposite Gilbraltar.

[68] The Emperor of Moroco.

69 Coimbra.
70 The Guadiana river.
71 The Battle of the "Horns of Hattin".
72 Sic in orig.
73 By D. Roderick the Goth.
74 Begins vehemently – *ex abrupto*.
75 The Lixus river, now Al-kús of Marocco.
76 Battle of Tarifa or Rio Salado, A.D. 1340.
77 Fourth of Portugal and eleventh of Castile.
78 i.e., Portuguese Afonso.
79 "Peace with honour."
80 Writing his name upon the tree-trunks and leaves.
81 In orig., Ministros, i.e., of wrath.
82 The famous Fonte-dos-Amores, near Coimbra.
83 E bem parece, — ambiguous.
84 Bryx or Brigus, whence Brangança.
85 Isla de Leon = Gades, Cadiz.
86 The Spanish Cuenca, concha, a shell.
87 Afonso I., son of D. Henrique (Canto III., 35).
88 The Castles were added in A.D. 1252.
89 Of Abrantes town; battle of Aljubarrota, A.D. 1385.
90 Sol in Libra.
91 Cape Rocca-de-Cintra.
92 Pompey, Canto III., 62.
93 Numidian.
94 Montes-Sete-Irmãos, near Tangier.
95 Around the Royal banner.
96 Battle of Valverde.
97 Canto III., 101.
98 "Saint" Ferdinand.
99 Octavius.

100 Pompey's tomb on Mount Casius (Baalzephon).
101 Explorer's epitaph!
102 That of the Moon.
103 The soldiers and sailors then being different services.
104 i.e., the ships.
105 Old chapel of Belem (Bethlehem).
106 The "Old Man of Belem" is the people personified.
107 Sol entering Leo (Northern Tropic).
108 The glorious Brazil.
109 Senegalese of "Sanagá" (Senegal).
110 The Cape Verd Islands.
111 Alias Gorgades: Fernando Po, etc.
112 N. Lat. 11° south of Sierra Leone.
113 S. Thomé.
114 Saint Elmo's Fire.
115 The moon moving faster than the sun.
116 Angra de Sancta Helena, S. Lat. 32° 40'.
117 Tropic of Capricorn.
118 In orig., bando, applied to birds.
119 Of Pedr' Alvares Cabral.
120 Bartholomeu Dias.
121 D. Francisco de Almeida.
122 D. Manoel de Souza.
123 Angra de Sam Braz (St. Blaise), 70 leagues E. of the Cape.
124 Sancta Cruz of Bart. Dias.
125 Off Cabo das Correntes.
126 Rio-dos-Reis; twelfth day O. S., Jan. 9.
127 The Cuama-Zambeze mouth.
128 i.e. to south-east.
129 The Archangel Raphaël.
130 Scurvy, first poetically described here.

131 Cleopatra (says Faria y Sousa).
132 Cleopatra.
133 Ino and Melicerta (Leucothea and Palæmon).
134 Glaucus, the fisherman.
135 Ambergris.
136 The Argonauts.
137 Æolus.
138 *Quarto da prima* = 6 to 9 p.m.
139 John of Gaunt.
140 = Macrinus, the "little lean one."
141 Bruges.
142 River of Bactria.
143 Venus rises, the storm falls, and India appears.
144 Mount Delli, near Cananor.
145 The Church.
146 Henry VIII.
147 Saladin.
148 François I.
149 River of Tripoli.
150 Carolus Magnus and St. Louis.
151 Poetic prophecy of the coming kingdom, Byzantinum.
152 Imaus = Híma-álaya = Snow-house.
153 The Samiry Rajah of Malabar.
154 Perimál Princes of Malayálam.
155 Pythagoras the Philosophos, not Sophos.
156 Kot-wál, captain of fort.
157 Semiramis.
158 Ruh Allah (the Breath of Allah).
159 Hezekiah.
160 Spurius Posthumius.
161 Slain at the capture of Lisbon.
162 Now Saint.
163 "Sans-peur," who captured Evora.
164 D. Pedro Fernandez de Castro.
165 Grand Master of Sant'Iago (Stanza 26).
166 Fernam Martinez de Santarem, Vasco Yannes and Gonçalo Ribeiro (Stanza 27).
167 Paio Rodriguez Marinho.
168 P. de Menezes, first Governor of Ceuta.
169 His son, D. Duarte, who saved D. Afonso V.
170 D. Joam I.
171 Southern Constellations.
172 Ursa Major.
173 The well Zemzem.
174 Of Egypt.
175 i.e., the capstan.
176 Mace.
177 The Moluccas.
178 Asia.
179 The Dove-nymph.
180 φιλαυτία, egoism opposed to altruism.
181 Myrrha.
182 Ninus and Amnon.
183 The peach (Malus persica).
184 Persia, famed for tapestry.
185 Narcissus.
186 Anemone (Adonis' blood).
187 Marjoram.
188 And thou shalt notice at the end of all *twixt ear and sickle how uprears the wall.*—PETRARCH.
189 The Pacific, west of "Tamistitam" (Tenochtitlan, Mexico).
190 The Magic Mirror (Canto VIII. 45).
191 Da Gama's second voyage.
192 Trimumpára, Rajah of Cochin.
193 "Conqueror of the Indies."
194 At the mouth of the Cochin Backwater.
195 Rajahship south of Cochin.
196 The Samorim.
197 Dom Francisco d'Almeida, first Viceroy.
198 Lucan, VI. 251, etc.
199 Chief Harbour of Bijapur.
200 Islet in the Gulf of Cutch, governed by Malik Iyáz.

[201] Mir Husayn, the Turk.
[202] Madagascar.
[203] On Ormuz or Hormuz Isle.
[204] Bahrayn Island.
[205] Nov. 25, 1510.
[206] The Malay "crease."
[207] Alludes to the hanging of Ruy Dias.
[208] Succeeded Soares, A.D. 1518.
[209] Hod. Masawwah Island.
[210] D. Duarte, A.D. 1522.
[211] D. Henrique, A.D. 1525.
[212] D. Pedro, A.D. 1526.
[213] Java.
[214] Lope Vaz S., the Usurper.
[215] The Moslem Admiral.
[216] D. Nuno, A.D. 1529.
[217] Bahádur Sháh, King of Cambay.
[218] D. Garcia, A.D. 1539.
[219] Estevam da Gama, A.D. 1540.
[220] Villegagnon, expelled by Martim (Martinho) Afonso de Souza, chosen A.D. 1542.
[221] Now Sadashivgarh.
[222] D. Joam de Castro (A.D. 1545) worthily ends the Viceroys.
[223] Commanding Diu fort.
[224] Bahádur Sháh of Gujarát.
[225] Elephants.
[226] Adil Sháh of Bijápúr.
[227] The Solar System (Ptolemeian).
[228] Or Imperial: No. II sphere, "sensorium of the Deity."
[229] A couplet for "The Spiritualist."
[230] First mover, i.e. source of motion: Sphere No. 10.
[231] i.e. moving the orbs from east to west.
[232] Crystalline Sphere (No. 9), revolving in 49.000 years.
[233] Firmament or Zodiac: Sphere No. 8.
[234] *In orig.* Posada, i.e., not a home.

[235] The Jesuit G. Da Silveira, A.D. 1561.
[236] The Zambeze.
[237] Rufiji River (of "sewn boats").
[238] Of vulgar error.
[239] Arab horses.
[240] Ras el-Hadd.
[241] D. Pedro de C., Governor of Hormuz.
[242] Paragoge for Lár.
[243] On the Zanzibar Coast.
[244] Sind; the "Bore" (flood-tide), and Cutch Gulf.
[245] Indus and Ganges.
[246] The Brahminical cord.
[247] Chittagong.
[248] Tavoy, in Tenasserim.
[249] Malaccan Pa-ang, and Patani.
[250] Burmans.
[251] The Karen tribe.
[252] The singer personifies himself as "Song."
[253] The seaboard of Cochin China.
[254] Hainan.
[255] Malasia.
[256] i.e., be applied to missions.
[357] Java.
[258] We now return westward to Sumatra.
[259] Styrax bezoin (gum benjamin).
[260] Adam's Peak.
[261] The Coco-de-mer.
[262] Ambergris.
[263] Magellan.
[264] S. Cruz (= The Brazil) found by Cabral, A.D. 1500.
[265] The Patagonians.
[266] Australia (?)
[267] Epilogue addressed to D. Sebastiam.
[268] Alii "Marroco's Moors" (Mouros).

THE COLLECTION

Collecting is choosing.
Choosing what we have that is most precious
and take care of it.
We only collect what we love.
What we want to inscribe in the memory that
survives us. What we wish to share with those
who are eternal to us.
We choose. We preserve. We share.
We choose authors, preserve literature, we share
it with the readers.
Because we have been, we are and will — always —
be a bookstore of today, retrieving to the present
and to the future the one that will always be,
to us and to you, the most beautiful bookstore
in the world.
This is a simple, magical, beautiful book that
fits in your pocket to be closer to your heart.
Just like Lello Bookstore enters your gaze
to stay alive in your emotions.
Through timeless authors, to our dedicated
readers, this is a gift from your Author's Bookstore,
which is, after all, your Reader's Bookstore.

Lello Bookstore
Author's Bookstore, Reader's Bookstore

An edition

LIVRARIA LELLO
PORTO